D0141028

Centro de Estudios Puertorriqueños

CENTRO JOURNAL
VOLUME XXXII • NUMBER III • FALL 2020

Photography courtesy of Por la Nuturaleza. Reprinted by permission.

ISSN: 1538-6279 (Print); ISSN: 2163-2960 (Online)
ISBN: 978-1-945662-43-0 (print); ISBN: 978-1-945662-44-7 (ebook)
©2020 Centro de Estudios Puertorriqueños
Hunter College / City University of New York
695 Park Avenue, E-1429, New York, NY 10065
212.772.5690 • Fax 212.650.3673 • http://centropr.hunter.cuny.edu

CENTRO Journal is indexed or abstracted in: Academic Search Complete (EBSCO host); Alternative Press Index; America: History and Life; Cabell's Whitelist; Caribbean Abstracts; CONUCO–Consorcio Universitario de Indización; Gale; HAPI—Hispanic American Periodical Index; Historical Abstracts; Left Index; MLA International Index; OCLC PAIS; Pro Quest; Scopus; Social Services Abstracts; Sociological Abstracts; Ulrich's Periodicals Service; H.W. Wilson Humanities Abstracts; Worldwide Political Science Abstracts.

Journal of the Center for Puerto Rican Studies
VOLUME XXXII • NUMBER III • FALL 2020

SPECIAL ISSUE: Post-Disaster Recovery in Puerto Rico and Local Participation
GUEST EDITOR: Edwin Meléndez

Post-Disaster Recovery in Puerto Rico and Local Participation: Introduction

EDWIN MELÉNDEZ

Puerto Rico has suffered the compounded effects of multiple disasters since the devastating impacts of hurricanes Irma and Maria in September 2017. At the end of 2019, the island was impacted with recurrent seismic activity in the southwest region, including a magnitude 6.4 earthquake on January 7, 2020. In early 2020, the current COVID-19 pandemic and the resulting health crises induced yet another economic contraction. All these disasters are underscored by a crushing debt crisis and a federally-mandated austerity regime since 2016. Multiple natural disasters have exacerbated vulnerability and poverty; and public energy, telecommunications, water, health, and transportation systems have deteriorated and become even more vulnerable, causing systematic failures in social safety nets.

Recent disasters have revealed serious vulnerabilities in Puerto Rico's preparedness planning, institutional response capacity and coordination, resource management at various levels of implementation, data availability, and the lack of suitable and accessible mechanisms to support adequate local community engagement. As Puerto Rico transitions to long-term recovery, the prospect of one of the largest disaster allocations in Community Development Block Grant funds in U.S. history is increasingly shaping state-level planning and decision-making processes. Used appropriately, these funds represent an opportunity for communities to secure decent housing, adequate infrastructure, and economic recovery.

The author (emele@hunter.cuny.edu) is a Professor of Urban Policy and Planning and the Director of the Center for Puerto Rican Studies at Hunter College, CUNY. In addition to numerous scientific papers and other publications, he is the author or editor of thirteen books including *State of Puerto Ricans* (Centro Press, 2017) and *Puerto Ricans at the Dawn of the New Millenium* (Centro Press, 2014), and served as guest editor of *CENTRO Journal*'s "Pathway to Economic Opportunity" (v.23 n.2, 2011) and "Puerto Rico Post-Hurricane Maria: Origins and Consequences of a Crisis" (v.30 n.3, 2018) issues.

The collection of studies included in this special volume of *CENTRO Journal* shows evidence of how post-disaster recovery is progressing in Puerto Rico, and the challenges and opportunities for local participation in reconstruction programs. To date, the available evidence leads to a portrait of an uneven recovery, a recovery characterized by the bifurcation of efforts from the civic sector and central and federal governments. Municipalities, the small business community, and nonprofit organizations had active engagement in the initial post disaster emergency phase to the benefit and welfare of victims and communities. For the most part, private and philanthropic donations supported local engagement and disaster relief. The Foundation Center estimates that philanthropic efforts alone raised more than $375 million for relief and recovery from the storms (Red de Fundaciones de Puerto Rico 2019).

In addition to donations from philanthropic organizations but with minimal support from the local or federal government, substantial donations and volunteerism from individuals and the private sector made it possible for the nonprofit sector to have an extensive and impactful participation in the immediate emergency phase of post-disaster recovery (García and Chandrasekhar 2020). In addition to civic sector engagement, federal disaster spending during the emergency phase reached $15 billion—about half of total federal spending for all disasters declared in 2017 in the United States and Puerto Rico.[1] This spending included, for example, the initial rehabilitation of the electrical grid, housing and other assistance to families, and loans and grants to small businesses.

Exacerbating the harshness of the immediate impact of the storms on the island people and economy, a close examination of common indicators stresses that the transition to long-term disaster recovery has been grueling and demanding. Census data for 2018 and 2019 indicate a very modest gain in population, from 3,193,354 in 2018 to 3,193,694 in 2019—an 0.01 percent population increase—definitely within the margin of error for the estimates. Yet the significance of these figures lay in a reversal of more than a decade of steady population decline spurred by a relentless exodus and the signaling of a first step toward recovery. Similarly, a modest increase of 1.6 percent in the Index of Economic Activity (IEA)[2] provides additional evidence of recovery in 2019, barely the second consecutive annual positive growth after five years of uninterrupted declines in the index.

However, because of the economic depression induced by the COVID pandemic, from January to September 2020 the IEA contracted by 5.7 percent. In this context, federal long-term recovery funding allocations to Puerto Rico for disasters declared in 2017 have stalled. From the $19.9 billion congressional allocation to HUD for disaster recovery and mitigation programs for Puerto Rico, as of the end of July 2020, only $96 million had been outlayed. In sum, three years after the 2017 storms that devastated the island, indicators such as economic activity and implementation of recovery programs point toward a stalled long-term recovery.

That said, local capacity for disaster recovery participation is largely a function of the policies and programs that facilitate or hinder civic participation and local engagement.

Local participation and engagement are critical elements for long-term economic recovery (FEMA 2017). The disaster recovery literature has established that community engagement, especially nonprofit and local government participation, is an important determinant of overall community recovery (Dyer 1999; Mileti 1999; Smith and Birkland 2012; Peacock, Morrow and Gladwin 1997; Scott and Murphy 2014; Welsh and Esnard 2009). The nonprofit sector capacity's to participate in the post-disaster economic recovery phase is constrained due to several factors. These factors are related to federal policies that regulate recovery programs and local implementation, and the various stages and capacity requirements for program participation, such as community planning for project development, competing for local and federal funding, and local management of programs. Additionally, there is limited experience in the nonprofit sector with federal housing and economic development, and disaster mitigation programs, which constitute the bulk of the post-disaster economic recovery phase. Even organizations with prior knowledge in community economic development have a limited capacity for real estate development and to meet the Notification of Funding Availability (NOFA) requirements and be competitive for federal disaster recovery and other ancillary funding. That said, local capacity for disaster recovery participation is largely a function of the policies and programs that facilitate or hinder civic participation and local engagement. Such is the dialectic that motivates the studies herein presented.

The studies included in this special volume of *CENTRO Journal* analyze challenges and opportunities for local participation in reconstruction programs and their potential to contribute to post disaster recovery in Puerto Rico. In the next section, I discuss indicators of disaster recovery or lack thereof three years after Hurricanes Irma and Maria ravaged the island. One critical indicator of recovery is business sector responses to the disaster, a topic addressed by Lobato, Álvarez and Aponte (2020) in this volume. Then, I discuss the challenges and opportunities for local participation in long-term recovery. Two studies included in this volume discuss nonprofit sector responses and grassroots innovative initiatives. The García and Chandrasekhar (2020) study focuses on the nonprofit sector response during the emergency recovery phase, and the Villarrubia-Mendoza and Vélez-Vélez (2020) study focuses on the emerging role of grassroots organizations in post-Maria recovery.

The third section of the introduction addresses challenges and opportunities in disaster recovery for the housing and community economic development industry. Meléndez (2020) identifies the absence of specific state-level policies benefiting community development, along with a weak support system, as important factors holding back the nonprofit sector participation in federal economic recovery programs. Borges-Méndez (2020) proposes that there is a disconnection between local implementation of disaster recovery programs, though many organizations already have a proven track record of project completion and are actively overcoming barriers to expand their participation in disaster recovery programs. In the final section of the introduction, Torres Cordero (2020) enumerates more equitable policies from other stateside jurisdictions aimed at producing a better and more just recovery, one that the Government of Puerto Rico can choose to implement in its CDBG-DR and CDBG-MIT governance.

The last section of the introduction is devoted to highlighting core findings from the studies and policy recommendations. Whether Puerto Rico takes advantage of this unique window of opportunity to restore its economy and infrastructure in a more resilient fashion, while strengthening the nonprofit sector's capacity for community planning, housing development, and neighborhood revitalization remains an open question. The studies included in this volume propose that the long-term benefits of federal disaster recovery programs are contingent on reforming public policy to encourage and support nonprofit developers' participation in developing reconstruction programs, strengthening nonprofit capacity, encouraging partnerships and collaborations, and providing professional development for economic recovery.

Where Is the Recovery Three Years After Hurricanes Irma and Maria?

Common indicators of post-disaster recovery found in the literature include the returning of population to the affected areas after natural disasters, the renewal of business activity, and the successful restoration of damaged infrastructure such as housing, public infrastructure, and government ser-vices. In this section I examine empirical indicators associated with these different aspects of disaster recovery.

Climate change and the devastating impact of more frequent and intense natural hazards in the United States and worldwide have induced a renewed effort in understanding post-disaster recovery and building community resil-ience—the idea that post-disaster reconstruction should go beyond restoring systems to their pre-disaster state and to seek systems' improvements that will mitigate potential damages from future hazard events. A recent review of the literature concluded that despite conceptual and methodological efforts across disciplines, to date we lack a comprehensive community resilience model that incorporates the interdependence of physical infrastructure, social and economic systems (Koliou et al. 2018). In this context, I use the resilience inference measurement (RIM) model to illustrate how different municipali-ties have adapted to the devastation caused by the 2017 Hurricanes Irma and Maria. The RIM model is adopted to measure community resilience in Puerto Rico because it was successfully used to "quantify resilience to climate-related hazards for 52 U.S. counties along the northern Gulf of Mexico (Lam 2016)," a region that resembles the storms (hazard events) that affected Puerto Rico. The RIM model uses exposure (the relative damage of a hazard event in a municipality), damage (the sum of all damages in a given period of time), and recovery (population change over the period of time) as indicators for the estimation of the index of community resilience. Given

Figure 1. Community Resilience (2016 to 2019) and Population Change (2017 to 2019) in Puerto Rico.

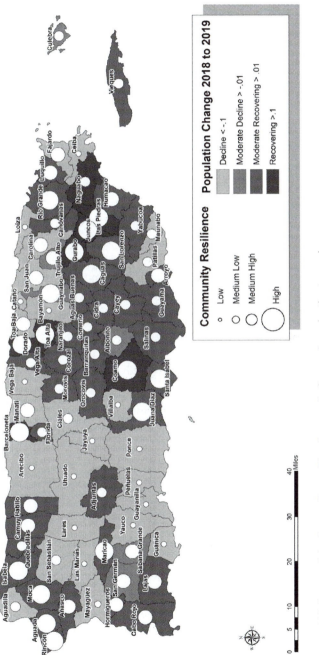

Source: U.S. Bureau of the Census, Puerto Rico Community Survey, Annual estimates, various years. FEMA Housing Assistance dataset.

Notes: Author's estimates and data available upon request.

these parameters, the RIM model ranks municipalities on four clusters raging from low to high community resilience.[3]

Figure 1 depicts the RIM classification of community resilience between 2016 to 2019, the period prior to and post hazard events, and population change from 2017 to 2019 in Puerto Rico by municipalities. After more than a decade of steady population decline, Puerto Rico experienced a modest one-tenth of one percent (0.01 percent) growth in population in 2019. As a reference point, the island lost more than two percent (-2.39 percent) population in 2017, and almost four percent (-3.97 percent) in 2018, the year immediately after the storms. Evidently the map shows that there is a high correlation between community resilience and municipalities that experienced population decline or modest growth after the storms. The data indicate that municipalities with higher resilience have (to some degree) stalled population losses, while communities with low resilience continue to experience population decline. Municipalities that experienced the highest percentage gains in population and are classified in the high community resilience group include Dorado (1.03 percent population growth), Barceloneta (1.12 percent), Juncos (1.15 percent), Coamo (1.25 percent), Las Piedras (1.30 percent), Naguabo (1.39 percent), Toa Alta (1.39 percent), and Gurabo (2.18 percent). Yet more than half of the municipalities depict low community resilience and a continuation of population loss. In sum, though there are signs of a modest overall recovery as measured by returning population to communities affected by the storms, most communities continue to experience the adverse impact of the disasters and continued population losses.

The loss and renewal of business activity follows a similar pattern to the one observed for post-disaster population losses and returning population across municipalities. Business activity before and after the hurricanes serve as an indicator of recovery. In a study sponsored by the Puerto Rico team of the Global Entrepreneurship Monitor (GEM) longitudinal research project, Lobato, Álvarez and Aponte show how, immediately after Hurricane Maria, Puerto Rico experienced "unusually high levels of closings of establishments and employment contraction" (2020, 39) But, by the beginning of 2018, from March 2018 to March 2019, business opening jumped 28 percent when compared to the same period the prior year, and the "effect on job creation was even stronger, with a raise of 39 percent in jobs created in newly opened establishments" (Lobato, Álvarez and Aponte 2020, 51). These rates of establishment closings and impact on employment in Puerto Rico are like those in Louisiana after Hurricane Katrina. However, in the case of Puerto Rico, "the rise of opening establishments lasted longer and was accompanied by an increase of expanding establishments from March 2018 on" (2020, 59).

In conclusion, Lobato, Álvarez and Aponte (2020, 62) state that:

Despite the fact that Puerto Rico's entrepreneurial activity suffered an initial strong negative effect, it reemerged with strength after the hurricanes. It may seem paradoxical, but the entrepreneurial activity performance observed in Puerto Rico and Louisiana could respond to entrepreneurial resilience behavior exposed in the literature. This hypothesis needs to be tested in future empirical research. Other possible reasons for the increase in business activity could be the injection of aid funds to individuals and businesses. After more than a decade of recession or stagnation, the economy of Puerto Rico is in urgent need of new sources of production and employment, but reports from GEM and other international research projects point out that domestic business activity faces an infertile context; several crucial factors hinder the birth and survival of entrepreneurial initiatives.

Within this frame of reference, it is important to examine in greater detail the implementation of federal disaster programs for Puerto Rico. FEMA's Public Assistance (PA) Program was deployed immediately after the storms and by the end of July 2020 had outlayed $13.8 billion of the $29.4 allocated, or 46.9 percent of the total (Table 1). Most of the remaining funds are obligated to FEMAs Hazard Mitigation Grant Program (HMGP, Section 404) to help rebuild the electrical grid system ($9.6 billion) and for the recovery of the education system ($2 billion). These new programs are funded under FEMA's Public Assistance Alternative Procedures, pursuant to Section 428 of the Robert T. Stafford Disaster Relief and Emergency Assistance Act. Under these procedures, intended to streamline projects while reducing costs, local jurisdictions could take advantage of a fast track for the approval and processing of small projects of up to $120,000 which may include mitigation projects on undamaged facilities.. In contrast to PA, 404 mitigation projects are considered to be part of the long-term recovery phase. This $3 billion mitigation program is supplemented with $1 billion from the CDBG-DR program to compensate for the local share of the program, for a program total of $4 billion. Though hundreds of submitted projects remain in the agency evaluation stage, in July 2020 FEMA approved "525 letters of intent (LOIs) from municipalities, agencies, and private non-profit organizations in Puerto Rico to be evaluated for risk mitigation" (Correa 2020). These LOIs move to the proposal preparation stage, which may take about a year, and if successful will move to project implementation. Pending LOIs continue the initial evaluation process, and it is expected that, depending on available funding, additional projects would be invited to move to the proposal preparation stage. Despite extraordinary measures imposed by President Trump's administration to federally funded programs in Puerto Rico (Fadulu and Walker 2020), FEMA's 404 mitigation program is slowly progressing towards implementation.

Table 1. Federal Disaster Spending Data for All Disasters Declared in 2017, United States, and Puerto Rico (Billions)

	Allocated	Obligated	Outlayed
United States (a)	118.6	81.3	42.1
(%)	100%	68.5%	35.5%
DHS-FEMA	49.4	49.4	29.6
HUD	35.4	12.7	0.950
Puerto Rico (b)	56.5	36.7	16.0
(%)	100%	65.0%	28.3%
DHS-FEMA	29.4	29.4	13.8
SBA	2	2	1.3
HUD	19.9	3.2	0.096
CDBG-DR (FA)	1.5	1.5	0.112
CDBG-DR	8.2	1.7	--
CDBG-MIT	8.4	--	--
CDBG-DR (EP)	1.9	--	--
DOD (CE)	2.5	0.095	0.041

Source: FEMA's Spending Explorer, Data as of September 30, 2020.
Notes:
   (a) Includes: FEMA and SBA for Harvey, Irma, Maria, 2017, CA Wildfires, and other 2017 Disasters;
   Harvey, Irma, Maria, 2017, CA Wildfires, and other 2017 Disasters (PL 115-123); Harvey, Irma, Maria, 2017,
   and CA Wildfires (PL 115-156); Harvey, Irma, Maria, 2017, and CA Wildfires (PL 115-72).
   (b) Includes DHS without FEMA and DOC.
   (FA) First Allocation February 9, 2018.
   (EP) Funding to be allocated specifically for enhancing and improving electrical power infrastructure and
   systems.
   (CE) Corps of Engineers-Civil Works.
Legend:
   •Allocated: Congress appropriated the funds;
   •Obligated: government has entered a binding agreement to award funding;
   •Outlayed: the money has actually been paid.

The situation with Congressional allocations to HUD for disaster recovery and mitigation programs to assist Puerto Rico is more daunting than the implementation of FEMA's long-term mitigation programs. Table 1 depicts federal data for all disasters declared in 2017 in the United States and Puerto Rico.[1] Congress made the first allocation to HUD for CDBG-DR programs for Puerto Rico in February 2018, just a few months after the 2017 hurricanes. The CDBG-DR action plan was initially approved by HUD in February of 2018 and since then has undergone four substantial amendments to date. The initial process of approval of the CDBG-DR action plan for Puerto Rico conforms to the timetable for other jurisdictions. Yet, the CDGB-MIT program, which with a $8.4 billion is the largest allocation for HUD programs for disaster mitigation in Puerto Rico, just completed the public comments phase of the action plan and is currently undergoing revisions for final approval.

HUD's disaster programs implementation in Puerto Rico lags in comparison to other jurisdictions. Of the initial allocation of $1.5 billion in February 2018, disbursed primarily for housing rehabilitation and assistance, only $96 million had been outlayed as of the end of July 2020. In a similar fashion, to date only $3.2 billion of the $19.9 billion has been obligated to program projects or administrative expenses. According to Martin (2018), the typical process "take 9–12 months after an Action Plan is approved (which typically occurs within months of HUD allocation notice) to hire staff, procure contractors and consultants, and develop management and information systems." By this standard, which is based on an examination of CDBG-DR grantees action plans for disasters from 2003 to 2014, so far program implementation in Puerto Rico is taking twice longer than the typical timeline for other jurisdictions across the United States. Based on the cumulative evidence from stateside jurisdictions, Martin asserts that in regard to typical disaster projects, "[w]ithin the same sample of grants, housing activities on average take 4.7 years to complete from the time a disaster is declared, and overall grants (including non-housing activities) on average take 5.1 years" (2018, 5). Considering CDBG-DR program implementation to date, we should expect Puerto Rico's program completion to exceed the typical CDBG-DR program implementation timeline elsewhere.

Housing rehabilitation, reconstruction, or facilitating relocation of disaster victims in Puerto Rico are activities tailor made for CDCs.

To date, the Puerto Rico Department of Housing CDBG-DR contracts totaling $723 million have gone entirely to the private sector, with 62 percent of this total awarded to foreign corporations (Meléndez 2020, 130, Table 3). These contracts are primarily for the Repair, Reconstruction, or Relocation (R3) housing program, which represents 24 percent of the total allocation of $3 billion to this program. Though the nonprofit sector capacity to bid for these contracts was restricted given the specifications of the Notification of Funding Availability (NOFA) of the Puerto Rico Department of Housing (PRDOH) as approved by HUD, other stateside jurisdictions have implemented more inclusive policies to support capacity building for municipalities and local nonprofit contractors. Housing rehabilitation, reconstruction, or facilitating relocation of disaster victims in Puerto Rico are activities tailor made for CDCs. Many of the CDCs are already implementing some of these activities in a modest scale with support from the private sector. Given the appropriate policy (i.e., a more inclusive NOFA), CDCs are positioned to participate as contractors in future allocations of the remaining three-quarters of funds in this program.

PRDOH's CDBG-DR program subrecipients agreements have earmarked Government of Puerto Rico agencies, municipalities, and nonprofit organizations. Of the total $679 million of PRDOH's agreements with CDBG-DR subrecipients from 2018 to 2020, 84 percent was allocated to government agencies and two newly created government-affiliated nonprofit organizations. Municipalities are earmarked to receive 5.5 percent, and nonprofits were allocated 12.7 percent (Meléndez 2020, 131, Table 4). Considering both contracts and agreements totaling $1.4 billion, $723 million (or 52 percent) are allocated to the private sector (of which two-thirds are assigned to foreign corporations), central government agencies are earmarked to receive $556 million (40 percent), non-government-affiliated nonprofit organizations are earmarked to receive $86 million (6 percent), and municipalities $38 million (2.7 percent). Despite the grim picture of CDBG-DR allocations supporting program activities implemented by nonprofit organizations and municipalities, it is important to consider that the CDBG-DR programs implementation is in its initial phases, and the CDBG-MIT action plan is still in the approval stage. A change in administrations in local government and stateside could lead to a policy framework more inclusive of nonprofit organizations and municipalities, and the bulk of federal disaster funding remains to be allocated.

In sum, three years after the Major Disaster Declaration by federal authorities in relation to the 2017 hurricanes in Puerto Rico, economic, population, and disaster program indicators offer a picture of an uneven and sluggish recovery. For one, despite the lack of coordination and erratic response from the federal and Puerto Rico governments to the catastrophic event and the collapse of the public infrastructure, the nonprofit sector, with support from the philanthropic and private sectors and local businesses, had a strong initial response during the emergency phase of recovery. But the transition to long-term recovery, which requires implementation of disaster recovery programs, has been sluggish and largely divorced from engagement of local resources. The next section examines the nonprofit sector in Puerto Rico and its ongoing and potential participation in economic recovery.

The Nonprofit Sector in Puerto Rico and Its Participation in Economic Recovery
The catalyst role of nonprofit organizations in mobilizing local resources, coordinating emergency services with government, and advocating for more resilient community infrastructure is well established in the literature (Eller et al. 2015; Luna 2013; Patterson et al. 2010; Robinson and Murphy 2014). However, one of the critical questions for disaster recovery policy in Puerto Rico is whether local nonprofit organizations are capable to implement programs effectively. This question is partially related to the sector's capacity in general, and specifically to its experience and ability to participate in federal recovery programs over a long period. I begin this section providing an overall portrait of the nonprofit sector in Puerto Rico, and then summarizing key findings from the García and Chandrasekhar (2020) study on the nonprofit sector response during the emergency recovery phase and the Villarrubia-Mendoza and Vélez-Vélez (2020) study on the emerging role of grassroots organizations in post-Maria recovery.

First, as depicted in Table 2, the nonprofit sector in Puerto Rico employs 40,676 (or 4.4 percent) of the civilian population aged 16 and

Table 2. Employment in Puerto Rico by Sector, 2019 (Civilian population aged 16 years and older)

Private	661,320	70.9%
Self-employed	26,671	2.9%
Nonprofit	40,676	4.4%
Government	204,510	21.9%
Total	933,177	100.0%

Source: U.S. Census Bureau, 2019 1-year American Community Survey, TableID: C24060.

older. To put in context, the nonprofit sector constitutes 10 percent of the American workforce[4] In short, though the nonprofit sector constitutes a significant portion of the Puerto Rico economy and workforce, it is about half the size of this sector for the average state.

Figure 2 illustrates the various types of non-governmental organizations (NGOs) comprising the nonprofit universe. Keeping in mind that the graphic is intended to illustrate a concept and not actual proportions of industry share, all nonprofit organizations are NGOs. We use this distinction to denote a significant group of international charitable organizations known typically as NGOs. This type of organization is active in the United States and includes well- recognized organizations such as the International Olympic Committee and Amnesty International among many others.[5] Conversely, there are U.S.-based NGOs with hefty international portfolios such as the Red Cross or the Salvation Army. The legal definition of a nonprofit in the United States is that they are charitable IRS Exempt Organizations.

For analytical purposes, as illustrated in Figure 2, I divide the nonprofit sector engaged in community development into two types of organizations: community-based organizations (CBOs) and community development corporations (CDCs). Both organization types are place-based, which distinguishes them from other nonprofit organizations. CBOs and CDCs have a focus on one or several neighborhoods, and they may operate at a local, regional, or national level. CDCs are the backbone of the community development industry. Many CDCs include social services, community planning and organizing, and programs typical of other types of CBOs or nonprofit organizations, yet they are distinct from other community organizations because they focus on affordable housing, business development and other revenue-generating economic development projects (Meléndez and Servon 2007).

Figure 2. Types of Non-Governmental Organizations

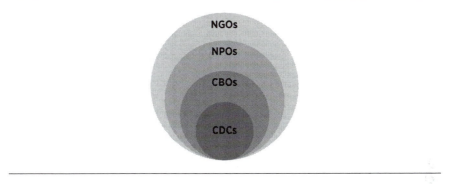

The nonprofit sector in Puerto Rico comprises 1,510 organizations registered with the Puerto Rico State Department and 114 cooperatives registered with the Corporación Pública para Supervisión y Seguro de Cooperativas de Puerto Rico (COSSEC). Of these 1,608 organizations,[6] 466 were IRS exempt organizations. In 2019, as depicted in Table 3, the 466 IRS exempt organizations in Puerto Rico that filed 990 returns (for calendar year 2018), arguably the more robust cohort within the nonprofit sector in Puerto Rico, reported $3 billion in total revenues and $7 billion in assets. Whether measured by average revenues or assets, health and education organizations represent the bulk of large nonprofit organizations. These sectors include the top hospitals and universities in the island, some of them exceeding annual revenues and assets of over one hundred million. The cooperative sector also includes large organizations. It is necessary to keep in mind that less than one-third of all the cooperatives filed 990 returns as IRS exempt organizations and therefore the average revenues and assets are not representative of the industry as a whole. According to the most recent financial filings submitted to the COSSEC in 2018, there were 114 cooperatives in Puerto Rico with $8.8 billion in assets, 996,132 members, and 2,899 employees (COSSEC 2018). A handful of credit unions are also CDFIs. Though the participation of coops in the affordable housing development industry is limited, a significant number of coops provide housing mortgages to their members.

However, whether nonprofit organizations can successfully navigate the dynamism and uncertainty of the disaster recovery process in Puerto

Table 3. IRS-Exempt Organization Returns Filed in Calendar Year 2019 (From 990 Forms)

Sector	Count	REVENUE Total	Average	ASSETS Total	Average
Arts, Culture, and Humanities	23	29,126,795	1,266,382	85,557,722	3,719,901
Cooperatives	16	141,527,602	8,845,475	2,525,222,028	157,826,377
Education	89	1,014,567,503	11,399,635	1,829,698,789	20,558,413
Health	81	1,378,082,922	17,013,369	1,495,944,636	18,468,452
Housing and Com. Devel.	58	46,655,404	804,404	173,006,470	2,982,870
Comm, Dev. Corp. (CDCs)	12	12,124,396	1,010,366	56,257,777	4,688,148
Human Services	117	176,099,476	1,505,124	200,975,876	1,717,743
Other Civic	53	167,839,988	3,166,792	158,677,918	2,993,923
Public Safety	29	76,149,905	2,625,859	514,656,348	17,746,771
TOTAL	466	3,030,049,595	6,476,234	6,983,739,787	50,566

Sources: https://www.irs.gov/statistics/soi-tax-stats-annual-extract-of-tax-exempt-organization-financial-data; and https://www.irs.gov/charities-non-profits/exempt-organizations-business-master-file-extract-eo-bmf/.

Rico remains an open question. Research shows that networking and communication can provide community organizations with new avenues of information and action (Quarantelli 1999), boost their diminished capacities, provide better means of community representation, and improve "cognition" of "emerging risk to which a community is exposed and to act on that information" (Comfort 2007). Evidence also suggests that neighborhoods that undertake social networking may be better able to respond to disasters because it facilitates information exchange, collective action, and access to new resources for recovery (Aldrich 2012). Community organizations play a critical role in disaster recovery, given their ability to motivate volunteerism, assess local needs, and distribute goods and aid (Patterson et al. 2010).

With support from the Center for Puerto Rican Studies, García and Chandrasekhar (2020) conducted a study to ascertain the role of nonprofits in disaster recovery, organizational and networking capacity, and to what extent they are implementing capacity-building measures. Selecting randomly from the universe of nonprofit organizations in Puerto Rico, they completed 235 telephone interviews as well as in-depth interviews with twenty-one residents and executive directors of agencies.

Table 4. Nonprofit Organizational Challenges in Puerto Rico Post-Maria

Category	Number	Percent
Affected buildings	105	45%
Loss of employees	16	7%
Loss of information or data	15	6%
More demand for services	34	14%
Lack of knowledge regarding reconstruction	9	4%
Other	55	24%
Total	234	100%

Source: García and Chandrasekhar (2020). Impact of Hurricane Maria to the civic sector and disaster recovery capacity in Puerto Rico Survey, 2019. Center for Puerto Rican Studies, Hunter College CUNY.

First, the survey requested organizations to identify the most frequent challenges that were faced since the hurricane. As depicted in Table 4 and might be expected, respondents reported the most frequent challenge faced since the hurricane were damages to their building infrastructure and facilities (45 percent). The second most frequent response was an increase in demand for services provided by the organization (14 percent). "Other" refers to loss of funding, lack of information on grants, greater bureaucracy, and lack of communication, among other answers. In terms of existing capacity, they found that the primary focus of organizations were education programs, with community development and health the next most prominent (Figure 3). Yet, it is noticeable that housing and economic development, the core activities of CDCs and the focus of reconstruction programs, were activities reported by a relatively small number of organizations, 20 percent or less of organizations.

Significant findings from the García and Chandrasekhar (2020) study are as follows:

1. the natural disaster had a significant impact in non-profit organizations physically and operationally, while interactions with other local nonprofits have increased substantially. But nonprofits organizations feel less connected to the government;

2. there is a lot of energy in the non-profit sector, as demonstrated by increased demand for services and changing missions to respond to this demand;

3. there has been intensified local interaction among non-profits; how-ever, non-profits are not "hooked" into formal recovery structures (funding or information) mainly relating to government, and it is somewhat of a surprise that disaster preparedness is not among the top choices for programmatic development; and

4. organizations want more help with capacity building across the board—from better understanding of recovery programs to grant-writing—to close a large gap between availability of funding and suc-cessful acquisition of grants.

The García and Chandrasekhar (2020) study indicates that local non-profit organizations are deeply embedded in communities and should be encouraged to participate in recovery efforts. Yet findings from the survey of nonprofit organizations in Puerto Rico indicate the urgent need to improve the capacity of local community organizations to participate more effec-tively in disaster recovery. There is a lack of organizations dedicated to or with the capacity to implement housing and economic development—which are key competencies required for local and federal recovery programs. Effective participation from nonprofit organizations would require access to government and federal recovery funding for community projects. In part, there is a great need for more inclusive policies that support local capac-ity building for reconstruction, and in part the allocation of funding needs to be more independent from the local political structure. According to responses to the survey, to date nonprofits participating in economic recov-ery are mostly being funded by private sources and members' contributions. Although nonprofit organizations might have knowledge about federal funding opportunities, they are not applying successfully for this funding or, when they apply, are not being successful in accessing these funds. Beside the need to have policies that encourage participation, these findings indi-cate that there is a clear need for technical assistance and capacity building for accessing federal funding. These findings from the survey are a first step torward an understanding of how nonprofit organizations have an interest and are eager to increase their capacity to engage in disaster recovery.

The Villarrubia-Mendoza and Vélez-Vélez (2020) study on the emerg-ing role of grassroots organizations in Post-Maria recovery, included as part

Figure 3. Objectives of Work Focus or Social Impact of Nonprofits in Puerto Rico

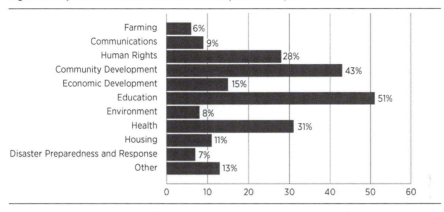

Source: García and Chandrasekhar (2020). Impact of Hurricane Maria to the civic sector and disaster recovery capacity in Puerto Rico Survey, 2019. Center for Puerto Rican Studies, Hunter College CUNY.

of this volume of *CENTRO Journal,* examines citizens grassroot participation and local engagement in disaster recovery in Puerto Rico through the prism of the emergence of community-based initiatives known as "centros de apoyo mutuo" (mutual support centers) or CAMs across the island. CAMs are projects based on principles of *"autogestión"* and are associated in the disaster recovery literature as grassroots community organizing, mutual aid (*"ayuda mutua," "apoyo mutuo"*), community empowerment and economic development, and social movements associated with resistance to top-down state initiatives.[7] The study involved over a year of ethnographic participant observation and conducted in-depth interviews with leaders and members of nine of the CAMs that emerged after the 2017 hurricanes. According to the Villarrubia-Mendoza and Vélez-Vélez (2020) study, CAMs engage in a wide range of projects and initiatives including community-coop housing programs, energy independence, sustainable agriculture, and entrepreneurship capacitation, among others. Through community engagement these organizations are redefining a vision of a more inclusive recovery process that encompasses a broader social transformation. They are confronting and raising awareness about pro-forma participation in CDBG funding hearings, denial of access to ownership deeds of abandoned schools and buildings, or the continued undermining of the basic needs of impacted communities.

Three years after Hurricane Maria devastated Puerto Rico, CAMs continue providing a grassroot model for reconstruction and community resilience, a model of a recovery process that questions how institutional structures have distributed the manifestation of damage. CAMs establish a framework that seek to improve socioeconomic conditions within their communities, producing a model for social transformation beyond the disaster context. As these grassroot groups engage in social entrepreneurship they are confronted with the challenges that nonprofit organizations in general confront—how to sustain these alternative models of recovery while continuing to challenge the current disaster recovery process and reconstruction programs. In the next section of this article I examine how nonprofit organizations and community development corporations (CDCs)—organizations that specialize in housing and community economic development—build capacity to be able to take advantage of the window of opportunity provided by the reconstruction process and disaster recovery

The Housing and Community Economic Development Industry and the Economic Recovery of Puerto Rico

There is a unique window of opportunity in Puerto Rico to capitalize on federal reconstruction funding to support the development of a more robust housing and community development industry, anchored on principles of social entrepreneurship as a foundation for neighborhood revitalization and local economic development. Social enterprises[8] and ventures are undertakings by private, nonprofit organizations or special units of local government that operate as businesses. Yet social enterprise, a core component of the stateside community development industry, which is also arguably the foundation of the most developed subsectors among nonprofits in Puerto Rico (e.g., cooperatives, education and health), is a critical need among community development and human services nonprofits in Puerto Rico, especially considering the critical role that the community development industry could play in economic reconstruction. There are numerous reasons for the existing capacity or lack thereof of the community development industry and the use of federal funding for the development of social projects in Puerto Rico. As I will discuss below, the absence of specific state-level policies benefiting and often impeding development, along with a weak support

Table 5. CDBG-DR Programs (Millions)

PROGRAM	ASSIGNMENT	PERCENTAGE
Planning	150	1.7%
Puerto Rico Geospatial Framework (GeoFrame) Program	50	
Municipal Recovery Planning Program	39	
Whole Community Resilience Planning Program	55	
Home Resilience Innovation Competition Program	6	
Housing	4,489	50.1%
Home Repair, Reconstruction, or Relocation Program	3,026	
Rental Assistance Program	10	
Homebuyer Assistance Program	350	
Title Clearance Program	40	
Social Interest Housing Program	33	
CDBG-DR Gap to Low Income Housing Tax Credits Program (LIHTC)	413	
Housing Counseling Program	18	
Community Energy and Water Resilience Installations Program	300	
Multi-family Reconstruction, Repair, and Resilience Program	300	
Economy	1,318	14.7%
Re-grow PR Urban-Rural Agriculture Program	93	
Small Business Incubators and Accelerators Program	35	
Small Business Financing Program	225	
Workforce Training Program	40	
Construction and Commercial Revolving Loan Program	100	
Economic Development Investment Portfolio for Growth Program	800	
Tourism & Business Marketing Program	25	
Infrastructure	1,475	16.5%
Non-Federal Match Program	1,000	
Community Resilience Centers Program	75	
Critical Infrastructure Resilience Program	400	
Multi-Sector	1,523	17.0%
City Revitalization Program	1,223	
Puerto Rico by Design Program	300	
Total	8,954	100%

Source: Puerto Rico Department of Housing, CDBG-DR Program. Accessed 10-6-20 from: https://cdbg-dr.pr.gov/en/.

system, are important factors holding back the nonprofit sector participation in federal economic recovery programs.

The distinction between community-based organizations (CBOs) and community development corporations (CDCs) is particularly relevant in the context of implementing federally funded recovery programs. Though both types of nonprofit organization are place-based, CDCs specialize in housing rehabilitation, affordable housing development, business development, and other revenue generating economic development projects (Meléndez and Servon 2007). These organizational capacities are necessary for most disaster recovery projects. Table 5 shows the CDBG-DR programs for Puerto Rico totaling $9 billion. Of this total, 50 percent of funding is devoted to housing, 15 percent to economic development, 14 percent to city (neighborhood) revitalization, and 1.2 percent to community planning. Besides having been incorporated under IRS Section 501(c)(3), affordable housing rehabilitation and construction program participation requires nonprofit organizations to be certified by the Department of Housing and Urban Development (HUD) as Community Housing Development Organization (CHDO), or to be certified as a Local Housing Counseling Agency (LHCA) to assist consumers to participate in HUD and other federal agencies housing subsidies programs. CDCs often obtain additional certifications from the U.S. Department of Treasury as a Community Development Financial Institution (CDFI) or a Community Development Entity (CDE). These certifications are a precondition for receiving federal funding for certain community development programs.[9] CBOs lacking these capacities face either a sudden capacity building challenge, or the need to partner with CDCs that possess these capacities and certifications to participate in federally funded reconstruction programs.

The relative size and strength of the housing and community development industry in Puerto Rico must be understood in the context of the nonprofit and cooperatives sectors. Assessing the housing and community development nonprofit subsector by the same metrics we used before, this subsector has the lowest averages for revenues and assets, except for the human services subsector (Table 3). If we consider the nonprofit sector to be inclusive of all the cooperatives, whether these are IRS exempt organizations or not, the total asset base of this sector as a whole in 2018 adds to over $13 billion in assets, of which the housing and community development sector and the CDC subsector represent a very small fraction. We have identified one dozen active CDCs, including some (currently or formerly) CHDOs, and about half a dozen CDFIs in Puerto Rico. In reference to Table 3, the CDCs in Puerto Rico rank as the organizations with the lowest average assets, and the second lowest average revenues. According to Borges-Méndez (2020), CDCs exhibit a wide range of capacity to implement development projects, most have limited capacity for housing and real estate development, and only few have undertaken any recovery-related projects other than housing rehabilitation and other emergency-related activities. As in the case of the community development industry in the United States, housing policy has had a determinant influence on the history of housing and community development in Puerto Rico, and it is perhaps the most significant element shaping the trajectory of the local industry.

In 2009 and 2010, nonprofit developers built more affordable housing using federal tax credits than private developers who up to that point (and after the ARRA program ended) dominated the industry.

In a study included in this special issue of *CENTRO Journal* and sponsored by the Center for Puerto Rican Studies, I identified three significant barriers that have hindered the development of the community economic development industry in Puerto Rico: the exclusionary role of federal and local recovery funding policy; the relative weakness of the industry ecosystem; and the relative scarcity of professionals with community development skills, especially professionals with the understanding of reconstruction programs (Meléndez 2020). The potential role that CDCs can play in the implementation of disaster recovery programs is illustrated by a case study of the impact of nonprofit developers in affordable housing construction after the American Recovery and Reinvestment Act (ARRA) of 2009 was enacted. In 2009 and 2010, nonprofit developers built more affordable housing using federal tax credits than private developers who up to that point (and after the ARRA program ended) dominated the

Figure 4. Community Economic Development Ecosystem

industry. During the four-year window provided by the ARRA funding, nonprofit developers built over 3,000 units of housing. This is a particularly important finding in the current context of post-disaster economic recovery and the use of CDBG-DR funding for housing rehabilitation, reconstruction, and new construction. Given an inclusive policy implementation, nonprofit developers were able to quickly respond to the challenge and developed as many units as the private sector, demonstrating a rapid deployment capability and surpassing private sector production in the initial years of the program (Meléndez 2020).

As illustrated in Figure 4, the community economic development ecosystem is integrated by CDCs, CDFIs and other financial intermediaries (such as capacity building and training vendors, often subsidiaries or affiliated with financial intermediaries), and other sector-specific networks that play a key role as regional and national advocacy coalitions for the advancement of the industry. Besides disaster mitigation and recovery funding, community economic development is financed through multiple federal programs, and often these programs are combined to finance different aspects of a project. programs broadly utilized in the industry include the LIHTC and HOME for subsidization of affordable housing, CDFIs for low interest community lending, New Market Tax Credits (NMTC) for commercial development, USDA programs for housing and other rural development, EDA programs for local economic development programs, SBA small business support programs, and many others. These federal programs are often paired with state and local subsidies. Yet, in Puerto Rico, many federal social purpose programs are grossly underutilized. The current window of opportunity for the island is given by the availability of reconstruction funding and of other underutilized non-disaster related federal programs. In Louisiana after Hurricane Katrina, for example, LIHTC 4-percent funding was combined with CDBG-DR for leveraging $1.1 billion for the development of 8,448 units, of which 63 percent were affordable (Severino 2018). In Puerto Rico, the current CDBG-DR program allocates $413 million to the LIHTHC-Gap program to provide gap funding for financing affordable rental housing units.

Puerto Rico has a relatively weak community economic development ecosystem. With the notable exception of Banco Popular, which holds a portfolio of affordable housing investments, the island has no significant community economic development financial intermediaries. However, disaster recovery programs offer an opportunity for emerging intermediaries to expand their portfolios. There are two nonprofit organizations that were created to serve as community development intermediaries with programs to support nonprofit and private organizations. Founded in 1984, the Puerto Rico Community Foundation (PRCF) is perhaps the oldest organization with an established program to support organizations' community-based economic development and social entrepreneurship, and to a far less extent, affordable housing. Founded in 2011, Foundation for Puerto Rico (FPR) is a nonprofit organization implementing an economic development initiative based on destination tourism in partnership with local governments and nonprofits organizations. Beginning in 2019, FPR received $37.5 million CDBG-DR funding from the Puerto Rico Department of Housing to lead the coordination of the Whole Community

Resilience Planning Program (Foundation for Puerto Rico 2019). According to the Foundation Center, in 2019, FPR and PRCF received $6 million in grants to support community organizations (Meléndez 2020, 143, Table 6).

Beside the FCPR and the FPR, there are two other important organizations that are initiating or renewing efforts for community development programs and potentially can have great impact on fostering social entrepreneurship in Puerto Rico. Two of the most important emerging community develop-ment intermediaries are established as public trusts. The Puerto Rico Science, Technology & Research Trust (PRTRT) has undertaken several social ventures and developed specific business development models that serve as capacity-building and financial intermediaries especially for technology companies. The PRDOH recently allocated $92.5 million from the CDBG-DR program to the PRTRT for the implementation of the Re-grow PR Urban-Rural Agriculture Program. Para la Naturaleza (PLN) is a nonprofit subsidiary of the Conservation Trust of Puerto Rico that oversees 42 natural areas throughout the island that are managed as social ventures, and implement fundraising, educational and volunteerism initiatives. These two public trusts have played a prominent role in reconstruction, implemented numerous programs with local community organizations, and have the revenues and assets capacity to evolve into anchors of the community development industry. Despite having a robust cooperative sector, evident gaps in the emergent community economic development indus-try eco-system are a specialized intermediary supporting and financing afford-able housing development, and a high-risk pre-development fund.

The development of CDCs and by implication the housing and com-munity development industry in Puerto Rico is in part a workforce devel-opment challenge (Meléndez 2020). In Puerto Rico, there is a wealth and abundant supply of well-trained, talented, and experienced nonprofit and business professionals but not enough professionals with the understand-ing of reconstruction programs and other federal programs supporting the housing and community development industry. A survey of professionals directly involved or overseeing programs that are part of or align with the economic and disaster recovery plans for Puerto Rico sponsored by the Center for Puerto Rican Studies documented a significant skills gap in criti-cal areas such as community engagement and planning, economic and hous-ing development, and disaster preparedness, recovery and resilience. Even among those most educated and actively engaged in the industry there is a recognition for the need for the development of professional skills in the industry moving forward (Meléndez 2020).

Too few CDCs with significant operational capacity are a tangible barrier to the potential expansion of financial intermediaries, the community economic development industry, and more specifically to the nonprofit sector participation in federally funded disaster recovery programs. CDCs typically maintain a steady pipeline of local development projects or the volume required for syndication and reasonable returns on the investment of financial intermediaries' organizational resources. In a study included in this volume and sponsored by the Center for Puerto Rican Studies, Borges-Méndez (2020) examines the organizational capacity and potential for participation in disaster recovery programs. Among the CDCs selected for the study, some were certified as CHDOs and CDFIs, but they operated other programs such as vocational education, special education, housing counseling, and others. This mix of education and social service, typical of CBOs, is related to the CDC's origins and mission. Many of them were created as CBOs and evolved into CDCs, while a smaller fraction were founded specifically for community economic development activities.

According to Borges-Méndez (2020), CDCs' experience with federal funding is limited and uneven. Though these CDCs have managed HUD (e.g., HOME, LIHTC) and FEMA (Public Assistance) contracts, they reported a limited capacity to prepare complex, multi-year projects, such as those of the CBDG-DR. Among the barriers for disaster recovery program participation they reported the following:

- The complexity of federal funding applications and the short project development cycle imposed by federal agencies;
- The limited project management and compliance expertise of the staff since every funding stream comes with its own reporting requirements;
- Limited outreach resources and methodologies to involve communities and other potential stakeholders in strategic planning, a salient requirement of federal applications.

In addition, CDC leaders were particularly critical of an opportunistic environment in the search for local and federal funding at the municipal level and would like disaster recovery programs to have greater autonomy from the island's political system and electoral cycle. Participating organizations recognized the imperative need to build organizational capacity in general and specifically for disaster programs participation but identified lack of funding and the "downtime" of senior staff while at training as practical impediments. They also would like to receive assistance for strategic planning and community engagement. In addition to these obstacles above, they identified several critical gaps in funding sources and project support:

1. "Lack of financial intermediaries to facilitate access to key pools of funding such as housing tax credits, new market tax credits, and the benefits and economic development incentives available through Opportunity Zones designations;

2. Difficulties in financing pre-development costs through the lengthy funding approval period, and compliance with project requirements;

3. Lack of information flows as a result of intentional political gatekeeping;

4. Lack of data, applied research, and information to document community needs, to elaborate proposals, and for project monitoring and evaluation" (Borges-Méndez 2020).

The experience of local CDCs with federal affordable housing and community development programs offers a foundation for scaling up non-profit sector participation in disaster recovery programs. Findings from the Borges-Méndez (2020) study indicate that there is a disconnection between local implementation of disaster recovery programs and CDCs with experience developing federally-funded housing and economic development programs. Collectively, these organizations have limited experience with recovery programs and require organizational capacity building to become competitive in the submission of proposals, and in the implementation and management of the projects. Yet a fraction of them already have a proven track record of project completion and are overcoming barriers to expand their participation in disaster recovery programs.

Policy, CDBG-DR Program Implementation, and Disaster Governance Models
In contrast to the example of ARRA stimulus funding presented earlier, we have documented that current recovery funding policy in Puerto Rico large-

ly excludes nonprofit developers. Puerto Rico's policy programs for disaster recovery are centralized into two agencies: the Puerto Rico Department of Housing (PRDOH) for the allocation of CDBG-DR and CDBG-MIT funding, and the Central Office of Recovery, Reconstruction and Resiliency (COR3) for the management of FEMA-funded programs. In a study included in this volume and sponsored by the Center for Puerto Rican Studies, Torres Cordero (2020) asserts that these two agencies function independently of each other and, in comparison to other U.S. jurisdictions, centralize decision-making, while the implementation of programs is restricting municipal and nonprofit sector participation in publicly sponsored reconstruction projects. The conventional practice in most states is to integrate reconstruction programs under one agency and set up governance structures that promote interagency collaboration and coordination with federal agencies and are more inclusive of local governments and nonprofit organizations. In light of these circumstances, Torres Cordero asserts that "current federal guidelines for the use of CDBG-DR funds allow for a certain measure of discretion and interpretation that the Government of Puerto Rico can elect to exercise or not in order to develop more equitable programs aimed at producing a better and more just recovery" (2020, 200).

Torres Cordero (2020) identified governance models in jurisdictions affected by hurricanes with experience managing federal disaster programs and a collection of practices that foster local involvement and equitable access to resources and programs. Case studies for CDBG-DR governance models in Puerto Rico, Louisiana, South Carolina, Florida, and Texas provide specific examples of local structural arrangements and policies that support local participation and build nonprofit organizations' capacity for community and economic development. Though the mechanisms for more inclusive participation vary, examples of local policy implementation within current federal law include:

- subrecipient agreements to provide direct allocations to local governments (Louisiana, post-hurricanes Gustav and Ike, 2008);
- multiple local grantees including partnerships with nonprofit housing developers and community development corporations (South Carolina, post-Hurricane Joaquin, 2015);
- regional differentiation through RFPs and joint ventures and part-

nerships between government agencies and for-profit and nonprofit organizations (Florida, post-Hurricane Irma, 2017); and

- supplemental action planning and amendments to the action plan to redistribute resources from the state to county and city levels (Texas, post-Hurricane Harvey, 2017).

Evidently, these examples highlight potential policy reforms in Puerto Rico that will lead to more inclusive practices for municipalities and nonprofit organizations. All these reforms are within the authority of the governor of Puerto Rico. Torres Cordero (2020, 220) concludes the study with a call to action:

The maneuvers referenced in this study are by no means easy to implement and might require significant structural and programmatic changes to the ways that disaster recovery is managed and resourced. The decision is not whether to change or not—the fact or reality is that change is inevitable. The decision is how to change in a manner that is equitable and that leads to a just recovery. The cases examined here show that incremental changes are possible; however, awareness and coalition building are crucial first steps toward the design and implementation of more inclusive and equitable policies. Further, what cannot be immediately changed, can be brought to light—and casting such a light on policy failures in clear and descriptive terms is a necessary precursor to change.

Conclusions and Recommendations

Post-disaster planning and federal funding for economic recovery offer Puerto Rico a unique window of opportunity—to restore its economy and infrastructure in a more resilient fashion. However, such an opportunity hinges on local participation to join government efforts in planning and then executing a comprehensive reconstruction and recovery program. Our main goal with this volume of *CENTRO Journal* is to provide an assessment of local participation in the economic recovery of Puerto Rico. The studies included in this volume provide an assessment of businesses and the nonprofit and municipal sectors' participation in the economic recovery of Puerto Rico to date, and the contingencies such as more inclusionary policies and capacity-building initiatives that may shape such participation in the future.

But nonprofit and grassroots organizing efforts are confronted with the challenge of how to build capacity to be able to take advantage of the window of opportunity provided by the reconstruction process and disaster recovery programs.

Findings from the aforementioned studies indicate that the nonprofit and business sectors had a wide participation in the immediate emergency phase of the post-disaster recovery, primarily supported by private donations and investments, with minimal support from the local or federal government. We also saw grassroot efforts for reconstruction and community resilience, such as the CAMs, that integrates natural disaster and social reconstruction. But nonprofit and grassroots organizing efforts are confronted with the challenge of how to build capacity to be able to take advantage of the window of opportunity provided by the reconstruction process and disaster recovery programs. Their capacity to participate in the post-disaster economic recovery phase hereon is constrained due to the limited experience in the sector with housing and economic development, and mitigation and resiliency-building programs, which constitute the focus of the long-term post-disaster federal economic recovery programs.

In this context, federal recovery programs implementation, and more specifically recovery funding policy, have resulted in the outright exclusion or minimal participation of nonprofit developers in publicly-sponsored reconstruction projects in Puerto Rico to date.

The recent awards for housing rehabilitation and reconstruction were solely awarded to the private sector, with 62 percent of the contracts awarded to foreign corporations. In contrast, CDCs and nonprofit developers demonstrated that, when given the opportunity during the ARRA program, they were able to build more than 3,000 units of housing using the LIHTC program and surpassed the number of housing units built by the for-profit sector. The Torres Cordero (2020) study introduces concrete examples of policies implemented in other jurisdictions benefiting from CDBG-DR and other federal disaster programs that are more equitable by supporting inclusiveness of local governments and nonprofit organizations.

These general findings from the studies included in this volume serve as a foundation for policy and community strategies recommendations.

Policy Reform

1. Enact local inclusionary policy reforms consistent with federal disaster recovery programs to support decentralization and municipal participation, and nonprofit developers and CDCs participation. These policies include subrecipient agreements to provide direct allocations to municipalities, promoting partnerships with nonprofit housing developers and community development corporations, regional differentiation through RFPs and joint ventures and partnerships between government agencies, for-profit and nonprofit organizations, and supplemental action planning and amendments to the action plan to redistribute resources from the state to county and city levels.

2. Development of a low-cost, high-risk predevelopment fund to support existing CDCs with some experience in housing and other community development activities. In addition to subsidizing predevelopment costs, CDCs require technical support for submitting competitive proposals to FEMA, CDBG-DR, and other economic recovery targeted funding, as well as for the combination of such funds with other traditional community development programs such as housing tax credits, new market tax credits, USDA programs, and opportunity zones.

Organizational Capacity-Building

3. Development of supports for non-profits to become CDCs though professional development for current staff on housing and community economic development, for understanding federal funding for economic recovery, and for partnerships with established CDCs or other intermediaries for implementing projects.

4. Development of professional training for post-disaster economic recovery that will be delivered as comprehensive continuing education courses, via online or other structured seminars.

Industry Ecosystem

5. Strengthening community development intermediaries to provide technical assistance to nonprofit organizations and developers. In particular, Puerto Rico needs a specialized Community Development Financial Institution (CDFI) for housing, financing, and development.

These financial intermediaries are important for understanding the plethora of federal programs available to nonprofit developers, including complex transactions involving syndication and the combination of funding required for most housing and commercial development projects, and the complexity of bidding, managing, and complying with federal recovery programs.

6. Creation of a hub for the exchange of information and networking to make available a directory of individuals and organizations, a calendar of activities, and opportunities for volunteerism and collaborations.

7. Creation of a data hub for easy access to interactive GIS maps available for each community and municipality in the island, to construct visualizations for community planning and contribute to crowd-sourcing data efforts, and for the training of community groups on the use of the platform for community planning and development for post-disaster economic recovery.

In sum, post-disaster federal funding for economic recovery offers Puerto Rico a unique window of opportunity to restore its economy and infrastructure in a more resilient fashion while strengthening the nonprofit sector's capacity for community planning, housing development, and neighborhood revitalization. However, such an opportunity is contingent on implementing a comprehensive strategy for reforming public policy to encourage and support nonprofit developers participation in reconstruction programs, building industry capacity by strengthening intermediaries and CDCs, encouraging intra-industry partnerships and collaborations, and providing professional development for economic recovery.

NOTES

[1] FEMA's Spending Explorer, Data as of 7/31/20. Figure includes various Congressional allocations though both FEMA and SBA for Hurricanes Harvey, Irma, Maria, 2017, CA Wildfires, and other 2017 Disasters; Harvey, Irma, Maria, 2017, CA Wildfires, and other 2017 Disasters (PL 115-123); Harvey, Irma, Maria, 2017, and CA Wildfires (PL 115-156); Harvey, Irma, Maria, 2017, and CA Wildfires (PL 115-72).

[2] The IEA correlates highly with the Gross National Product and is used as an early indicator of economic activity.

[3<7>] To estimate these elements—damage, exposure, and recovery—we used 28 indicator variables in a linear discriminant analysis (LDA) to calculate the RIM index, and then classified counties into the RIM's four categories (susceptible, recovering, resilient, and usurper counties) corresponding to low, medium- low, medium-high, and high community resilience.

[4] The Charitable Sector <https://independentsector.org/about/the-charitable-sector/#:~:text=The%20nonprofit%20sector%20%E2%80%93%2010%20percent,2.7%20percent%20increase%20from%202015/>.

[5] Differences Between NGOs and Nonprofits <https://www.the-balancesmb.com/differences-between-ngos-and-nonprofits-4589762#:~:text=Nonprofits%20can%20be%20called%20non,disaster%20relief%20and%20human%20rights/>.

[6] Subtracting cooperatives that are registered as nonprofits with the IRS, which are counted as nonprofits.

[7] *Autogestión* is defined as a perspective on development and social organizing that centers peoples' right to self-determination and participation in the socioeconomic and political sphere of their communities.

[8] A social enterprise is an organization that applies commercial strategies to maximize improvements in financial, social, and environmental well-being — this may include maximizing social impact alongside profits for external shareholders. See <https://en.wikipedia.org/wiki/Social_enterprise/>.

[9] In addition, some states and state-wide associations of CDC require local certifications for local program participation. In Puerto Rico, there is no specific legal definition for CDCs at the state level, yet nonprofit organizations seeking federal funding from specific programs will need to comply with various required certifications (e.g., as CHDO or LHCA).

REFERENCES

Aldrich, D. P. 2012. *Building Resilience: Social Capital in Post-Disaster Recovery*. Chicago: University of Chicago Press.

Lobato, Manuel, Marta Álvarez and Marinés Aponte. 2020. Entrepreneurial dynamics in Puerto Rico before and after Hurricane María. *CENTRO: Journal of the Center for Puerto Rican Studies* 32(3), 39–66.

Borges-Méndez, Ramón. 2020. Community Development Corporations and Reconstruction Policy in Puerto Rico. *CENTRO: Journal of the Center for Puerto Rican Studies* 32(3), 157–98.

Comfort, L. 2007. Crisis Management in Hindsight: Cognition, Communication, Coordination, and Control. *Public Administration Review* 67, 189–97.

Correa, Pedro. 2020. FEMA approves 500-plus hazard mitigation proposals for evaluation. *The San Juan Daily Star*. Accessed 26 November 2020. <https://www.sanjuandailystar.com/post/fema-approves-500-plus-hazard-mitigation-proposals-for-evaluation/>.

COSSEC, Corporación Pública para Supervisión y Seguro de Cooperativas de Puerto Rico. 2018. Total de activos, número de socios y de empleados, por cooperativa. 30 junio. Accessed 30 August 2020. <http://www.cossec.com/cossec_new/est/Junio18/Anejo_9_Total_de_Activos,_Socios_y_Empleados_Tiempo_Completo_Por_Cooperativa_jun_2018.pdf/>.

Dyer, Christopher L. 1999. The Phoenix Effect in Post-Disaster Recovery: An Analysis of the Economic Development Administration's Culture of Response after Hurricane Andrew. In *The Angry Earth: Disaster in Sociological Perspective*, eds. A. O.-S. a. S. Hoffman. New York: Routledge.

Eller, Warren, Brian J. Gerber and Lauren E. Branch. 2015. Voluntary Nonprofit Organizations and Disaster Management: Identifying the Nature of Inter-Sector Coordination and Collaboration in Disaster Service Assistance Provision. *Risk, Hazards & Crisis in Public Policy* 6(2), 223–38.

Fadulu, Lola and Mark Walker. 2020. Trump Attaches Severe Restrictions to Puerto Rico's Long-Delayed Disaster Aid. *The New York Times* 15 January. <https://www.nytimes.com/2020/01/15/us/politics/trump-puerto-rico-disaster-aid.html/>.

Federal Emergency Management Agency (FEMA). 2017. Pre-Disaster Recovery Planning Guide for Local Governments. FEMA Publication FD 008-03, February.

_____. 2018. Puerto Rico One Year after Hurricanes Irma and María. <https://www.fema.gov/news-release/2018/09/06/puerto-rico-one-year-after-hurricanes-irma-and-maria/>.

Foundation for Puerto Rico. 2019. Foundation for Puerto Rico Begins Phase One Of Whole Community Resilience Program. 15 January. Accessed 31 August 2020. <https://static1.squarespace.com/static/59e4cf35a8b2b019331ce112/t/5c3e08c203ce640330cd5e0e/1547569347160/FOUNDATION+FOR+PUERTO+RICO+BEGINS+PHASE+ONE_ENGLISH_01-15-19-converted.pdf/>.

García, Ivis and Divya Chandrasekhar. 2020. Impact of Hurricane María to the Civic Sector: A Profile of Non-Profits in Puerto Rico. *CENTRO: Journal of the Center for Puerto Rican Studies* 32(3), 67–88.

Koliou, Maria, John W. van de Lindt, Therese P. McAllister, Bruce R. Ellingwood, Maria Dillard and Harvey Cutler. 2018. State of the Research in Community Resilience: Progress and Challenges. *Sustain Resilient Infrastructure* 10.

Lam, Nina S. N., Margaret Reams, Kenan Li, Chi Li and Lillian P. Mata. 2016. Measuring Community Resilience to Coastal Hazards along the Northern Gulf of Mexico. *Natural Hazards Review* 17(1).

Luna, Emmanuel M. 2013. Community-Based Disaster Risk Reduction and Disaster Management. *Disaster Management*. 12 November. <https://doi.org/10.4324/9780203082539-15/>.

Martín, Carlos. 2018. The Evidence Based on how CDBG-DR Works for State And Local
   Stakeholders. Statement of Carlos Martín, Senior Fellow, Urban Institute,
   before the Subcommittee on Oversight and Investigations, Committee on
   Financial Services, United States House of Representatives. 17 May.
Meléndez, Edwin. 2020. Puerto Rico Housing and Community Development
   Industry's Capacity for Disaster Recovery. *CENTRO: Journal of the Center
   for Puerto Rican Studies* 32(3), 118–56.
Meléndez, Edwin and Lisa J. Servon. 2007. Reassessing the Role of Housing in
   Community-Based Urban Development. *Housing Policy Debate* 18(4), 751–83.
Mileti, Dennis S. 1999. *Disasters By Design: A Reassessment of Natural Hazards in
   the United States.* Washington: Joseph Henry Press.
Office of Economic Studies. 2020. The Puerto Rico Economic Activity Index
   ("EDB-EAI"). Economic Development Bank for Puerto Rico, September.
Patterson, O., F. Weil and K. Patel. 2010. The Role of Community in Disaster
   Response: Conceptual Models. *Population Research and Policy Review* 29(2),
   127–41.
Peacock, Walter Gillis, Betty Hearn Morrow, and Hugh Gladwin. 1997. *Hurricane Andrew:
   Ethnicity, Gender, and the Sociology of Disasters.* New York: Routledge.
Red de Fundaciones de Puerto Rico. 2019. Philanthropy and Puerto Rico After
   Hurricane Maria: How a Natural Disaster Put Puerto Rico on the
   Philanthropic Map and Implications for the Future. San Juan, Puerto Rico.
Quarantelli, E. L. 1999. The disaster recovery process: What we know and do not
   know from research. Preliminary Paper #286. University of Delaware:
   Disaster Research Center.
Robinson, Scott E. and Haley Murphy. 2014. Frontiers for the Study of Nonprofit
   Organizations in Disasters. *Risk, Hazards & Crisis in Public Policy* 4(2), 128–34.
Severino Kathya. 2018. Rebuild Puerto Rico: A Guide to Federal Policy and
   Advocacy. New York: Center for Puerto Rican Studies. <https://
   centropr.hunter.cuny.edu/sites/default/files/data_briefs/CENTRO_
   POLICYGUIDE_PB2018-02.pdf/>.
Smith, Gavin and Thomas Birkland. 2012. Building a Theory of Recovery: Institutional
   Dimensions. *Journal of Mass Emergencies and Disasters* 3092), 147–70.
Torres Cordero, Ariam L. 2020. What Is Possible? Policy Options For Long-Term
   Disaster Recovery in Puerto Rico. *CENTRO: Journal of the Center for
   Puerto Rican Studies* 32(3), 199–223.
Villarrubia-Mendoza, Jacqueline and Roberto Vélez-Vélez. 2020. Centros de Apoyo
   Mutuo: reconfigurando la asistencia en tiempos de desastre. *CENTRO:
   Journal of the Center for Puerto Rican Studies* 32(3), 89–117.
Welsh, Mark G. and Ann-Margaret Esnard. 2009. Closing Gaps in Local Housing
   Recovery Planning for Disadvantaged Displaced Households. *Cityscape:
   A Journal of Policy Development and Research* 11(2), 195–212.

Entrepreneurial Dynamics in Puerto Rico Before and After Hurricane María

MANUEL LOBATO, MARTA ÁLVAREZ AND MARINÉS APONTE

ABSTRACT

Entrepreneurship is crucial for the future of Puerto Rico. Hurricane María hit the Island on September 2017, in the midst of a long recession, a period of employment loss and very low rates of new business creation. This paper studies the effect of the Hurricane on the entrepreneurial activity of the island by comparing important entrepreneurial indicators before and after the event. The research is based on data from the Bureau of Labor Statistics, the Global Entrepreneurship Monitor (GEM) and the Puerto Rico Community Survey. The immediate effect of the hurricane and its aftermath was unusually high levels of closings of establishments and employment contraction. After the first impact, this dynamic was combined with a sudden increase of new entrepreneurial initiatives, as entrepreneurs identified business opportunities in this new scenario. These dynamics are similar to those observed in Louisiana after Hurricane Katrina. [Key words: entrepreneurship, Puerto Rico, hurricane, economic development]

Manuel Lobato (manuel.lobato@upr.edu) is a professor at the Department of Finance, School of Business, University of Puerto Rico, Río Piedras, and co-manager of the Center to Foster Innovation and Commercialization (UPR i+c). He is also researcher of Global Entrepreneurship Monitor (GEM) Puerto Rico. Lobato has a PhD in International and Development Economics and conducted several surveys on innovation and R&D activities.

Introduction

This paper focuses on the dynamics of entrepreneurial initiatives in Puerto Rico after Hurricane María hit the island in September 2017. This is a crucial subject, because the rates of entrepreneurial ventures in this economy are very low when compared to other countries or states. Current structural changes and future growth in Puerto Rico are conditioned by this fact. The focus of public attention in Puerto Rico is usually directed towards the entries and exits of multinational corporations and their impact on employment, but the undergoing process of economic transformation relies on domestic entrepreneurs. In this context, the dynamics of entrepreneurial initiatives deserve special attention. The proper understanding of these dynamics can lead to strategies that strengthen the network of small and medium entrepreneurial ventures or support the emergence of domestic startups.

Entrepreneurship is herein understood as a behavioral characteristic of individuals, not an occupation. It refers to the ability and willingness of individuals to perceive and create new economic opportunities (alone or with others), and to introduce their ideas into the market (Wennekers and Thurik 1999; Carree and Thurik 2010). Entrepreneurial initiatives include formal and informal ventures, even just temporary or part-time activities.

The hurricane and its aftermath affected everyone on the island. Families and companies struggled with damaged infrastructures, the interruption of communications and a blackout that lasted for months. Although this

Marta Álvarez (marta.alvarez1@upr.edu) is a professor at the Institute of Statistics and Computer Information Systems, School of Business, University of Puerto Rico, Río Piedras. She has a PhD in Statistics from Texas A&M University. She has been Director of the School of Business Research Center and a member of the Board of Directors of the Institute of Statistics of Puerto Rico. She is data manager and researcher for the Global Entrepreneurship Monitor Puerto Rico team.

Marinés Aponte (marines.aponte@upr.edu) is a professor at the Department of Finance, School of Business, University of Puerto Rico, Río Piedras Campus. She has a PhD in Entrepreneurship and Management from the Autonomous University of Barcelona, Department of Economics and Business. She has been the director of the Finance Department, the Entrepreneurial Program and the Cooperative Institute. She is the Puerto Rico National Team Leader and PI in the Global Entrepreneurship Monitor (GEM) international research study.

translated into an immediate contraction in the entrepreneurial activity, the adverse conditions led many people to behavioral adaptation and lifestyle changes. As will be seen in this paper, after one quarter the trend on business creation reversed, and one year after the hurricane the number of entrepreneurial ventures was growing at its highest rates.

Entrepreneurs are agents of change, but the link between entrepreneurship and economic growth is not linear. The outcome of the entrepreneurial dynamics depends on factors such as the local environment, the internal culture of corporations, and the institutional framework in the society and within firms, among others. These will define the incentives system for entrepreneurs and the barriers that hamper their initiatives (Carree and Thurik 2010).

Before getting into the analysis of entrepreneurial activity, the next section will present a background of the economic policy in Puerto Rico during the last decades, and how it turned into a very long recession. The number of establishments and other indicators of entrepreneurial activity dropped when the recession began and remained low until recent times.

Section 3 goes into the numbers of pre- and post-María entrepreneurial activity. The section begins with an analysis of the changes in the context of the entrepreneurial activity, as the hurricane affected not only business, but also the factors that promote or hinder the initiatives of the entrepreneurs. Then, detailed data of changes in establishment openings and closings, their survival rate and several indicators of early-stage entrepreneurship are presented. This data includes information about the profile of the entrepreneurs and the variations observed after the hurricane.

The entrepreneurial dynamics may be better understood after María. This experience is not an isolated episode or anecdotic for entrepreneurial studies. Section 4 compares what happened in Puerto Rico after Hurricane María with the changes in entrepreneurial activity observed in Louisiana after Hurricane Katrina in 2005. The final section discusses the findings of the whole research and presents some concluding remarks.

Background

Puerto Rico is a modern economy. Its production is led by the manufacturing of pharmaceuticals, chemicals and electronic products[1]; investment in R&D

activities amounts to 0.43 percent of the GDP[2]; and 30 percent of the population between 25 and 64 years old has a bachelor's degree or higher[3]. To a large extent, this is a result of its particular political economy over decades.

In the 1950s and 60s, the Puerto Rican government defined an innovative strategy to foster industrialization and accelerate economic growth. Initially it had sketched a program to spur and protect domestic corporations in strategic sectors, guided by the example of other governments in Latin America. Discouraged by the difficulties to implement it and the early results, it soon decided to shift the economic policy towards foreign corporations. Puerto Rico managed to provide extraordinary tax benefits to U.S. companies that built subsidiary factories in its territory. This drew the attention of multinational firms, who were also attracted by the island's low salaries and the political link between Puerto Rico and the U.S. (which, from a business perspective, meant protection by the U.S. law, political stability and absence of customs). Operation Bootstrap was born. This "industrialization by invitation" strategy effectively led to high growth rates, but also posed sensitive weaknesses in the long term over the economic structure (Dietz 1989; Martínez, Máttar and Rivera 2005).

The termination of section 936 was the deathblow, even with its 10-year transitional period until the full implementation of this decision.

Policy makers expected the development of a network of domestic entrepreneurs. It would spontaneously emerge as the multinational corporations settled in Puerto Rico looked for suppliers or hired local managers, which in turn would develop the skills to create their own world-class business. This happened, but not at the scale that was expected. Large U.S. corporations led the growth and transformations of the economy of Puerto Rico until the end of the 20th century (Martínez et al. 2005; Caraballo-Cueto and Lara 2018).

In 1996, the U.S. Congress decided to terminate section 936 of the U.S. Internal Revenue Code, which provided tax exemptions to U.S. corporations with subsidiaries in Puerto Rico. At that time, the erosion of the other factors underlying Operation Bootstrap was evident. Salaries were no longer competitive with low-cost economies, international agreements between the U.S. and other countries in Latin America reduced the burden of customs in trade, and many other countries had developed fiscal policies to attract large corporations. Under the new scenario of globalization, the uniqueness of Puerto Rico vanished (Martínez et al. 2005; Caraballo-Cueto and Lara 2018). The termination of section 936 was the deathblow, even with its 10-year transitional period until the full implementation of this decision.

The new century began under the pressure of private companies' divestment. Public policy efforts were hesitant between defining new fiscal incentives to foreign companies and embarking on a new economic model. Meanwhile, government spending sustained the economy, but in 2006 Puerto Rico finally entered in a long recession period. The deindustrialization process mixed with the failure of the government to define and implement new development strategies led to an inevitable production decline, even with increasing levels of governmental debt (Caraballo-Cueto and Lara 2018; Gluzmann, Guzmán and Stiglitz 2018; Meléndez 2018). The domestic private sector was not ready to become the new engine. An economy with low rates of entrepreneurial activity and employment was not able to cope with the structural changes (Álvarez, Aponte and Lobato 2018).

The long recession

Puerto Rico's real Gross National Product growth experienced negative rates every year between 2006 and 2017, as can be seen in Table 1, except in 2012, when the rate was 0.5 percent. It is one of the longest recessions ever registered in any economy. According to the Puerto Rico Planning Board, GNP was $57.9 billion in 2006 and $70.0 billion in 2017 in current prices, but when measured in constant prices (of 1954), it went from $7.4 billion to $6.0 billion, which is an 18-percent decrease in those 11 years. After the hurricane, it dropped to $5.7 billion, setting the total loss on 22 percent when compared to 2006 numbers.

Table 1 also shows that labor market provided employment to 1.25 million in 2006 and peaked in 2007 with 1.26 million, according to data from the Puerto Rico Department of Labor and Human Resources. The participation rate then was 48.6 percent, which was very low compared

Table 1. Indicators of production and employment in Puerto Rico, 2006 to 2017

							Fiscal Year						
	2006	2007	2008	2009	2010	2011	2012	2013	2014	2015	2016	2017	2018
Gross National Product (GNP)													
Gross National Product (GNP) (in millions of dollars, current prices)	$57,854	$60,643	$62,703	$63,618	$64,295	$65,721	$68,086	$68,945	$68,798	$69,602	$69,985	$70,000	$68,049
Gross National Product (GNP) (in millions of dollars, constant prices of 1954)	$7,351	$7,262	$7,054	$6,784	$6,542	$6,432	$6,466	$6,458	$6,344	$6,292	$6,192	$6,007	$5,727
GNP's growth rate, real terms	0.5	-1.2	-2.9	-3.8	-3.6	-1.7	0.5	-0.1	-1.8	-0.8	-1.6	-3.0	-4.7
Employment													
Employment, total (in thousands of persons)	1,254	1,263	1,203	1,144	1,075	1,043	1,024	1,012	987	977	989	982	971
Participation rate	48.6	48.6	46.6	45.5	44.1	42.8	41.7	40.9	40.3	39.6	40.0	40.1	40.1
Number of employed persons in establishments, by major industrial sector (in thousands of persons)													
Mining, Logging & Construction	66	65	60	49	36	32	35	34	28	27	24	22	23
Manufacturing	113	108	104	97	88	86	84	79	75	75	74	73	71
Trade, Transportation & Utilities	189	184	181	176	173	174	174	177	177	175	174	174	165
Information				23	23	23	21	20	19	19	19	19	20
Financial Industries	50	49	48	49	46	44	44	44	43	43	42	43	42
Professional and Business Services	107	109	108	103	103	106	109	113	115	113	113	116	119
Educational and Health Services					104	105	109	110	111	114	118	122	123
Leisure and Hospitality	75	74	73	71	71	71	73	77	79	81	81	81	75
Other Services	24	22	21	20	19	18	18	18	18	18	17	18	17
Government	302	302	302	302	302	302	302	302	302	302	302	302	302

Data sources: Economic reports to the Governor, Government of Puerto Rico Planning Board.

to the rates in the United States (66%) and other countries. Afterwards, the number of jobs shrunk every year. In 2017, there were 982,000 persons employed, a 22-percent decline compared to 2007. In 2018, it was 971,000. The participation rate went down to an unprecedented 40 percent (and even below 40 percent in 2015)[4].

Feliciano (2018) links the U.S. Congress's decision to end Section 936 with a large, direct negative impact on employment in manufacturing sectors, and this dynamic extended to the whole economy as the recession expanded and developed. News of closing plants of multinational corporations came on a monthly basis. Between 2008 and 2010, there was a steep decline in employment in construction, information and other services sectors. The number of people employed by the government was stable these first years of the recession, but since 2010 it shrunk, going from 300,000 to 213,000 in 2018.

The recession had a profound effect also on domestic entrepreneurial activity, as will be seen in the following section. Nevertheless, Álvarez et al. (2018) point out the reduction was not due to unusual rates of existing establishment closings, but to the lack of new establishments.

These adverse economic conditions led thousands of people to migrate to the United States. The decline in fertility rates made things even worse. According to the U.S. Census Bureau estimates, in 2006 there were 3.93 million residents in Puerto Rico and 3.94 in 2007; it went down to 3.33 million in 2017, which is 16 percent less than in 2007. Hurricane María and its aftermath pushed migration flows, and the population dropped to 3.2 million in 2018.

Caraballo-Cueto and Lara (2018) claim that the deindustrialization process and the prolonged recession led to the bankruptcy of the government of Puerto Rico. Even before the recession began, the government sustained its public expenditures through public debt, but this strategy could not last forever. As the recession extended over the years, public finances tightened, and finally the credit of Puerto Rico collapsed (Meléndez 2018; Gluzmann et al. 2018).

In 2014, the main bond credit rating agencies gave non-investment grades to the general obligations and other bonds of the Puerto Rican government and its agencies. Governor García-Padilla announced in 2015 that Puerto Rico's debt was unpayable. The U.S. Congress enacted the Puerto Rico Oversight, Management and Economic Stability Act (PROMESA) in

2016, in order to provide a legal framework for the public debt restructuring process. A Financial Oversight and Management Board for Puerto Rico was set up to oversee Puerto Rico's finances and lead the way back to capital markets. According to Meléndez (2018), this is still insufficient, and long-term economic development depends on further Congressional action: "austerity alone will not solve the problem. Puerto Rico cannot simply cut its way into solvency" (Meléndez 2018, 99).

Pre and post-María entrepreneurial activity

In general terms, recessions involve contradictory dynamics in entrepreneurial activity. Lack of demand in the markets and financial constraints have a cleansing effect, cause business bankruptcies and disable new initiatives (Caballero and Hammour 1994; Rampini 2004; Klapper and Love 2011). On the other hand, lack of employment opportunities pushes people to self-employment initiatives (Evans and Leighton 1990); Parker (2009) calls this the "recession push" and considers that this effect encourages marginal types of entrepreneurship.

Adding to the effects of the recession, the aftermath of Hurricane María led to sudden changes in the economic situation of many people, and at the same time business opportunities arose. In this context, new ventures were born. Bosma and Harding (2007) distinguish between necessity-driven and opportunity-driven initiatives to highlight that some people are pulled into entrepreneurship when they have no other means of making a living, while others identify an opportunity and at the same time desire independence or to increase their income. Nevertheless, Williams (2008) suggest that in the case of entrepreneurial activity in the informal economy, both necessity and opportunity drivers are involved in making the decision to start a venture. Also, the motivations of these entrepreneurs shift from necessity-oriented to opportunity-oriented as their initiatives become more established.

The net effects of a recession over entrepreneurial activity depend on many factors. Some contexts are more prone to entrepreneurial initiatives than others. How the different factors in Puerto Rico influence entrepreneurial activity is not only relevant to understand the dynamics during the recession, but also to compare the situation before and after the hurricane impacted the island.

An infertile context

Before Hurricane María, Puerto Rico was already perceived as an infertile place for entrepreneurs, as different studies highlight.

The Global Entrepreneurship Monitor (GEM) is the world's leading research project in entrepreneurship. It is an international, longitudinal investigation that studies the emergence and development of entrepreneurial activity in participating economies. The project, which began in 1999 with ten economies, has grown to include 50 to 60 economies each year. Puerto Rico has been participating consecutively since 2013.

GEM administers two surveys and uses secondary sources, enabling a comparison of the rates, conditions, and factors that influence business creation among participating countries. The Adult Population Survey (APS) is delivered to a randomly selected sample of at least 2,000 adults aged 18 to 64 in each country. The National Experts Survey (NES) collects the assessment of a group of national experts about contextual factors and framework conditions that may influence entrepreneurial activity in an economy.

For the year 2017, the mean of the scores provided by all Puerto Rico experts were under 5, in a Likert scale from 1 to 9, in all factors except physical infrastructure. This means that the factors' contribution to the promotion of entrepreneurship is considered insufficient. The lowest scores were assigned to taxes and bureaucracy, and to entrepreneurial education at school level. All mean scores, except that of entrepreneurial education at post-school levels, were also under average compared to all participating countries in GEM. In fact, these negative results have been repeated year after year since GEM conducted its first survey in Puerto Rico in 2013, even when the experts change every year (Aponte, Álvarez and Lobato 2018). The Global Entrepreneurship Monitor (GEM) 2018-2019 Global Report ranks Puerto Rico's entrepreneurial context among the less favorable for businesses, in the 51st position out of 54 economies (Bosma and Kelley 2019).

The Ease of Doing Business 2020 report ranks Puerto Rico in the 65th position out of 190 countries, a drop from the 64th position in 2018 and the 55th in 2017 (World Bank Group 2017).

"Ease of Doing Business" is aligned with this perspective. In this annual report, the World Bank measures and compares the performance of countries across different parameters related to the activities of small and mid-sized companies, including starting a business and dealing with permits, taxes, electricity, property registration, credit availability, export activities, contract enforcement, investor protection and insolvency. It is widely used for academic research and public policy evaluation. The Ease of Doing Business 2020 report ranks Puerto Rico in the 65th position out of 190 countries, a drop from the 64th position in 2018 and the 55th in 2017 (World Bank Group 2017). This result is a combination of very good evaluations in some factors (such as "Getting credit" or "Resolving insolvency," where Puerto Rico ranks among the first 10 countries) and very poor in others (such as "Paying taxes" [162], "Registering property" [159] and "Dealing with construction permits" [141]) (World Bank Group 2019).

The hurricane worsened some of the key factors for entrepreneurship. The infrastructure was severely affected, and public policy focused on other priorities. In order to gain a better perspective of the changes, the GEM Puerto Rico team conducted in 2018 the experts' survey with experts that had already participated in previous years (2013 and 2014). Figure 1 shows the mean results in 2018 in a Likert scale of 5 points and compares them with the scores given by the same experts in 2013 and 2014. The difference in four factors—"Physical infrastructure," "Government Policies: Support and Relevance," "Government Entrepreneurship Programs" and "R&D Transfer"—was significant at a 0.05 level, with 2018 mean scores being lower—or worse—than in 2014.

The detailed analysis of the experts' mean responses, shown in Table 2, provides some additional insights. In the statements—presented in descending order from largest to lowest statistically significant difference—the mean scores assigned in 2018 were also worse than in 2014, with the exception of the following statement: "In my country, there is sufficient funding available from informal investors (family, friends and colleagues) who are private individuals (other than founders) for new and growing firms."

Entrepreneurial activity before and after María
In sum, domestic entrepreneurs were facing an adverse context before the hurricane struck the island, both because of the long economic recession and of the inadequacy of factors that affect them.

Figure 1. Mean scores for NES factors, 2014 and 2018

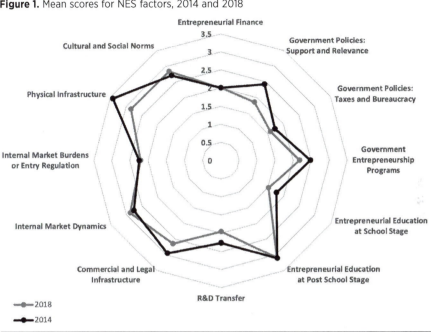

5-point Likert scale: 1= highly insufficient to 5=highly sufficient
Data source: Global Entrepreneurship Monitor (Aponte et al. 2017, 2018).

Table 3 shows several indicators of entrepreneurial activity in selected years. At the beginning of the century, 97,000 people were self-employed or business owners, which is equivalent to 4.2 percent of the population aged 16 to 64; there were also 44,000 establishments. In the following years, the number of self-employed persons and establishments raised both in absolute and relative terms. In 2006, the year the recession began, 145 thousand people were self-employed or business owners (6.0% of the population aged 16 to 64), and there were 46,000 establishments. Even at this peak point, the indicators of entrepreneurial activity were weak compared to that of the United States and other countries. The same data sources show that in 2006 there were 25.4 establishments per 1,000 inhabitants in the United States, more than twice than in Puerto Rico (11.8); and self-employed rates were equivalent to 7.8 percent of the population aged 16 to 64.

During the recession, all absolute numbers decreased, mainly due to the migration flows and the stagnation of natural growth rates. The popu-

Table 2. Mean scores for items with significant differences between 2014 and 2018

	2018	2014	Difference (2018-2014)	Better or worse in 2018?
In my country, the physical infrastructure (roads, utilities, communications, waste disposal) provides good support for new and growing firms	2.24	3.62	-1.38***	Worse
In my country, the support for new and growing firms is a high priority for policy at the local government level.	1.97	2.85	-.88***	Worse
In my country, the support for new and growing firms is a high priority for policy at the national government level.	1.81	2.61	-.81***	Worse
In my country, there is sufficient funding available from informal investors (family, friends and colleagues) who are private individuals (other than founders) for new and growing firms.	2.79	2	.79**	Better
In my country, there are enough subcontractors, suppliers, and consultants to support new and growing firms.	2.92	3.57	-.65**	Worse
In my country, new or growing firms can get good access to utilities (gas, water, electricity, sewer) in about a month	3.03	3.68	-.65*	Worse
In my country, the science and technology base efficiently supports the creation of world-class new technology-based ventures in at least one area.	2.64	3.24	-.61*	Worse
In my country, it is not too expensive for a new or growing firm to get good access to communications (phone, Internet, etc.)	3.16	3.68	-.51*	Worse
In my country, a wide range of government assistance for new and growing firms can be obtained through contact with a single agency.	1.54	2.03	-.49**	Worse
In my country, new and growing firms can afford the cost of using subcontractors, suppliers, and consultants.	1.76	2.24	-.49*	Worse
In my country, taxes and other government regulations are applied to new and growing firms in a predictable and consistent way.	1.64	2.08	-.44*	Worse
In my country, there is sufficient debt funding available for new and growing firms.	1.81	2.24	-.43**	Worse

Notes: (i) The responses are measured in a 5-point Likert scale, where 1=completely false, and 5=completely true; (ii) The means were calculated with a paired sample; subjects that answered the questions in both 2014 and 2018; (iii) *** significant at 0.001, ** at 0.01, * at 0.05 level.

Table 3. Indicators of self-employment and establishments in Puerto Rico in 2000, 2006, 2016 and 2017

	Puerto Rico				U.S.A.	
	2000	**2006**	**2016**	**2017**	**2006**	**2017**
Total population	**3,808,610**	**3,927,776**	**3,411,307**	**3,337,177**		
Population, 16 to 64 years	2,294,816	2,407,727	2,070,663	2,021,631		
Civilian employed population 16 years and over	930,865	1,213,749	1,052,154	1,002,763		
Self-employed, total	**97,452**	**145,091**	**127,748**	**123,266**		
Self-employed, % of population 16 to 64 years	4.2%	6.0%	6.2%	6.1%	7.8%	7.1%
Self-employed, % civilian employed population 16 years and over	10.5%	12.0%	12.1%	12.3%	10.7%	9.6%
Self-employed in own incorporated business workers	28,271	39,478	26,540	28,480		
Self-employed in own not incorporated business workers	69,181	105,613	101,208	94,786		
Households with self-employment income	**97,846**	**120,876**	**105,201**	**96,229**		
Households, total	1,261,816	1,240,456	1,208,438	1,191,305		
Households with self-employment income, % of total	7.8%	9.7%	8.7%	8.1%	12.1%	10.9%
Number of establishments, total	**44,015**	**46,300**	**43,325**	nd		
Number of establishments per 1,000 persons	11.6	11.8	12.7	nd	25.4	24.0*
Number of establishments per 1,000 persons 16 to 64 years	19.2	19.2	20.9	nd	39.3	37.1*

Note: Households with self-employment income data of 2000 corresponds to 1999.
Note: Self-employed, total and in own not incorporated business workers of 2006 includes non-paid family workers.
*Note: Number of establishments per 1,000 persons rates in U.S.A. correspond to 2016.
Data sources: Puerto Rico Community Survey, U.S. Census Bureau (population and self-employment); County Business Patterns, U.S. Census Bureau (establishments).

lation in Puerto Rico decreased from 3.9 million in 2006 to 3.3 million in 2017. Accordingly, the number of self-employed and of establishments also waned. Paradoxically, most entrepreneurship rates grew, as the population decreased at a faster pace than self-employment and establishments. In 2017, there were 123,000 self-employed persons or business owners in Puerto Rico, equivalent to 6.1 percent of the population aged 16 to 64. The

Table 4. Private sector establishment births and deaths by quarter in 2005-2007 and 2015-2019, seasonally adjusted

	Establishments			Employment in these establishments		
Year 3 months ended	**Births**	**Deaths**	**Net**	**Births**	**Deaths**	**Net**
2005 March	1,387	1,028	359	11,827	9,520	2,307
June	1,310	1,103	207	9,564	9,634	(70)
September	1,390	1,222	168	8,508	7,374	1,134
December	1,115	1,053	62	6,274	5,032	1,242
2006 March	982	1,215	(233)	6,806	8,417	(1,611)
June	1,250	1,142	108	7,150	7,377	(227)
September	1,035	2,011	(976)	5,743	9,079	(3,336)
December	1,393	1,559	(166)	6,168	7,215	(1,047)
2007 March	1,211	1,322	(111)	6,729	6,697	32
June	1,254	1,263	(9)	9,001	7,180	1,821
September	1,324	1,252	72	7,634	6,047	1,587
December	880	1,203	(323)	3,817	6,134	(2,317)
2015 March	927	1,161	(234)	4,510	5,143	(633)
June	809	1,170	(361)	5,163	5,051	112
September	935	982	(47)	4,685	4,368	317
December	910	925	(15)	4,627	4,306	321
2016 March	919	980	(61)	4,459	3,761	698
June	876	865	11	4,632	3,794	838
September	918	855	63	5,187	4,267	920
December	808	969	(161)	4,012	4,771	(759)
2017 March	995	1,020	(25)	5,075	3,759	1,316
June	905	735	170	4,384	3,029	1,355
September	512	1,081	(569)	3,687	4,944	(1,257)
December	804	1,411	(607)	6,452	6,499	(47)
2018 March	979	1,338	(359)	7,085	5,109	1,976
June	1,070	860	210	7,013	4,386	2,627
September	1,237	na	na	8,004	na	na
December	1,046	na	na	4,843	na	na
2019 March	1,252	na	na	6,104	na	na

Data source: Bureau of Labor Statistics, U.S. Department of Labor.

number of establishments decreased to 43,325 in 2016, but that represents 12.7 establishments per 1,000 inhabitants (it is still almost half the rate observed in the United States, 24.0).

When Hurricane María struck, the trend in net creation of establishments in Puerto Rico was weak or negative, as can be seen in Table 4 and figure 2. The data stems from the Quarterly Census of Employment and Wages and is provided by the Bureau of Labor Statistics. It only covers formal entrepreneurial activity. Table 4 shows that before September 2017 less than 1,000 new establishment were being opened every quarter, according to the Bureau of Labor Statistics. After the hurricane, the first reaction was an even weaker number of establishment openings, while the establishment closings increased 35 percent from September 2017 to March 2018, compared to the same period in the previous year. This rate of establishment closings was nevertheless lower than the rate registered from September 2006 to March 2007, when Puerto Rico was in the first year of its long recession. The impact of these establishment closings over job loss was also higher at that time.

The aftermath of Hurricane María led to lower establishment openings and higher closings, but after the first quarters there was a swing effect. The number of establishments opened in the 12-month period from March 2018 to March 2019 was 28 percent higher than those opened in the same 12-month period previous to the 2017 hurricane season (from March 2016 to March 2017). The effect on job creation was even stronger, with a raise of 39 percent in jobs created in newly opened establishments.

On the other hand, the remarkable raise in establishment closings in the quarter of September 2017 and the following quarters affected the domestic entrepreneurial network. How relevant were these effects, from a historical perspective?

Figure 2 shows the long-term series of survival rates of private sector establishments in Puerto Rico and the United States. In March 2018, 77.5 percent of the establishments that had opened one year earlier were still open; they had survived Hurricane María and its aftermath. Although this number is lower than the survival rate in previous years, it is not too far from the average (82% from 2013 to 2017) and was close to the survival rate registered in the United States (79.1%). In an interesting turning of events, the following year the result was inverse: 86 percent of the establishments had survived

Figure 2. Survival of private sector establishments opened 1, 3, 5 and 10 years earlier, in Puerto Rico and United States

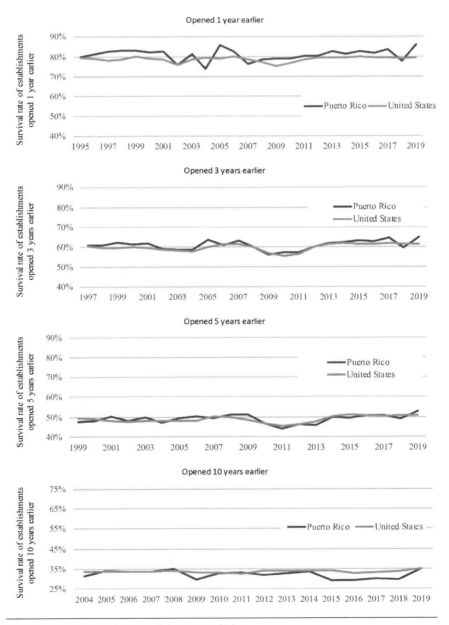

their first year as of March 2019. The durability of new businesses increased after Hurricane María and its aftermath.

Similar observations can be made looking at the survival rates of establishments opened three years earlier. The survival rate of establishments opened in Puerto Rico in 2015 was 59.5 percent, lower than the rate registered in previous years (63% from 2013 to 2017) and in the United States that same year (61.4%). Again, afterwards, the trend reversed: 64.9 percent of establishments that had opened in 2016 had survived as of March 2019.

The negative effect of the hurricane and its aftermath on the survival rates of establishments vanishes as the age of the establishment increases: 49.0 percent of establishments that opened in 2013 were still open as of March 2018, close to the average (49.6% in the previous five years); and 29.6 percent of establishments that opened in 2008 were still open in March 2018 (30.8% in average in the previous five years). Nevertheless, in all cases, a positive swing can be observed: in 2019 the survival rate increased to 52.8 percent for five-year-old establishments and 34.8 percent for 10-year-old establishments. Therefore, not only new businesses had better survival rates in 2019, but also older ones. This might result from the improvement of economic conditions, but also could be an evidence of the increased resilience of entrepreneurs after the hurricane experience. Future research should test the hypothesis that the strengthening of entrepreneurial activity in Puerto Rico is due to the resilience developed by entrepreneurs. Other possible reasons for the increase in business activity could be the injection of aid funds to individuals and businesses.

The analysis of the effects of Hurricane María and its aftermath on entrepreneurial activity can be expanded using data from the Global Entrepreneurship Monitor (GEM). These data result from a yearly survey to a representative sample of the adult population, and therefore covers both formal and informal activities. Table 5 compares the results of several indicators of entrepreneurial activity in 2017 and 2018, according to GEM surveys. The surveys are conducted from May to July each year, and therefore results from 2017 are prior to Hurricane María.

The most important change between 2017 and 2018 is the increase of new business ownership rate, from 1.4 percent to 2.6 percent. Since the initial population survey conducted by GEM Puerto Rico in 2013, this is the first time that new business ownership rate is over 2.0 percent, as shown in Figure 3. This indicator refers to the proportion of the population that has an entrepreneurial initiative (of less than three years and a half) that allows them to pay salaries or wages, including to themselves, for at least 3 months prior to the survey. Every year Puerto Rico ranked among the lowest rates of all economies in this indicator. The consequence of repeated very low rates of new business creation is very low numbers in another crucial indicator: the established business ownership rate. This refers to the proportion of the population with an entrepreneurial initiative of more than three years and a half. In Puerto Rico, only 1.6 percent of the population in 2017 and 1.9 in 2018 owned an established business; that is the lowest rate among all GEM participants. It must be recalled that once the establishments open, their survival rates are similar to those of the United States.

The paradox is that Puerto Rico has a high rate of nascent entrepreneurship, that is, of people who are actively involved in starting a new venture, but still have not received salaries or wages for at least 3 months. In 2017, this rate was 9.5 percent and in 2018, it was 9.1 percent. Why there is such a huge difference in Puerto Rico between nascent and new entrepreneurship rates is yet to be determined, but probably the answer lies in the infertile context and historical economic policies previously described. This is a very relevant matter, from a public policy perspective, and requires further in-depth research. As we mentioned previously, the experts' assessment in the GEM studies repeatedly suggest that new business face hindrances related to taxes and bureaucracy and highlight the lack of entrepreneurial education at the school level.

A new business ownership rate of 2.6 percent is still low when compared to other countries, but it represents a very important leap for Puerto Rico's economy. This result goes hand in hand with an increase in opportunity-driven entrepreneurial activity among nascent and new entrepreneurs, as can be seen in Table 5. Accordingly, we also observe higher proportions of the population that identify good opportunities to start an entrepreneurial venture (from 28.0% in 2017 to 35.2% in 2018), as well as those who declare their intention to begin a new venture in the next three years (from 18.3% in 2017 to 22.9% in 2018). Interestingly, the proportion of early-stage entrepreneurs who expect to create more than five jobs in the next five years also increased, from 22.9 percent in 2017 to 24.2 percent in 2018.

Table 5. Entrepreneurial activity indicators in Puerto Rico in 2017 and 2018, according to the Global Entrepreneurship Monitor

	2017	Rank out of 54 econo- mies, 2017	2018	Rank out of 49 economies, 2018
Self-perceptions about entrepreneurship				
Perceived opportunities	28.0%	47	35.2%	34
Entrepreneurial intentions	18.3%	22	22.9%	22
Entrepreneurial activity				
Total early-stage Entrepreneurial Activity (TEA)	10.6%	28	11.6%	22
Nascent entrepreneurship rate	9.5%	14	9.1%	12
New business ownership rate	1.4%	52	2.6%	42
Established business ownership rate	28,271	39,478	26,540	28,480
Self-employed in own not incorporated business workers	1.6%	51	1.9%	49
				22
Motivation				
Necessity-driven entrepreneurial activity (% of TEA)	31.7%	11	22.9%	24
Opportunity-driven entrepreneurial activity (% of TEA)	67.1%	45	71.2%	26
Improvement-driven opportunity entrepreneurial activity (% of TEA)	42.3%	39	39.7%	38
Motivational index: Improvement-Driven Opportunity / Necesity Motive	1.3%	44	1.7%	31
Entrepreneurship impact	11.6	11.8	12.7	nd
Job expectations (6+)	22.9%	22	24.2%	17

Data source: Global Entrepreneurship Monitor (GEM 2018, Bosma and Kelley 2019, Aponte et al. 2017, 2018).
The rank is out of the total of economies that administered the Adult Population Survey (APS) in their country: 54 in 2017 and 49 in 2018.
Definitions (Global Entrepreneurship Monitor 2018/2019 Global Report):
Perceived opportunities – Percentage of the 18-64 population who see good opportunities to start a firm in the area where they live.
Entrepreneurial intentions – Percentage of the 18-64 population (individuals involved in any stage of entrepreneurial activity excluded) who intend to start a business within three years.
Total early-stage Entrepreneurial Activity (TEA) – Percentage of the 18-64 population who are either a nascent entrepreneur or owner-manager of a new business.
Nascent entrepreneurship rate - Percentage of the 18-64 population who are currently nascent entrepreneurs, i.e., actively involved in setting up a business they will own or co-own; this business has not paid salaries, wages, or any other payments to the owners for more than three months.
New business ownership rate – Percentage of the 18-64 population who are currently owner-manager of a new business, i.e., owning and managing a running business that has paid salaries, wages, or any other payments to the owners for more than three months, but not more than 42 months.
Established business ownership rate – Percentage of the 18-64 population who are currently owner-manager of an established business, i.e., owning and managing a running business that has paid salaries, wages, or any other payments to the owners for more than 42 months.
Necessity-driven entrepreneurial activity (% of TEA) – Percentage of those involved in TEA who are involved in entrepreneurship because they had no better options for work.
Opportunity-driven entrepreneurial activity (% of TEA) – Percentage of those involved in TEA who state they are driven by opportunity as opposed to having no better options for work.
Improvement-driven opportunity entrepreneurial activity (% of TEA) – Percentage of those involved in TEA who (i) state they are driven by opportunity as opposed to having no better options for work; and (ii) who indicate the main driver for being involved in this opportunity is being independent or increasing their income, rather than just maintaining their income.
Motivational index: Improvement-Driven Opportunity / Necessity Motive – Improvement-Driven Opportunity rate divided by Necessity Motive rate.
Job expectations (6+) – Percentage of TEA who expect to employ more than 5 employees five years from now, minus the current number of employees.

Figure 3. Nascent and new business entrepreneurship rates in Puerto Rico, 2013 to 2018

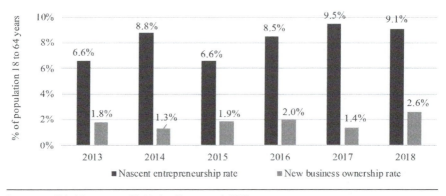

Data source: Global Entrepreneurship Monitor (Aponte et al., 2018).

Table 6. Proportion of early-stage entrepreneurs by sociodemographic group in Puerto Rico in 2017 and 2018, according to the Global Entrepreneurship Monitor

	2016	2017	2006	2017
Age	9.9%	26	12.4%	18
18 - 24 years	16.1%	21	19.0%	13
25 - 34 years	12.5%	28	13.8%	19
35 - 44 years	9.7%	29	8.3%	30
45 - 54 years	4.6%	36	4.6%	32
55 - 64 years				
Gender	13.2%	25	15.2%	17
Men	8.3%	29	8.4%	25
Women	101,208	94,786		

Data source: Global Entrepreneurship Monitor (Aponte et al., 2018, 2019).
The rank is out of the total of economies that administered the Adult Population Survey (APS) in their country: 54 in 2017 and 49 in 2018.

Table 6 details the sociodemographic characteristics of the entrepreneurs with new or nascent initiatives in Puerto Rico. The results show that the reactions to the new scenario have differed by group. The proportion of early-stage entrepreneurs has increased remarkably among young adults (19% of people aged 25 to 34 are starting a venture), but it decreased among people over 45 years of age. Men also showed higher levels of entrepreneurial activity in 2018, while the proportion of women involved remained stable.

Comparison with Louisiana after hurricane Katrina

The short-term entrepreneurial dynamics described in the previous section can be compared with data and results from other research studies on economies that suffered unexpected external shocks.

Louisiana had a comparable experience when Hurricane Katrina struck in September 2005. Figure 4 shows the dynamics hof establishments in Louisiana and Puerto Rico based on their employment trend, before and after hurricanes Katrina and María, respectively. The number of *closing* establishments (those with zero employment in the last month of the quarter)[5] jumped in September 2005 in Louisiana, increasing by more than 200 percent when compared to the numbers of the same quarter of the previous year. In Puerto Rico there was also a leap in closing establishments in September 2017, although it peaked in the following quarter, when not only the numbers of *closing* establishments, but also of *contracting* establishments (those with a net decrease in employment in that quarter) increased.

It is interesting that both Louisiana and Puerto Rico experienced a sudden increase in opening *establishments in the quarter following the hurricanes' impact.*

It is interesting that both Louisiana and Puerto Rico experienced a sudden increase in *opening* establishments in the quarter following the hurricanes' impact. In the case of Puerto Rico, the rise of opening establishments lasted longer and was accompanied by an increase of expanding establishments from March 2018 on.

Could entrepreneurial resilience represent an important aspect in the reconstruction of economies that suffer unexpected external shocks?

The term *resilience* means adapting to change, especially to sudden shocks in the external environment. Initially it was used in engineering and ecology, but recently other fields such as psychology, geography, environmental economics and business are doing research on resilience. The concept is being explored in the context of disturbances such as hurricanes, floods, tsunamis, terrorist attacks, earthquakes, etc. (McNaughton and Gray

Figure 4. Change in private sector establishments by direction of employment change, seasonally adjusted, in Louisiana (2003-2007) and Puerto Rico (2015-2019)

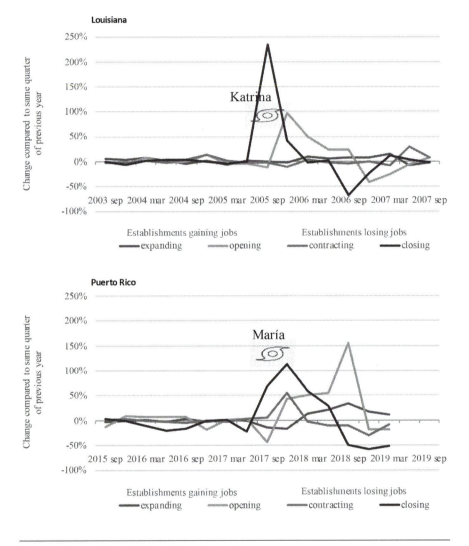

Data source: Bureau of Labor Statistics, U.S. Department of Labor.

2017) and it contributes to explain the paradoxical observation that enterprise activities often flourish under extreme adversity, as in the cases of Puerto Rico after Hurricane María and Louisiana after Katrina.

Korber and McNaughton (2018) in a systematic literature review identified 144 papers that study the intersection of entrepreneurship and resilience. Entrepreneurial resilience connotes the ability to bounce back from adverse events by adapting business models, strategies, work routines and/or organizational structures to the new environmental conditions created by the disaster (Linnenluecke 2015, McNaughton and Gray 2017, Williams and Vorley 2014).

This conduct has also been called "disaster entrepreneurship." Linnenluecke and McKnight (2017) define it as attempts by the private sector to create or maintain value during and in the immediate aftermath of a natural disaster by taking advantage of business opportunities and providing goods and services required by community stakeholders. Entrepreneurial business continuity, scaling of organizational response, improvising and emergence of new entrepreneurial activity have been identified in the context of disasters. Linnenluecke and McKnight (2017) propose that each of these factors are related to community-level resilience. Branzei and Abdelnour (2010) extend the analysis beyond natural disasters and explain how terrorism conditions (outbreak, escalation and reduction) may create psychological incentives for enterprise resilience. They show that, controlling for ex ante terrorism conditions, enterprise resilience yields more favorable economic payoffs at higher levels of terrorism, especially for informal entrepreneurs. From the perspective of the entrepreneur's decision-making, Bernard and Barbosa (2016) show that a resilience dynamic can play an important role in triggering the decision to become an entrepreneur, although they emphasize that this in no way excludes other factors that may contribute to this decision. As a result, policy debates are considering entrepreneurship as a key element to build more resilient economies, as William and Vorley (2016) highlight. As mentioned before, future research should test the hypothesis that the strengthening of entrepreneurial activity in Puerto Rico is due to the resilience developed by entrepreneurs as well as its impact on the economy.

Discussion and Concluding Remarks

Hurricane María brought destruction of infrastructure, interruption of communications and a lengthy blackout, which caused serious difficulties for established business in Puerto Rico. The number of establishments that closed grew by 35 percent in the months following the hurricane[6]; in fact, the hurricane was a main reason[7] for ending a business venture in Puerto Rico in 2018. At the same time, the number of establishments opened immediately after the hurricane was reduced—16 percent less when compared to the same period of the previous year. Altogether, the difference between the post-hurricane period and the same period of the previous year throws a net balance of 1,412 establishments less.

After the first months after the hurricane, the unusual rates of establishment closings stopped, and births raised above their average numbers. Between March 2018 and March 2019 the number of new establishments was 4,605, which is 1,008 more (28%) than in the same period of 2016-2017 (before the hurricane).

It may seem paradoxical, but the entrepreneurial activity performance observed in Puerto Rico and Louisiana could respond to entrepreneurial resilience behavior exposed in the literature.

The survival rates figures show the same dynamic. Initially, the survival rate of one-year-old establishments went down to 77.5 percent in 2018, from 83.3 percent the previous year; in 2019 it jumped to 85.9 percent, the highest rate recorded since this measurement began in 1994. Similar changes happened among three-year-old establishments (64.6 percent in 2017, 59.5 percent in 2018 and 64.9 percent in 2019). The effect was detectable also in older establishments, although the initial negative effect diminished with its age.

Despite the fact that Puerto Rico's entrepreneurial activity suffered an initial strong negative effect, it reemerged with strength after the hurricanes. It may seem paradoxical, but the entrepreneurial activity performance observed in Puerto Rico and Louisiana could respond to entrepreneurial resilience behavior exposed in the literature. This hypothesis needs to be tested in future empirical research. Other possible reasons for the increase in business activity could be the injection of aid funds to individuals and businesses.

Will the renewed entrepreneurial activity become a long-term trend in Puerto Rico? Can this effect reinforce and accelerate the reconstruction and transformation of the economic structure? After more than a decade of recession or stagnation, the economy of Puerto Rico is in urgent need of new sources of production and employment, but reports from GEM and other international research projects point out that domestic business activity faces an infertile context; several crucial factors hinder the birth and survival of entrepreneurial initiatives.

The proportion of people who take some steps to begin an entrepreneurial venture is relatively high in Puerto Rico; lack of initiative has never been a problem. The rising numbers of new entrepreneurs are encouraging, but they need a proper scenario to thrive. Additional research is needed to understand why entrepreneurial intentions do not translate into actual entrepreneurial undertakings more often and to properly identify discouraging factors. Nevertheless, we have enough signs that point to bureaucracy, taxes and entrepreneurial education, among others, and changes should not be postponed. This is the time to undertake serious, long-term reforms.

NOTES

[1] 2018 Economic Report to the Governor, Government of Puerto Rico Planning Board.
[2] 2014-15 Survey on Science and Technology: R&D, Institute of Statistics of Puerto Rico.
[3] 2017 American Community Survey 1-Year Estimates.
[4] 2018 Economic Report to the Governor, Government of Puerto Rico Planning Board.
[5] The publication *Business Employment Dynamics* provides the following definitions of establishment-level employment changes:
Openings. These are either establishments with positive third-month employment for the first time in the current quarter, with no links to the prior quarter, or with positive third-month employment in the current quarter following zero employment in the previous quarter.
Expansions. These are establishments with positive employment in the third month in both the previous and current quarters, with a net increase in employment over this period.
Closings. These are either establishments with positive third-month employment in the previous quarter, with no positive employment reported in the current quarter, or with positive third-month employment in the previous quarter followed by zero employment in the current quarter.
Contractions. These are establishments with positive employment in the third month in both the previous and current quarters, with a net decrease in employment over this period.
All establishment-level employment changes are measured from the third month of each quarter. Not all establishments change their employment levels; these establishments are included in total employment, but do not affect counts of gross job gains and gross job losses.
Source: Business Employment Dynamics, Overview: https://www.bls.gov/bdm/bd-mover.htm#concepts
[6] Establishment deaths in three quarters, ending September 2017, December 2017 and March 2018. Bureau of Labor Statistics, Business Employment Dynamics.
[7] 27.3 percent of the entrepreneurs who discontinued their venture in 2018 pointed to a "single incident" (the hurricane) as the reason for discontinuation, according to Global Entrepreneurship Monitor Puerto Rico (Aponte et al. 2019).

REFERENCES

Álvarez, Marta, Marinés Aponte and Manuel Lobato. 2018. Panorama de la actividad emprendedora en Puerto Rico. San Juan, Puerto Rico: School of Business Administration. Accessed 1 December 2019. <https://gem.uprrp.edu/index.php/panorama-empresarial-en-puerto-rico/>.

Aponte, Marinés, Marta Álvarez and Manuel Lobato. 2018. Informe de Puerto Rico GEM 2017. San Juan, Puerto Rico: School of Business Administration. Accessed 1 December 2019. <https://gem.uprrp.edu/index.php/gem-puerto-rico-2017/>.

_____. 2019. Informe de Puerto Rico GEM 2018. San Juan, Puerto Rico: School of Business Administration. Accessed 1 December 2019. <https://gem.uprrp.edu/index.php/gem-puerto-rico-2018/>.

Bernard, Marie-Josée and Saulo Dubard Barbosa. 2016. Resilience and Entrepreneurship: A Dynamic and Biographical Approach to the Entrepreneurial Act. *M@n@gement* 19(2), 89–123.

Bosma, Niels and Rebecca Harding. 2007. Global Entrepreneurship Monitor: GEM 2006 Results. London: London Business School. Accessed 1 December 2019. <https://www.gemconsortium.org/report/>.

Bosma, Niels and Donna Kelley. 2019. Global Entrepreneurship Monitor: 2018/2019 Global Report. Babson Park: Global Entrepreneurship Research Association. Accessed 1 December 2019. <https://www.gemconsortium.org/report/>.

Branzei, Oana and Samer Abdelnour. 2010. Another Day, Another Dollar: Enterprise Resilience under Terrorism in Developing Countries. *Journal of International Business Studies* 41(5), 804–25.

Caballero, Ricardo J. and Mohamad L. Hammour. 1994. The Cleansing Effect of Recessions. *American Economic Review 84*(5), 1350–68.

Caraballo-Cueto, José and Juan Lara. 2018. Deindustrialization and Unsustainable Debt in Middle-income Countries: The Case of Puerto Rico. *Journal of Globalization and Development* 8(2), DOI: https://doi.org/10.1515/jgd-2017-0009.

Carree, Martin A. and A. Roy Thurik. 2010. The Impact of Entrepreneurship on Economic Growth. In *Handbook of Entrepreneurship Research: An Interdisciplinary Survey and Introduction*, eds. Zoltan Acs and David Audretsch. 557–94. New York: Springer.

Dietz, James. 1989. *Historia económica de Puerto Rico*. Río Piedras, PR: Huracán.

Evans, David S. and Linda S. Leighton. 1990. Small Business Formation by Unemployed and Employed Workers. *Small Business Economics* 2, 319–30.

Feliciano, Zadia M. 2018. IRS Section 936 and the Decline of Puerto Rico's Manufacturing. *CENTRO: Journal of the Center for Puerto Rican Studies* 30(3), 30–42.

Global Entrepreneurship Monitor. 2018. Global Entrepreneurship Monitor: 2017/2018 Global Report. Babson Park: Global Entrepreneurship Research Association. Accessed 1 December 2019. <https://www.gemconsortium.org/report/>.

Gluzmann, Pablo A., Martín M. Guzmán and Joseph E. Stiglitz. 2018. An Analysis of Puerto Rico's Debt Relief Needs to Restore Debt Sustainability. *CENTRO: Journal of the Center for Puerto Rican Studies* 30(3), 104–46.

Klapper, Leora and Inessa Love. 2011. The Impact of the Financial Crisis on New Firm Registration. *Economics Letters* 113(1), 1–4.

Korber, Stefan and Rod B. McNaughton. 2018. Resilience and Entrepreneurship: A Systematic Literature Review. *International Journal of Entrepreneurial Behavior & Research* 24(7), 1129–54.

Linnenluecke, Martina K. and Brent McKnight. 2017. Community Resilience to Natural Disasters: The Role of Disaster Entrepreneurship. *Journal of Enterprising Communities: People and Places in the Global Economy* 11(1), 166–85.

McNaughton, Rod B. and Brendan Gray. 2017. Entrepreneurship and Resilient Communities—Introduction to the Special Issue. *Journal of Enterprising Communities: People and Places in the Global Economy* 11(1), 2–19.

Martínez, Jorge Mario, Jorge Máttar and Pedro Rivera, eds. 2005. *Globalización y desarrollo: desafíos de Puerto Rico frente al siglo XXI*. México: CEPAL.

Meléndez, Edwin. 2018. The Economics of PROMESA. *CENTRO: Journal of the Center for Puerto Rican Studies* 30(3), 72–103.

Parker, Simon. 2009. *The Economics of Entrepreneurship.* Cambridge, UK: Cambridge University Press.

Rampini, Adriano A. 2004. Entrepreneurial Activity, Risk, and the Business Cycle. *Journal of Monetary Economics* 51, 555–73.

Wennekers, Sander and Roy Thurik. 1999. Linking Entrepreneurship and Economic Growth. *Small Business Economics* 13(1), 27–55.

Williams, Colin C. 2008. Beyond Necessity-driven versus Opportunity-driven Entrepreneurship: A Study of Informal Entrepreneurs in England, Russia and Ukraine. *The International Journal of Entrepreneurship and Innovation* 9(3), 157–65.

Williams, Nick and Tim Vorley. 2014. Economic Resilience and Entrepreneurship: Lessons from the Sheffield City Region. *Entrepreneurship & Regional Development* 26(3-4), 257–81.

World Bank Group. 2017. Doing Business 2017: Equal Opportunity for All. International Bank for Reconstruction and Development / The World Bank. Accessed 1 December 2019. <http://documents.worldbank.org/curated/en/172361477516970361/Doing-business-2017-equal-opportunity-for-all/>.

_____. 2019. Doing Business 2019: Training for Reform. International Bank for Reconstruction and Development / The World Bank. Accessed 1 December 2019. <https://elibrary.worldbank.org/doi/book/10.1596/978-1-4648-1326-9/>.

_____. 2020. Doing Business 2020: Comparing business regulations in 190 economies. International Bank for Reconstruction and Development / The World Bank. Accessed 1 December 2019. <https://openknowledge.worldbank.org/handle/10986/32436/>.

Impact of Hurricane María to the Civic Sector: A Profile of Non-Profits in Puerto Rico

IVIS GARCÍA AND DIVYA CHANDRASEKHAR

ABSTRACT

Non-profit organizations can play a critical role in disaster recovery owing to their ability to motivate volunteerism, assess local needs, distribute goods, and aid. But few such organizations can successfully navigate the dynamism and uncertainty of disaster recovery. This is particularly true of locally embedded, non-profit organizations that typically have a smaller staff, fewer resources, fewer extra-local connections, and much less experience in disaster recovery. In this study, we first created a profile of non-profits in Puerto Rico. Then, we capture the activities that relate to responding and improving their capacity to engage in recovery actions after Hurricane María. Data were collected through phone surveys of 235 responses of non-profit organizations as well as in-depth interviews with 21 executive directors of agencies, residents, and community leaders. We discuss four relevant themes in this article: (1) disaster impact on organization, (2) changes in interaction with other organizations, (3) knowledge and use of traditional recovery funding mechanisms, and (4) need for education, capacity building, and collaboration. We conclude with observations on the impact that Hurricane María had on the operations of these non-profit organizations, their knowledge-seeking behavior, new opportunities for collaboration, and access to resources in the post-disaster context. [Keywords: non-profits, Puerto Rico, Hurricane María, disaster recovery]

Introduction

On September 20, 2017, María, a Category 4 hurricane with sustained winds of over 140 miles per hour, devastated the Island's housing, infrastructure, agriculture, transportation networks, and communications systems (Hinosa, Román and Meléndez 2018; Puerto Rico Department of Housing 2020). Hurricane María was one of the deadliest natural disasters in U.S. history, with an official death toll of close to 3,000 individuals in Puerto Rico alone (Fink 2018). It was the tenth-most intense Atlantic hurricane on record in the world (Willie 2018). Hurricane María was also the third-costliest storm in U.S. history—$90,000 billion, after Katrina ($160 billion) and Harvey ($125 billion) (Ramsey 2012). The most severe loss of life and infrastructure damages was in Puerto Rico, where it is estimated to be about $100 billion (The Associated Press 2018).

A record worldwide was achieved in Puerto Rico: the second-largest blackout in the world after Super Typhoon Yolanda hit the Philippines in 2013 (Doug 2018). According to a FEMA report, it was also (1) the lengthiest air mission delivering food and potable water in U.S. history, (2) the most massive delivery of commodities due to a natural disaster, (3) the largest sea-bridge operation of federal disaster aid, (4) the largest disaster generator installation mission in the United States, (5) one of the largest disaster medical response missions, and (6) one of the largest disaster housing missions in the history of the organization (FEMA 2018).

Ivis García (ivis.garcia@utah.edu) is an Assistant Professor in City & Metropolitan Planning at the University of Utah. Dr. Garcia chairs Planners for Puerto Rico and it is involved with the National Puerto Rican Agenda, the Disaster Housing Recovery Coalition of the National Low-income Housing Coalition, and Centro's IDEA-Común—all of which promote Puerto Rico's recovery. Dr.García has a Ph.D. in urban planning and Policy from the University of Illinois at Chicago.

Divya Chandrasekhar (D.Chandrasekhar@utah.edu) is an Associate Professor in the Department of City & Metropolitan Planning at the University of Utah with expertise in community recovery from disasters. Her research has examined post-disaster community participation and capacity building, networking and coordination among recovery institutions, and disaster recovery policy in South and Southeast Asia, the Caribbean, and in the United States. She is an affiliate of the Global Change and Sustainability Center at the University of Utah.

Help from traditional actors such as the Federal Emergency Management Agency (FEMA) was slow in reaching the Island, and this, combined with the large scale of destruction, raised local community organizations into prominent recovery roles. FEMA had been ill-prepared for the widespread impact of María (FEMA 2018). According to researchers, a disaster of this magnitude is so big that no government could deliver all of the aid needed during the first weeks or even months (Patterson, Weil, and Patel 2010; Olshansky and Johnson 2010). This has been the case in many disasters around the world. One might present emergency relief efforts in Kobe, Gujarat, Indonesia, India, Japan, Trinidad, Tobago, Haiti, Turkey, Nepal, New Orleans, New York, Houston, and Florida (Borges-Méndez et al. 2018).

Puerto Rico, in this sense, was no different. People expect the government to be there. However, the number of people who work for the government is minimal compared to the number of citizens. During this period of crisis, usually, non-profits step in and help neighbors (Sylves 2008). This is true disaster after disaster, no matter if we are talking about a weak state or a strong state, a local government, the federal government in the case of the U.S., or national governments in the case of international disasters (Benson, Twigg and Myers 2001; Izumi and Shaw 2012; Nolte and Boenigk 2011). Non-profits become first respondents (Sylves 2008; Simo and Bies 2007; Bisri 2013). They fill the gap that government agencies cannot fill.

As described above, community organizations play a critical role in disaster recovery, owing to their ability to motivate volunteerism, assess local needs, distribute goods and aid (Patterson, Weil, and Patel 2010). However, few organizations can successfully navigate the dynamism and uncertainty of the disaster recovery process (Liberatore et al. 2013). Non-profits are key actors in disaster recovery, but how are they impacted after a disaster? Do they have the capacity to do this critical work? What actions do they take to enhance their post-disaster operations?

In this study, we employed a mixed-methods approach. We conducted 21 interviews and a random survey to, first, create a profile of registered non-profit organizations in Puerto Rico, and, second, understand their engagement in recovery-related activities. Data were collected through phone surveys of 235 responses of non-profit organizations. We interviewed 11 executive directors of organizations as well as 10 residents, community leaders, and activists—for a total of twenty-one interviews. This research study feeds into the capacity building action work that the Center for Puerto Rican Studies (Centro) is conducting in Puerto Rico through IdeaComún, a collaborative initiative of civic and community organizations, the private sector, academics, and other collaborators for the coordination of projects of integral and sustainable economic development that pursue a social purpose.

Literature Review

The function of non-governmental organizations, particularly in disaster-prone regions, is gaining importance as a study of researchers (Izumi and Shaw 2012; Kapucu 2006; Sylves 2008). In a recovery scenario, non-governmental organizations provide services to those affected, build infrastructure, empower individuals to get involved in recovery, and advocate for change and sustainable development (Lewis 2009; Streeten 1997; LeRoux and Feeney 2014; Robinson and Murphy 2013). A variety of non-governmental organizations are associated with a range of disaster prevention and mitigation activities relevant to training, readiness, housing, microfinance, microenterprises, health, and environment (Benson, Twigg and Myers 2001; Robinson and Murphy 2013).

This means that the state recognizes the need for non-profits to get involved in emergency response and recovery.

As described in the introduction, non-profits often act as first respondents, getting involved in cleaning-up, providing food, emergency health care, and fulfilling the most immediate needs of their neighbors (Sylves 2008; Simo and Bies 2007; Bisri 2013). However, non-profit organizations also lead the local community rebuilding efforts that are necessary for long-term recovery—they train staff, partners, and others associated with them to build their capacity, engage in advocacy, and impact policy decision-making related to disaster prevention, mitigation, and recovery (LeRoux and Feeney 2014). Additionally, a rising number of non-profit organizations are getting into partnerships with the government in recovery efforts and disaster risk management programs (Luna 2013; Kapucu 2006).

Some non-profit organizations have focused on pre-disaster methods such as readiness and disaster risk reduction, for example, employing the Community-Based Disaster Risk Reduction (CBDRR) framework (Shaw 2012). As Shaw explains, many jurisdictions have used this framework since the late 1990s as a substitute for top-down planning. This means that the state recognizes the need for non-profits to get involved in emergency response and recovery. Jones and colleagues (2013) argue that the activities of non-profits working in collaboration with the state and employing the CB-DRR are more effective than when government institutions lead the actions by themselves. Furthermore, a public-private strategy when non-profits are involved improves focus on disaster risks by using indigenous expertise, knowledge, and skills within existing local organizations (Shaw 2012; Jones, Aryal and Collins 2013). We can conclude then that the expertise, knowledge, and skills of community organizations, including non-profits, is needed in preparedness, mitigation, response, and recovery activities.

Unfortunately, most non-profit organizations have the usual inadequacies related to offering services, finding volunteers, getting political support, and applying for competitive funding (Dolnicar, Irvine and Lazarevski 2008; Keyes et al. 1996). These include not finding funding that matches their mission (Dolnicar, Irvine and Lazarevski 2008), having a small staff, relaying in volunteer work, and having staff or volunteers with insufficient skills for the scale and nature of the work needed (Streeten 1997). Another challenge is that long-term pursuits, such as recovery, might have never been experienced in the affected region (Arabasz, Smith and Richins 1980). Thus, all non-profit organizations in the area might be ill-prepared and trained for what is ahead of a recovery effort. To engage in disaster-related work, which provides a long-term source of funding, these organizations need to transcend these difficulties (Kapucu 2007). Non-profit organizations need to actively deal with organizational improvement and technological concerns to increase their effectiveness (Kapucu 2006; Sylves 2008).

To overcome their deficiencies, many non-profit organizations chose to work together to assume duties and responsibilities to work on mutual actions (Creech and Willard 2001). In the disaster recovery environment, non-profit organizations might organize training, expertise, sectorial or multi-sectoral collaborations (Simo and Bies 2007; Liebler and Ferri 2004;

Liberatore et al. 2013). Concerning humanitarian aid in a disaster scenario, inter-organizational organizations are either strengthened or created in response to the disaster crisis (Doerfel, Chewning and Lai 2013). For example, the United Nations agencies, local governmental agencies, academics, non-profits, and community-based organizations work on mutual goals and objectives that could not be achieved by one single institution (Abelson 2003).

Formal and informal groups of stakeholders can improve organizations' capability by motivating them to fulfill and discuss experience and knowledge (Allen, James and Gamlen 2007). They function as spaces where organizations can share knowledge, mutually build capacity, discuss problems, and work with each other to develop plans, programs, and strategies (Doerfel, Chewning and Lai 2013; Simo and Bies 2007; Izumi and Shaw 2012). The deliberate collaboration among various stakeholders also offers non-profit organizations with a unifying force and the chance to influence recovery decisions and actions as well as call the attention from other vital organizations to that specific sector, when otherwise it might have been ignored (Manring 2007; Weisbord 1992). Inter-organizational collaboration can make non-profit organizations capable of articulating civic sector recovery ideas and how they can be implemented (Manring 2007; Doerfel, Chewning and Lai 2013; Carlson et al. 2017).

As previously described, this article seeks to understand the role, characteristics, accomplishments, and shortcomings of non-profit organizations. We aim to examine the activities of the non-profit sector in Puerto Rico after Hurricane María. To this end, our questions are: (1) How non-profit organizations were affected?, (2) How they have changed after the disaster?, and (3) What are the development activities that would improve their work? The next section provides information about the interviews and surveys conducted to measure those activities.

Methods

To create a profile of the non-profit sector in Puerto Rico and understand their disaster recovery activities, a random sample telephone survey was conducted in Spanish by Metrika—which is a research company in San Juan, Puerto Rico. A total of 537 out of 1,422 master list entries were contacted using various resources to arrive at a comprehensive list: (1) a 2005-2017 database on registered non-profits in Puerto Rico compiled by the Non-Profit

Evaluation & Resource Center Inc., (2) an Internal Revenue Service (IRS) Form 990 data set compiled by the National Center of Charitable Statistics (NCCS), (3) organizations that have attended Centro conferences, and (4) a computer program that searches online organizations for phones, emails, and other information.

Researchers designed the survey, and Metrika, a contractor, was hired to collect responses. Metrika obtained 235 responses (68 percent response rate) in 15 days in 2019. The questionnaire only used close-ended questions, and it took less than 12 minutes to complete. Screening questions were asked to make sure that those who answered had a non-profit status. We also asked screening questions to access the executive director, vice-president, or higher ranked personnel. The survey asked about organization characteristics (year of foundation, budget, number of employees, etc.) as well as pre- and post-disaster operations (mission, funding, capacity, etc.). Finally, we asked questions about relationships and knowledge of other organizations' efforts.

We conducted interviews with 11 executive directors of non-profit organizations as well as with 10 residents, community leaders, and activists—for a total of 21 interviews. The University of Utah IRB approved the protocol. We only contacted for interviews organizations that volunteered to be called in the survey. We asked questions related to organization characteristics, the impact of the hurricane, how they found information, need, networking activities, and suggestions they had for a recovery network. Interviews were conducted using Zoom.com, a video conference software, and lasted from 25 to 60 minutes. The interviews were conducted in Spanish by one of the researchers and a graduate assistant. The audio recordings were transcribed using Sonix software, and then they were edited twice by a graduate assistant and one of the researchers. Quotes that spoke directly to the quantitative data were added to this manuscript using four codes: disaster impact on the organization, changes in interaction with other organizations, knowledge, and use of traditional recovery funding mechanisms and capacity building and collaborations. The qualitative analysis was conducted using Dedoose, a web-based collaborative software.

This particular study uses the qualitative data to elaborate on the descriptive survey findings. The quantitative data were analyzed using Excel. Researchers do not employ quantitative methodologies and, therefore, did not use software packages like SPSS to conduct statistical analysis. The next section discussed the findings, which included: (1) a general profile of the non-profit organizations in Puerto Rico, (2) a description of the disaster impact on the organization, (3) a report changes in interaction with other organizations, (4) the portrayal of knowledge and use of traditional recovery funding mechanisms, and (5) the presentation of a need for education, capacity building, and collaboration.

Findings

General Profile of Non-Profits
The survey asked 20 questions that identified the organization's areas of interest, current institutional capacity to undertake recovery action, as well as willingness to participate in a networking initiative. The results of the survey were analyzed using descriptive statistics and used to understand the existing capacities and needs of local organizations. A profile of respondents is presented below:

- 100 percent incorporated in Puerto Rico
- 80 percent incorporated at the federal level (criteria to receive federal funds)
- 99 percent have a board
- Median number of board meetings per year: six
- Median year of establishment: 1994
- Median number of employees: six
- 62 percent directly involve community members in operations
- Organizations were based in 57 municipalities; most were located in San Juan (72), followed by Ponce (16), Bayamón (15), Caguas (11), Guaynabo (11), and Mayagüez (8).

We asked about the primary mission, purpose, and scope of the organizations we surveyed. We provided ten categories, which are listed in the figure below. The top three categories were Human Services (24 percent), Education (17 percent), and Health Care (17 percent). Our survey allowed respondents to report up to three areas of focus. Some common responses to requests for clarification of "other" included religious purposes, violence prevention, and cultural services.

We asked respondents to report the amount of capital their organizations managed in the prior year, providing them with the categories below. The most frequent response (32 percent) was $100,000 to $499,000 (Figure 2). It is also interesting to note the diversity of funding amounts reported by our sample of organizations. While a small number of organizations (14 percent) reported managing less than $10,000 in the previous year, on the other end of the spectrum, three organizations managed over $10 million. Most organizations (45 percent) depend on member donations, followed by donations from private entities (32 percent), and grants from the central government (16 percent) (Figure 3).

Disaster Impact on the Organization

As might be expected, our respondents report affected buildings (45 percent), including structural or flooding damage, to be the most frequent challenge faced since the hurricane. The second most frequent specific response is an increase in demand for services provided by the organization (14 percent) (Figure 4). As one interview participant simply said, "Demand increased because now there is a greater need." "Other" refers to a loss of funding, lack of information on grants, greater bureaucracy, and lack of communication, among other evident categories.

An executive director of a non-profit organization stated, "Our administrative offices were damaged due to leaks, and our services could not be provided for a week. Despite not having electricity, the employees who were able to arrive at the office were in the street helping people in the shelters." Another participant described the environment that resulted from damage:

The hurricane affected a part of our office that was made of glass—it broke, letting water in. The water damaged some of our archives and information. Thankfully we had some digital backups. In regards to how the hurricane-affected employment...due to PTSD (post-traumatic stress disorder), there were employees that left the organization and preferred to move to the United States or simply abandoned the work—the burden was very heavy throughout the nation to feel apt to help other people.

We also asked if their mission changed after the disaster; 46 percent of respondents changed the organization's mission after the disaster. As the

Figure 1. Primary Mission

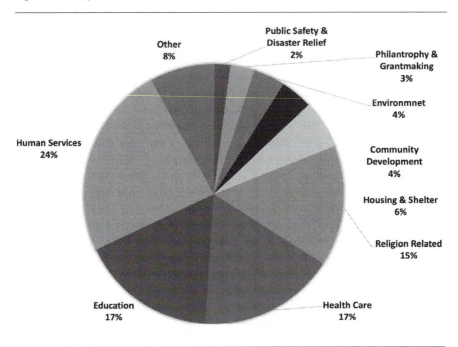

Figure 2. Annual Budget

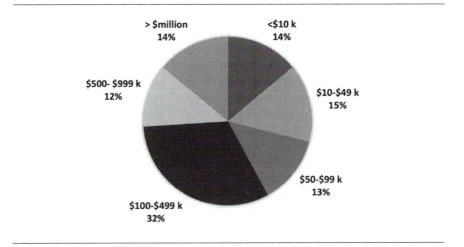

Figure 3. Sources of Funding

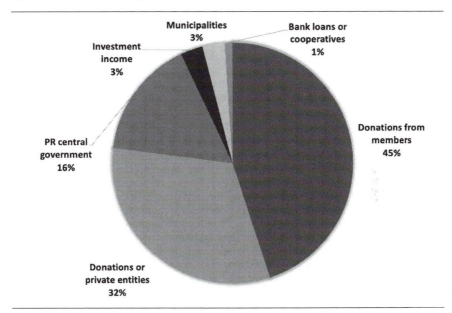

graph notes below, there has been an increase across all sectors (community development, education, health, etc.), but especially in disaster prepared-ness. An interviewee explained, "Everyone was involved with the disaster and aide. We were trying to do our best to provide help. We did what was needed. Our staff banned together and did things that we would not nor-mally do, but now we still need to keep being involved in the recovery."

In particular, staff that responded to the survey on behalf of the non-profit organiza-tions felt less connected to the government and Puerto Rican diaspora organizations.

Changes in Interaction with other Organizations

We asked several questions to understand how networking and capacity among staff at non-profits have changed since the disaster. The question was posed on a Likert scale with values of "much less," "less," "same," "more," and "much more" available for selection by our respondents. For simplified

Figure 4. Annual Budget

Category	Number	Percent
Affected buildings	105	45%
Loss of employees	16	7%
Loss of information or data	15	6%
More demand for services	34	14%
Lack of knowledge regarding reconstruction	9	4%
Other	55	24%
Total	234	100%

reporting, we have combined the counts for "much less" and "less" into the category "decreased," and combined the counts for "more" and "much more" into the category "increased" (Figure 6). We see that staff interaction with other local non-profit staff has increased substantially, while interaction with all other categories has either stayed about the same or diminished. In particular, staff that responded to the survey on behalf of the non-profit organizations felt less connected to the government and Puerto Rican diaspora organizations. In regard to changes in interactions with staff at other non-profit organizations, a participant said:

We worked without light, without water, we worked outside, we had a table set up outside, everything was very "old school" using paper intake forms. We did community outreach one on one, walking throughout the community to see what was going on and what was needed. From there, we formed connections with [staff at] other organizations to buy food supplies and emergency supplies for various communities.

Executive directors of organizations discussed their interactions with staff at other non-profits. One participant expressed their opinion, "I would say [the disaster] increased our communication [with staff at other organizations]....Various [staff of] organizations have called us and asked us to help with projects and tasks.... I would say that I communicate with [staff at] organizations within my network almost daily." Another director agrees, "Our connec-

Figure 5. Changes in the mission after the disaster

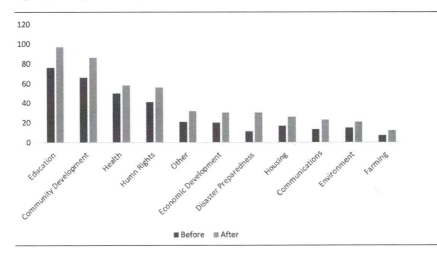

Figure 6. Changes in interactions with organizations

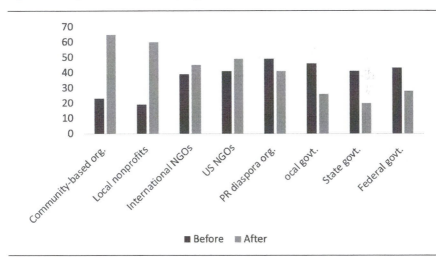

tion and relationship with [staff at] non-profits have been strengthened [since the hurricane]. Before, we really didn't have any communication with other non-profits, and now we are creating more connections, networks." However, organizations staff feel less connected with the government staff:

Figure 7. Knowledge & experience with a recovery financing mechanism

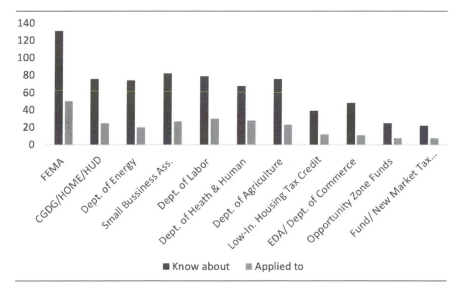

Services and communication with government [staff] have been practically zero...What
we did was with private organizations...as far as the government [staff] we couldn't get
ahold of them after the hurricane. They [the government staff] haven't shown much
interest in helping us, and I don't know about other organizations [staff], but at least in
our case, with our organization [staff], there hasn't been much communication.

Another executive concurred,

My personal position in regard to how the government [staff] has handled the disaster
is that they've obviously handled it very poorly...They haven't been a government
[staff] that involves stakeholders in making decisions of how to use the funds...which is
essential in improving the situation, deeply, not just cosmetically.

Knowledge and Use of Traditional Recovery Funding Mechanisms

Of the funding sources listed, FEMA registers as both the funding source of
which respondents are most familiar as well as the source with which they
are most successful in securing funding (Figure 7). One participant expressed,

Figure 8. Knowledge & experience with a recovery financing mechanism

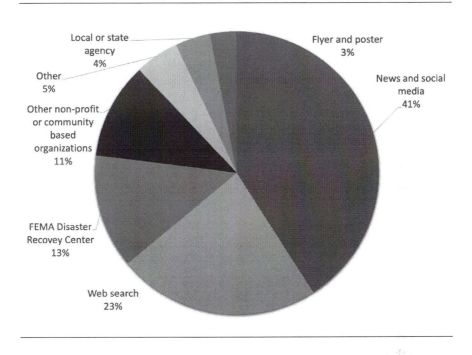

Knowing about the funds is one thing, but being able to apply is something else. You might not be capable of applying because really you need to know a lot of things. It is not simple because you are just getting started. Basically, you do not know anything practical is all theoretical.

Another administrator said,

I think it all depends on your staff and administration. If they have expertise, then you know they can do a good job applying, and they might get the funding. A lot of people think it is very complicated. They think they need many things and it is not really like that. Is more about feeling comfortable with the language and ability to communicate what you are trying to do. Past sometimes indicates the future too, so if you have applied before and manage funds, then this indicates that you are of less risk. People are then willing to invest in you.

Generally, we see a large gap between the frequency in reporting of knowledge of a specific grant opportunity (e.g., FEMA, CDBG, etc.) and successful funding acquisition. This might come as no surprise, as financing is competitive, and it is common that grant proposals do not result in funding for organizations. Moreover, many of the staff in organizations might know about a particular funding source, but that doesn't mean that they have tried to obtain financing. This demonstrates that non-profit organization staff needs organizational capacity building to apply and secure funding.

Need for Education, Capacity Building, and Collaborations

We asked non-profits staff from where they get information, such as opportunities to apply for grants, engagement events, and the like (Figure 8). Many (41 percent) expressed getting information from the news (television and newspaper reporters) and social media users. About a quarter (23 percent) conducted web searches to find the information they needed from content creators. Some 13 percenr receive it from FEMA Disaster Recovery Center personnel, followed by staff at other non-profits or community-based organizations (11 percent). Very few staff of organizations (4 percent) got their information from personnel of a local state agency. One research participant said,

A lot of the activism occurs in social media. Facebook and email have allowed us to have direct communication with the people we interact with, clients, and other organizations. We organize and share information in a fast manner. I think it has had a key role in sharing information about the recovery and what is going on.

We asked about what organizations need. The staff of non-profit organizations reported needing the following in order of importance: information, technical assistance for projects and proposals, training in recovery issues, social networking and support groups, access to data, and advocacy for their mission. A participant shared their point of view:

There are a lot of things we need... greater knowledge of how to receive funds from the government. There are a lot of funds given to improve the community, community development, but the process to get the funds is very long and requires a lot...I would also say that here in Puerto Rico we need more courses specialized in teaching program management. There are a lot of people here who work in construction or as workers who would have an interest in growing, but that doesn't know about program management.

Another director said,

A little of everything, right? We are in a position of growth. We need more resources on how to have a greater reach. Perhaps courses educating about different issues and then how to address those issues...Also to know what federal funds are being offered to the island...and how to access them.

We also asked if people were connected to a network and have attended conferences. The vast majority (74 percent) reported that they have not. Those who attended conferences (25 percent) also provided the names of those networks, which included: Centro de Nueva Economia, Coalición de Lideres Comunitarios, Foundation for Puerto Rico, Fundación Comunitaria, Fundación Ángel Ramos, Red de Fundaciones, Ayuda Legal Huracán María, Hispanic Federation, Enterprise, NeighborWorks, Unidos por Puerto Rico, and Center for Puerto Rican Studies.

An interviewee expressed, "Many of the [staff at] organizations have contacted us to do training and work together.... [The networks] are there to help prepare and train people so they can respond quickly and effectively to whichever issue comes up." "Many of the organizations have contacted us to do training and work together.... [The networks] are there to help prepare and train people so they can respond quickly and effectively to whichever issue comes up." A very well-connected executive director shared with us, "In our network, we have funders, funders here and in the U.S. We are also connected to [staff at other] non-profit organizations...for example, we are working with [staff at] el Centro de Estudios Puertorriqueños, Enterprise, NeighborWorks, and Hispanic Federation. We have a very ample network. We are different organizations that together can help different causes or issues." However, some expressed concerns with helping hands who might be interested mostly motivated by financial gain:

We know that it is a reality that there are people with bad intentions. They see a big opportunity to make a profit out of this disaster. And we are aware of this. We are working with the best alliances we can, but we have to keep our eyes open on who we are making deals with. Because we know that intentions can be mixed, and that's something we are working on constantly. That's kind of stressful. Cause you see that there are a lot of agencies coming to Puerto Rico but which ones are really going to help and which ones are just going to take advantage of the opportunities.

Discussion and conclusion

Above, we discussed four relevant themes: (1) disaster impact on organization, (2) changes in interaction with other organizations, (3) knowledge and use of traditional recovery funding mechanisms, and (4) need for education, capacity building, and collaboration. We can highlight four findings: (1) the natural disaster had a significant impact in non-profit organizations physically and operationally, (2) there is a lot of energy in the non-profit sector, as demonstrated by increased demand for services and changing missions to respond to this demand, (3) there has been intensified local interaction among non-profits; however, non-profits are not "hooked" into formal recovery structures (funding or information) mainly relating to government, and (4) organizations want more help with capacity building across the board—from better understanding recovery to grant-writing.

The participation of the different sectors that encompass the civic sector in Puerto Rico opened a space for dialogue and finding solutions to the challenge of developing Puerto Rico. The transcendent thread between the needs of non-profit organizations can be summarized in three areas: (1) the need for technical assistance in developing long-term sustainable strategies, (2) the need to understand the process to acquire federal funds designated for Puerto Rico, and (3) collaboration between the different non-profit organizations to work together in the reconstruction of Puerto Rico.

Organizations that bring together other organizations are a valuable tool in a recovery scenario, and they have the potential to strengthen the activities of partners.

Organizations that bring together other organizations are a valuable tool in a recovery scenario, and they have the potential to strengthen the activities of partners. IdeaComún is a new organization that seeks to bring people together to work in educational training and to connect people that work in recovery. So much of its impact outside of its current members and partners will take place in the future. IdeaComún has the opportunity of playing a central role in shaping the non-profit sector and becoming active agents in capacity building. IdeaComún can keep sharing knowledge among organizations, developing training courses, and helping organizations to apply for grants, meet regularly, and create a database where data can be used to create projects.

Given that local community organizations are more deeply embedded in the communities they represent, they must continue to be represented in local recovery. This study aims to improve local community organizations' capacity to participate and participate more effectively in disaster recovery. This study is expected to be used by IdeaComún to support local community organizations in Puerto Rico while also providing knowledge and insight into how such organizations can increase their capacity to address disaster recovery. As demonstrated by this study, non-profit organizations are needed to allow an equitable and effective recovery process. In the words of a study participant, "In every agency, there are people who genuinely want to help that genuinely want to see the Island recover and to become what it once was or even better."

REFERENCES

Abelson, Adam. 2003. NGO Networks: Strength in Numbers? Bureau of Democracy, Conflict, and Humanitarian Assistance U.S. Agency for International Development. <https://reliefweb.int/report/world/ngo-networks-strength-numbers/>.

Allen, James, Andrew D. James and Phil Gamlen. 2007. Formal versus Informal Knowledge Networks in R&D: A Case Study Using Social Network Analysis. *R&D Management* 37 (3), 179–96. <https://doi.org/10.1111/j.1467-9310.2007.00468.x/>.

Arabasz, W. J., R. B. Smith and W. D. Richins. 1980. Earthquake Studies along the Wasatch Front, Utah: Network Monitoring, Seismicity, and Seismic Hazards. *Bulletin of the Seismological Society of America* 70(5), 1479–99.

Benson, Charlotte, John Twigg and Mary Myers. 2001. NGO Initiatives in Risk Reduction: An Overview. *Disasters* 25(3), 199–215.

Bisri, Mizan B. F. 2013. Examining Inter-Organizational Network during Emergency Response of West Java Earthquake 2009, Indonesia. Procedia Environmental Sciences, The 3rd International Conference on Sustainable Future for Human Security, SUSTAIN 2012, 3-5 November 2012, Clock Tower Centennial Hall, Kyoto University, JAPAN, 17 (January): 889–98. <https://doi.org/10.1016/j.proenv.2013.02.107/>.

Borges-Méndez, Ramón, Ariam Torres-Cordero, Ivis Garcia, Robert Olansky, Nazife Ganapati, Anuadha Mukherji, Divya Chandrasekhar, Tisha Holmes and Laura Geronimo. 2018. Roundtable: Organizing Community & Nonprofit Networks for Community Rebuilding. <https://www.planning.org/events/activity/9157175/>.

Carlson, Elizabeth J., Marshall Scott Poole, Natalie J. Lambert and John C. Lammers. 2017. A Study of Organizational Reponses to Dilemmas in Interorganizational Emergency Management. *Communication Research* 44(2), 287–315. <https://doi.org/10.1177/0093650215621775/>.

Creech, Terry and Heather Willard. 2001. *Strategic Intentions : Managing Knowledge Networks for Sustainable Development*. First Edition edition. Winnipeg: International Institute for Sustainable Development/Institut International du De.

Doerfel, Marya L., Lisa V. Chewning and Chih-Hui Lai. 2013. The Evolution of Networks and the Resilience of Interorganizational Relationships after Disaster. *Communication Monographs* 80(4), 533–59. <https://doi.org/10.10 80/03637751.2013.828157/>.

Dolnicar, Sara, Helen Irvine and Katie Lazarevski. 2008. Mission or Money? Competitive Challenges Facing Public Sector Nonprofit Organisations in an Institutionalised Environment. *International Journal of Nonprofit and Voluntary Sector Marketing* 13(2), 107–17. <https://doi.org/10.1002/nvsm.311/>.

Doug, Chriss. 2018. Puerto Rico's Power Outage Is Now the Second-Largest Blackout in History. *CNN* 16 April 2018. <https://edition.cnn.com/2018/04/16/us/puerto-rico-blackout-second-largest-globally-trnd/index.html/>.

FEMA. 2018. Puerto Rico One Year after Hurricanes Irma and María. 2018. <https://www.fema.gov/news-release/2018/09/06/puerto-rico-one-year-after-hurricanes-irma-and-maria/>.

Fink, Sheri. 2018. Puerto Rico: How Do We Know 3,000 People Died as a Result of Hurricane Maria? *The New York Times* 13 September. <https://www.nytimes.com/2018/06/02/us/puerto-rico-death-tolls.html/>.

Hinosa, Jennifer, Nashia Román and Edwin Meléndez. 2018. Puerto Rican Post-Maria Relocation by States. Center for Puerto Rican Studies, March. <https://centropr.hunter.cuny.edu/sites/default/files/PDF/Schoolenroll-v2-3-3-2018.pdf/>.

Izumi, Takako and Rajib Shaw. 2012. Effectiveness and Challenges of an Asian NGO Network for Disaster Reduction and Response. *Risk, Hazards & Crisis in Public Policy* 3(2), 1–15. <https://doi.org/10.1515/1944-4079.1106/>.

Jones, Samantha, Komal Aryal and Andrew Collins. 2013. Local-Level Governance of Risk and Resilience in Nepal. *Disasters* 37(3), 442–67. <https://doi.org/10.1111/disa.12006/>.

Kapucu, Naim. 2006. Public-Nonprofit Partnerships for Collective Action in Dynamic Contexts of Emergencies. *Public Administration* 84(1), 205–20. <https://doi.org/10.1111/j.0033-3298.2006.00500.x/>.

_____. 2007. Non-profit Response to Catastrophic Disasters. *Disaster Prevention and Management: An International Journal* 16(4), 551–61. <https://doi.org/10.1108/09653560710817039/>.

Keyes, Langley C., Alex Schwartz, Avis C. Vidal and Rachel G. Bratt. 1996. Networks and Non-profits: Opportunities and Challenges in an Era of Federal Devolution. *Housing Policy Debate* 7(2), 201–29. <https://doi.org/10.1080/10511482.1996.9521219/>.

LeRoux, Kelly and Mary K. Feeney. 2014. *Non-profit Organizations and Civil Society in the United States.* 1 edition. New York: Routledge.

Lewis, David. 2009. *Non-Governmental Organizations and Development.* 1st edition. London: New York: Routledge.

Liberatore, F., C. Pizarro, C. Simón de Blas, M. T. Ortuño and B. Vitoriano. 2013. Uncertainty in Humanitarian Logistics for Disaster Management. A Review. In *Decision Aid Models for Disaster Management and Emergencies*, edited by Begoña Vitoriano, Javier Montero and Da Ruan. 45–74. Atlantis Computational Intelligence Systems. Paris: Atlantis Press. <https://doi.org/10.2991/978-94-91216-74-9_3/>.

Liebler, Claudia, and Marisa Ferri. 2004. NGO Networks: Building Capacity in a Changing World. Bureau for Democracy, Conflict and Humanitarian Assistance Office of Private and Voluntary Cooperation.

Luna, Emmanuel M. 2013. Community-Based Disaster Risk Reduction and Disaster Management. Disaster Management. November 12, 2013. <https://doi.org/10.4324/9780203082539-15/>.

Manring, Susan L. 2007. Creating and Managing Interorganizational Learning Networks To Achieve Sustainable Ecosystem Management. *Organization & Environment* 20(3), 325–46. <https://doi.org/10.1177/1086026607305738/>.

Nolte, Isabella M. and Silke Boenigk. 2011. Public–Nonprofit Partnership Perfor-
     mance in a Disaster Context: The Case of Haiti. *Public Administration*
     89(4), 1385–402. <https://doi.org/10.1111/j.1467-9299.2011.01950.x/>.
Olshansky, Robert B. and Laurie A. Johnson. 2010. Chapter 1: The Hurricane
     Katrina Catastrophe. In *Clear As Mud: Planning for the Rebuilding of New
     Orleans.* 3–20. Np: American Planning Association.
Patterson, Olivia, Frederick Weil and Kavita Patel. 2010. The Role of Community
     in Disaster Response: Conceptual Models. *Population Research and Policy
     Review* 29(2), 127–41. <https://doi.org/10.1007/s11113-009-9133-x/>.
Puerto Rico Department of Housing. 2020. Action Plan Amendment 4 (Substantial
     Amendment). <https://www.cdbg-dr.pr.gov/en/action-plan/>.
Ramsey, K. 2012. Residential Construction Trends in America's Metropolitan Re-
     gions. Washington, D.C.: Office of Sustainable Communities, U.S. Environ-
     mental Protection Agency.
Robinson, Scott E. and Haley Murphy. 2013. Frontiers for the Study of Nonprofit
     Organizations in Disasters. *Risk, Hazards & Crisis in Public Policy* 4(2),
     128–34. <https://doi.org/10.1002/rhc3.12038/>.
Shaw, Rajib. 2012. *Community Based Disaster Risk Reduction.* Np: Emerald Group
     Publishing.
Simo, Gloria and Angela L. Bies. 2007. The Role of Non-profits in Disaster Response:
     An Expanded Model of Cross-Sector Collaboration. *Public Administration
     Review* 67(s1), 125–42. <https://doi.org/10.1111/j.1540-6210.2007.00821.x/>.
Streeten, Paul. 1997. Non-governmental Organizations and Development. *The An-
     nals of the American Academy of Political and Social Science* 554, 193–210.
Sylves, R. 2008. Public Managers, Volunteer Organizations, and Disasters: Emer-
     gency Managers Need Clear Working Relationships with Non-Profits
     and Charitable Organizations That Assist Disaster Victims. *The Public
     Manager* 37(4), 76.
The Associated Press. 2018. Nearly 3,000 Deaths in Puerto Rico Now Blamed on
     Hurricane Maria. *CBC News.* 28 August. <https://www.cbc.ca/news/
     world/puerto-rico-hurricane-death-3000-1.4801826/>.
Weisbord, M., ed. 1992. *Discovering Common Ground.* Np: Berrett-Koehler Publishers.
Willie, Drye. 2018. Worst Hurricanes on Record in Order of Wind Strength. *National
     Geographic* 12 October. <https://www.nationalgeographic.com/environ-
     ment/2018/10/strongest-hurricanes-in-history/>.

Centros de Apoyo Mutuo: reconfigurando la asistencia en tiempos de desastre

JACQUELINE VILLARRUBIA-MENDOZA AND ROBERTO VÉLEZ-VÉLEZ

ABSTRACT

Weeks after Hurricane Maria hit Puerto Rico, the emergence of community-based initiatives known as "centros de apoyo mutuo" (mutual support centers) across the island was evident. Based on over a year of fieldwork studying the emergence and work of CAMs, it is evident that breaking away from the dependency cycle born out of state assistantship programs represents the biggest challenge to be faced. Our work addresses the following questions: How do CAMs transform people's expectations regarding assistance? How do CAMs create a movement toward autonomy and *autogestión* after approximately a century of policies that foster paternalism and dependency? Our study reveals that more than promoting a critique towards assistensialism, CAMs promote the assertion of autogestión as a vehicle of social transformation. [Key words: Hurricane María, self-management, assistentialism, mutual support, disasters, recovery]

Introducción

Tras el paso del huracán María el 20 de septiembre del 2017, se hizo patente que el Estado, tanto a nivel federal como a nivel local, estaba fallando en su misión de proveer asistencia humanitaria a las comunidades más impactadas por la devastación causada —parcialmente— por el huracán. Este fenómeno natural develó para muchos las condiciones de precariedad marcadas por una crisis socioeconómica que han aquejado a Puerto Rico por más de una década (Cabán 2018; LeBrón 2016).

Paralelo a esto, surgieron a lo largo del archipiélago iniciativas comunitarias conocidas como Centros de Apoyo Mutuo (CAM), que fueron centrales en los procesos de auscultar y asistir las comunidades impactadas. Los CAM buscan remover los modelos tradicionales de respuesta y recuperación que mantienen intactas las estructuras de poder que fomentan la dependencia y la marginalización. Aprovechando así la coyuntura histórica del huracán María y la crisis fiscal, los CAM buscan hacerle frente al asistencialismo a través del potenciamiento de la autogestión y el empoderamiento de las comunidades marginadas.

A casi tres años del paso del huracán y dentro del lento proceso de recuperación, un número significativo de CAM siguen operativos e impulsando agendas a largo plazo. Su enfoque se ha centrado en la transformación de las expectativas de las comunidades afectadas por el huracán sobre el proceso de recuperación pos-María. Guiadas por una crítica a las nociones tradicionales de la asistencia y por principios cementados en una visión participativa e

Jacqueline Villarrubia-Mendoza (jvillarrubia@colgate.edu) is an associate professor in the Sociology and Anthropology Department at Colgate University. Her research focuses on Latin American/Caribbean migration to the United States. Villarubia-Mendoza's work has been published in *Latino Studies*, *Current Sociology*, and the *Journal of Migration and Integration*, among others.

Roberto Vélez-Vélez (velezr@newpaltz.edu) is an associate professor of Sociology at SUNY New Paltz. His research has concentrated on the antimilitary movement in Vieques; the intersections among memory, identity, and politics; and US–Latin American political dynamics. Vélez-Vélez's work has been published in *Mobilization*, *Social Movements Studies*, and the *American Journal of Cultural Sociology*.

Both are currently collaborating on a National Science Foundation-funded project related to the emergence of Centros de Apoyo Mutuo (mutual support centers) in the aftermath of Hurricane Maria in Puerto Rico (ID #1917961/1917980).

inclusiva del desarrollo, los CAM han puesto en práctica una serie de ejercicios organizativos para cultivar en los residentes una visión hacia la autonomía comunitaria. Una examinación de las narrativas de los organizadores y las iniciativas puestas en marcha nos muestran cómo, por medio de una reconfiguración de la asistencia, estas organizaciones buscan crear conciencia de las limitaciones del asistencialismo, involucrar a los residentes en actividades de desarrollo comunitario autogestionado y demostrarles los beneficios de la autogestión para la resolución de sus problemas.

Nuestro análisis comienza con una exposición de la perspectiva social del desastre y la consideración del cambio social en este contexto por medio de fenómenos emergentes y el apoyo mutuo. Desde este marco teórico, presentamos un acercamiento a los CAM, que sugiere una subversión a la asistencia partiendo de parámetros alternativos sobre el rol y el involucramiento de la comunidad en la recuperación. El análisis entonces se centra en la discusión de los ejercicios organizativos de los CAM que buscan cultivar la autogestión como alternativa al asistencialismo. El texto concluye con una contextualización del fenómeno del CAM como uno de transformación social profunda que trasciende la recuperación posdesastre.

La dimensión social del desastre

En el pasado, los desastres se entendían como procesos desencadenados por la naturaleza o "actos de Dios", desvinculando así el rol humano (Picou y Marshall 2007). En la actualidad, el consenso descansa en que "todas y cada una de las fases y aspectos del desastre... el contorno del desastre y la diferencia entre quién vive y quién muere es en mayor o menor medida un cálculo social" (Smith 2006, 1). Con este argumento se busca reconocer que los desastres, aunque sean de origen meteorológico o geológico, tienen impactos que van a lo largo de las fisuras estructurales de la sociedad (Cutter 2006; Martínez Martínez 2013). De aquí que los desastres no afectan a todos por igual, ya que la vulnerabilidad es informada por condiciones estructurales, tales como pobreza, raza y género, entre otros, que dominan el entorno social.

Más allá de reconocer la causa social de los desastres, estos reflejan las desigualdades estructurales, y de igual forma exacerban las condiciones de precariedad y desigualdad que las comunidades experimentan, sobre todo durante el periodo de respuesta y recuperación (Hartman y Squires 2006;

Kleiner et al. 2007; Oliver-Smith 1994; Padilla et al. 2016). La exacerbación de la vulnerabilidad de las comunidades resulta en experiencias más agudas de daños cuando estas se enfrentan a desastres. (Lavell 2000; Padilla et at. 2016). De aquí que podemos argüir que la vulnerabilidad a desastres "remite a procesos generadores de esa condición", es decir, las relaciones sociales que contribuyen y determinan esta vulnerabilidad (Macías 1992, 6). Por ende, hay que auscultar las relaciones sociales que sostienen y se afianzan de esta dinámica de poder para atajar estas vulnerabilidades. Solo por medio de la eliminación de los factores condicionales de la vulnerabilidad social se puede infundir en los sectores sociales empobrecidos la capacidad de recuperarse y mostrar una disposición institucional a reducir el riesgo (Macías 1992).

La respuesta del Estado al desastre

Desde la prevención hasta la respuesta y recuperación, toda acción del Estado ante el desastre tiene que entenderse como una informada por fuerzas económicas, políticas y sociales. La expectativa de que, en un desastre, algún tipo de respuesta es competencia del Estado se sustenta en que este ha asumido "tener la autoridad" para atenderlo (Schneider 2018). El proceso de estructuración de un "estado catastrófico", encargado de responder a desastres, fue uno guiado por patentes principios de gubernamentalidad. Esta interpretación asume que "el estado tenía la autoridad de regular a sus habitantes según lo que, a su juicio, era el bien común" (Schwartz 2018, 288). De esta manera, el acercamiento del Estado para con la respuesta al desastre es guiado por una visión estadocentrista (Taylor-Gooby 1981).

A dos años del paso del huracán Katrina, el barrio más pobre de Nueva Orléans —el Lower Ninth Ward— aún no se había rehabilitado, miles de personas continuaban desplazadas y los índices de pobreza continuaban altos (Hartman y Squires 2006).

Esta perspectiva implica que lo social —problemas, actores y soluciones— es definido desde la prerrogativa del Estado. De aquí que las políticas sociales se enfoquen en el razonamiento gubernamental sobre la carencia, la necesidad y el merecer (Taylor-Gooby 1981). Por ende, la respuesta posdesastre es una caracterizada por el intervencionismo desde arriba, regulatorio, "plagado de un lenguaje paternalista", y reproduciendo las dinámicas de poder correspondientes a este (Schwartz 2018, 290). Esta convicción estadocentrista es asumida por la ciudadanía, que mira hacia el Estado y sus figuras públicas como fuente de dirección durante la crisis (Schneider 2018). La forma en que esta intervención del Estado se produce depende de cómo este entienda su rol: si es uno de benefactor —acercamiento desde arriba— o de facilitador —desde abajo— (Schneider 2018).

La ausencia de una respuesta institucional al desastre que considere la desigualdad social en el diseño de planes de prevención, mitigación y recuperación expone a las poblaciones vulnerables a mayores riesgos e impactos (Padilla et al. 2016). Por ejemplo, el huracán Katrina develó al mundo cómo los altos niveles de pobreza y desempleo, combinados con una extrema segregación racial, falta de acceso a transportación privada y una mayor probabilidad de vivir en áreas susceptibles a inundaciones, dificultaron significativamente el desalojo y/o la preparación adecuada por parte de los residentes empobrecidos de Nueva Orléans (Dyson 2006). A dos años del paso del huracán Katrina, el barrio más pobre de Nueva Orléans —el Lower Ninth Ward— aún no se había rehabilitado, miles de personas continuaban desplazadas y los índices de pobreza continuaban altos (Hartman y Squires 2006). "El huracán Katrina no solamente expuso las deficiencias principales en las áreas de planificación de la preparación para emergencias y desastres. De igual manera expuso las desigualdades a nivel social, físico y económico entre los grupos de la población" (Padilla et al. 2016, 148).

De igual manera, tanto la *calidad* y la *forma* como el *qué* y el *cómo* se entienden y experimentan la respuesta al desastre se suscriben a las dinámicas de la economía política dominante. En el contexto de Puerto Rico, la respuesta institucional al paso del huracán María, así como a desastres anteriores, ha sido concebida tanto desde la colonialidad como del neoliberalismo (Pérez-Lizasuain 2018). Estos marcos discursivos sugieren, por un lado, dependencia a la metrópolis y su política asistencial y, por el otro, un acercamiento a la respuesta y la recuperación desde arriba, guiado por las tendencias del mercado, medidas de austeridad y privatización de los servicios.

Fenómenos emergentes y ayuda mutua

Drabek (1986), Drabek y McEntire (2003) y Oliver-Smith (1994), entre otros, visualizan las etapas de respuesta y recuperación como unas dominadas por "fenómenos emergentes". Esto se refiere al surgimiento de nuevas organizaciones y comportamientos que responden a condiciones cambiantes (Stallings y Quarantelli 1985). Cuando las estructuras existentes no cumplen con sus roles y responsabilidades, o la comunidad entiende que es necesario responder a la crisis, podemos anticipar el surgimiento de fenómenos emergentes (Wenger 1992). Los fenómenos emergentes abarcan al "grupo emergente", que se caracteriza como una organización recién formada que atiende problemas asociados con las emergencias posdesastre (Dynes 1970). Estos grupos están compuestos de ciudadanos que, aunque no están constituidos como organización, producen una respuesta, ya sea a la ausencia total de organizaciones formales o a la ausencia de una respuesta temprana y eficiente (Stallings y Quarantelli 1985, 84; Stallings 1978, 91). Drury y colegas (2009, 489) arguyen que bajo condiciones de desastre surge una solidaridad en función del "destino compartido" entre los individuos que encaran la emergencia como grupo. Muchos de estos procesos organizativos toman lugar a nivel de comunidad, donde, a la vez que incrementa la "solidaridad interna", surge un "liderato local" que tiene un "mejor y más profundo" entendimiento de cuáles son sus necesidades y las maneras de atenderlas (Mileti et al. 1975; Schuller 2012, 63). En el proceso, se priorizan las acciones, los recursos y las formas de producción que tengan "funciones de apoyo mutuo" (Wenger 1992).

La literatura de desastres ha identificado la "asistencia mutua" o el "apoyo mutuo" como denominador común en la gestión de respuesta y recuperación posdesastre en virtud de fomentar la autogestión y/o la resistencia (Chamlee-Wright 2010; Jon y Purcell 2018). Chamlee-Wright (2010) identificó la "asistencia mutua" como una entre varias estrategias utilizadas por los residentes en Nueva Orléans en su proceso de recuperación. "La asistencia mutua es una estrategia por la cual los sobrevivientes de la tormenta se apoyaron unos a otros por medio del intercambio de trabajo, refugio, herramientas, entre otras..." (2010, 45). Esta provee apoyo material a los residentes y restaura sus relaciones sociales, a la vez que "indica" a otros el inicio de la recuperación. Esto infunde en los residentes un sentido de compromiso al regreso y a la restauración de los vecindarios, lo cual activa la acción colectiva. Esta señal de que la comunidad ha regresado también sirve de precursor a la acción institucional, para incentivar la inversión y atención de necesidades por parte del gobierno.

Jon y Purcell (2018) sugieren una visión de la recuperación desde la resistencia y la autogestión que se entiende como "resiliencia radical". Esta no tan solo es emergente de entre los afectados por el desastre, o sea, desde abajo, sino que también produce una "agenda transformativa que abre oportunidades de voz política, de resistencia, y que reta la estructura de poder" (2018, 237). Desde una síntesis de las literaturas de la planificación radical-anarquista y la sociología del desastre, se propone una conceptualización de la resiliencia que asume el empoderamiento de las comunidades y su rol central en el proceso de recuperación como elemento integral en las fases posdesastre. Aunque los modelos que describen Jon y Purcell (2018) no se presentan explícitamente como unos basados en la ayuda mutua como lo hace Chamlee-Wright (2010), las descripciones de colectivización de recursos, la orientación de diseño y decisión desde abajo, y el énfasis en el modelo participativo y local remiten a gestiones compatibles y comparables al uso del apoyo mutuo.

En el contexto posdesastre, uno de los retos de los movimientos sociales y de las organizaciones enfocadas en cultivar una visión colectiva y de empoderamiento es figurar cómo atajar externalidades de la asistencia que reproducen el individualismo y la actitud pasiva entre los ciudadanos (Bacallao-Pino 2016, Rivera y Kliksberg 2007). La vertiente teórica dominante argumenta que los desastres tienen una capacidad muy limitada para gestar cambio social transformativo (Drabek 1986). No tan solo los cambios en política pública tras un desastre son una respuesta a corto plazo y no representan "un cambio de prioridades a gran escala ni duradero", sino que tienden a afianzar el poder de las élites políticas (Drabek 1986 cf. Passerini 2000, 67). Cabe resaltar que, opuesto a esto, la temporalidad que producen los desastres sirve como un espacio donde surgen "sociabilidades alternativas" (Pérez-Lizasuain 2018, 44) donde los movimientos sociales pueden expandir su campo político (Passerini 2000). Considerando la literatura de los fenómenos emergentes en conjunto con la perspectiva de la ayuda mutua y la autogestión en el proceso de respuesta y recuperación posdesastre, podemos establecer un acercamiento mejor informado de la respuesta de los CAM al huracán María.

Figura 1: Descripción de Muestra de CAMs por Localización, Geografía y Área Programática

Nombre	Localización	Foco geográfico	Agricultura	Alimentación	Cultura	Economía	Educación	Geriatría	Salud	Sustentabilidad	Reconstrucción	Vivienda
Brigada Solidaria del Oeste (BSO)	Varios	Mixto		✓		✓				✓	✓	
CAM Bucarabones Unidos (CAMBU)	Las Marias	Rural		✓		✓				✓		
CAM Bartolo	Lares-Castañer	Rural	✓		✓	✓						✓
CAM Caguas	Caguas	Urbano		✓		✓			✓			
CAM Las Carolinas	Caguas	Urbano		✓				✓	✓			
CAM Jíbaro-Lares (CAMJI)	Lares	Rural	✓			✓				✓		
CAM-Utuado (CAM-U)	Utuado	Mixto	✓				✓			✓		
Caminando la Utopía	Comerio-Cidra	Mixto						✓	✓			
La Olla Común	Río Piedras	Urbano		✓								

Metodología

Este proyecto es el resultado de 18 meses de trabajo en el cual teníamos como objetivo recopilar datos relacionados a las experiencias y motivaciones de individuos y colectivos que se organizaron en CAM. Nuestro diseño metodológico se compone de dos elementos principales: observación partícipe y entrevistas. En cuanto a la observación partícipe, durante un año participamos como voluntarios —cuyo rol de investigadores era conocido— en eventos de repartición de suministros, reconstrucción de hogares, eventos comunitarios y reuniones convocadas por los CAM. Este rol como voluntarios y etnógrafos nos proveyó un mejor entendimiento sobre las motivaciones, las experiencias y los retos de los CAM. Esto también trajo consigo consideraciones de índole ética que nos llevaron a un proceso reflexivo sobre la necesidad de establecer delimitaciones entre ambos roles. Estas consideraciones eran importantísimas para poder mantener una visión crítica como investigadores, sobre todo cuando nuestras familias fueron afectadas por el huracán y nuestro rol como voluntarios en los CAM requirió, en ocasiones, de un gran compromiso de tiempo que dificultaba tomar notas con detenimiento. Llevamos a cabo 31 entrevistas con miembros de CAM alrededor de Puerto Rico. De los CAM activos durante el periodo de trabajo de campo que fueron invitados a participar en el proyecto, se lograron entrevistas con miembros de nueve centros (figura 1). Las entrevistas tuvieron una duración promedio de dos horas y fueron realizadas en persona, grabadas y transcritas. Los participantes fueron seleccionados mediante un muestreo de bola de nieve deliberado en el cual les hicimos un acercamiento a coordinadores de distintos CAM para entrevistarlos. Una vez entrevistamos a estas personas, les preguntamos si nos podían referir a otros coordinadores que pudiesen estar disponibles e interesados en participar en nuestro proyecto.

Las entrevistas siguieron una guía semiestructurada que establecía una serie de preguntas base alrededor de temas que arrojaran luz sobre el trabajo de organizar comunidades y sus objetivos organizativos y de acción a corto y largo plazo. Más aun, se abordaron temas relacionados a la conceptualización y puesta en marcha de la autogestión por parte de los coordinadores de los CAM, su entendimiento sobre la precariedad y la crisis en Puerto Rico previo al huracán y cómo relacionan su trabajo actual con procesos de transformación social más allá de la emergencia inmediata producida por el huracán María. Todas las entrevistas fueron grabadas y transcritas en español para luego ser codificadas usando un programa cualitativo, MAXQDA, para su análisis. El proceso de codificación siguió un acercamiento inductivo dividido en dos partes: primero, basado en las preguntas de investigación, la literatura que la informa y la guía de entrevista semiestructurada, se crea un grupo de categorías de análisis primario (nivel superior); y segundo, por medio de una lectura minuciosa y reflexiva de las entrevistas, se identifican patrones que se entiendan relevantes y que no estén capturados por las categorías a nivel superior, produciéndose un grupo de categorías secundarias (nivel inferior). De igual forma, todas las notas de observación partícipe, junto a materiales adquiridos en el trabajo de campo, fueron digitalizadas en MAXQDA para su codificación.

Centros de apoyo mutuo en contexto

Unas dos semanas antes del paso del huracán María, el huracán Irma pasó a 60 millas al noreste de Puerto Rico como una tormenta categoría 5, dejando a un millón de personas sin electricidad (*Primera Hora* 2018). Esta experiencia llevó a reflexionar sobre la posible catástrofe que podría experimentar Puerto Rico de ser azotado directamente por un huracán mayor e influyó en la formación de los CAM. Estos surgieron como iniciativas de rescate y recuperación en la inmediatez de la emergencia, así como en respuesta al mal manejo y la distribución de ayuda por parte de agencias gubernamentales a nivel local y federal (Sosa y Mazzei 2017).

Inicialmente, estos se enfocaron en una variedad de tareas atadas al estado de emergencia: (1) distribución de donativos y suministros, (2)

Figura 2: Distribución de CAMs en Puerto Rico (2017-2019)

organización de brigadas para ayudar en la limpieza de escombros y (3) asistencia a individuos con necesidades urgentes de vivienda y alimentación. Con el paso a la recuperación, los CAM expandieron sus agendas de trabajo para incluir proyectos a largo plazo que enfatizaban principios de autogestión (Vélez-Vélez y Villarrubia-Mendoza 2018).

La adopción del nombre Centro de Apoyo Mutuo tenía el propósito de llevar un mensaje claro de que la organización se iba a regir por el apoyo mutuo y la autogestión (Roberto 2018).

El primer CAM en surgir fue CAM-Caguas, unos nueve días tras el paso del huracán (entrevista con Giovanni Roberto). Sus orígenes datan de los comedores sociales que se establecieron en distintos recintos de la UPR desde 2013. La adopción del nombre Centro de Apoyo Mutuo tenía el propósito de llevar un mensaje claro de que la organización se iba a regir por el apoyo mutuo y la autogestión (Roberto 2018). A poco tiempo de haberse establecido CAM-Caguas, surgieron a lo largo de Puerto Rico otros grupos que tomaron —en su mayoría— la decisión de mantener el nombre y la misma narrativa política antisistémica con base en el apoyo mutuo y la autogestión (figura 2).

Cabe resaltar varios puntos sobre los CAM que los caracteriza como producto de las mismas condiciones emergentes del desastre que propiciaron la solidaridad que los moviliza. Primero, es notable la cantidad de CAM en la región centro-rural de la isla. Aunque todo el archipiélago puertorriqueño sufrió daños por el paso del huracán María, la región central experimentó tanto los daños más severos como una respuesta más tardía en el proceso de recuperación. Segundo, cada CAM se enfoca en una serie de áreas programáticas que responden a las prioridades delineadas por las comunidades (figura 1). Tercero, aun cuando los CAM han coordinado una serie de encuentros en los cuales buscan forjar vínculos y compartir experiencias, ya que comparten una visión de apoyo mutuo y autogestión, estos no son un grupo homogéneo. Los CAM funcionan de forma independiente y cada uno articula sus estrategias de acción basado en el capital social y los recursos a su disposición. A casi tres años del paso del huracán María por Puerto Rico, la mayoría de los CAM siguen en pie, gestando proyectos relacionados a la recuperación pos-María, pero también en otros que buscan potenciar el desarrollo integral socioeconómico de sus comunidades[8].

Desmantelando el asistencialismo

Inmediatamente después de que el huracán María impactara a Puerto Rico, los CAM eran conscientes de que había una gran necesidad de proveer asistencia a las comunidades más impactadas. Tal como nos cuentan Giovanni y Fabiola:

...después del desastre, pues, pues rápido lo que viene es toda esta perspectiva de asistir a la población, que se entiende y hasta cierto punto uno no la puede criticar, porque la gente tiene necesidad y hay que proveer para esa necesidad. Pero a la misma vez, uno sabe que lo que está atado a esa asistencia es una manera de ver las cosas, tú sabes, es una manera de dejar las cosas como están. (Giovanni – CAM-Caguas)

Porque no podíamos esperar ayuda política, sino que nosotros mismos tuvimos que darle cara a la situación, porque no había de otra forma. Si nos quedamos esperando, pues es la hora que no se hubiera hecho nada. (Fabiola – Olla Común)

Estas reflexiones —representativas de respuestas similares— hacen patente que los CAM buscan cuestionar el discurso que sitúa al Estado como el único ente a resolver los retos tras el desastre. En esta gesta, se busca romper con la noción de que las comunidades son actores pasivos dispuestos a recibir lo que se les dé sin incorporarlos en la toma de decisiones.

Los CAM buscan presentar una visión alternativa al estado catastrófico, problematizando así las relaciones sociales que informan esta manera de responder al desastre.

Nosotras estábamos bien claras desde el principio que no queremos actuar como el gobierno, como una agencia gubernamental... No queríamos convertirnos en un ente de asistencialismo. (Sandra – BSO)

Entre las fallas del estadocentrismo y la necesidad en tiempos de crisis, los CAM han buscado resignificar lo que involucra la labor de responder al desastre. Esto implica romper con visiones esencialistas que suelen normalizar la intervención del Estado (Guardiola 2012; Schneider 2018). Organizaciones como los CAM buscan proveer asistencia basada en la creación de prácticas democráticas participativas que se enfoquen en el bienestar del colectivo y en el empoderamiento del sujeto (Bacallao-Pino 2016).

La gestión de asistencia por parte de los CAM sugiere promover una dinámica oposicional al asistencialismo. Entendiendo que todas las relaciones de asistencialismo también son intersecadas por "puntos de resistencia" que promueven la autonomía y la autogestión (Cotto-Morales 2006, 126), los CAM proponen crear un espacio para ejecutar versiones alternativas de la asistencia.

Cuando uno se siente parte de una comunidad, pues ya no tiene esa perspectiva jerárquica de arriba-abajo, y tiro toallas o tiro semillas o tiro comida, o lo que sea, sino que me conviene que mi comunidad sea fortalecida. [...] Porque yo creo que al fin y al cabo lo que buscamos es empoderar la gente de su entorno. (Damary – BSO)

En este espacio, la introducción de nuevas relaciones entre beneficiario y proveedor de asistencia inicia una ruptura en el ciclo de las relaciones de dominio y dependencia. O sea, tal como Pérez-Lizasuain (2018) sugiere, los CAM, reconociendo una zona de contacto, crean en la recuperación la pauta para cultivar nuevas nociones sobre la responsabilidad, el colectivo y la autonomía por medio de una subversión de la respuesta.

Esta visión de respuesta y recuperación ante el desastre es también informada desde la precariedad de un Estado en quiebra y desmantelado por el neoliberalismo. En el contexto de Puerto Rico, tal como expone Kinder (2016) sobre Detroit, las iniciativas autogestionadas, como los CAM, vienen a llenar el espacio que dejó el Estado benefactor y que la recuperación desde el modelo neoliberal promovió, lo que inspira los imaginarios de la autogestión y del apoyo mutuo.

Subversión de la respuesta en práctica

Para producir una visión alternativa sobre la recuperación, hay que proveer parámetros igualmente alternativos que sitúen al individuo en un nuevo contexto de gestionar sus necesidades y soluciones. Al examinar los objetivos y la misión de los CAM, podemos identificar los fundamentos filosóficos que sostienen su visión de autogestión: el acercamiento "desde abajo y desde adentro" y el principio de "apoyo mutuo, esfuerzo propio".

"Desde abajo y desde adentro" sugiere un acercamiento al desarrollo desde la base, así como un énfasis en la comunidad como eje y gestor del proceso de desarrollo socioeconómico:

Porque ahí viene también un proceso de formación desde adentro y desde abajo. Desde adentro, nosotras que estamos aquí pues estamos viendo en trabajar un proceso de sanación para compartirles de mejor manera a las futuras generaciones unas ideas de progreso [...] vemos cómo compartir unas ideas que rompen con la narrativa actual, ¿verdad? Y vamos sustituyendo con una contra narrativa ese poder hegemónico que [se] ha creado... (Omar – CAMBU)

Bajo la premisa de "desde abajo y desde adentro" se busca configurar nuevas relaciones sociales de poder para las comunidades marginadas. Para los organizadores, esta reconfiguración del poder es un cambio en dirección, ya sea "poder desde abajo" (Pluma y Marisel) o transformación social "de abajo hacia arriba" (Damary). El centrar a la comunidad en los procesos de recuperación propone una subversión a las narrativas tradicionales de respuesta al desastre donde estas son definidas como receptores de proyectos o políticas de desarrollo determinadas a priori y desde arriba, usualmente sin consulta (Molinari 2018; Noboa-Ortega 2018).

Bacallao-Pino (2016) argumenta que los movimientos sociales tienen la capacidad de examinar la articulación entre desarrollo y democracia, y poner en práctica nuevas dinámicas organizativas y relaciones sociales que promueven la horizontalidad, la equidad y la autonomía. Jesef, de CAM-Utuado, nos describe la manera en que un acercamiento desde abajo produce esa reconfiguración que Bacallao-Pino propone:

Pues, yo diría que esto mismo que se está haciendo [taller de salud] como que son estos enlaces comunitarios, identificar las personas que ya, ¿verdad?, están conscientes de que no quieren depender más de la... del asistencialismo de arriba, sino de crear como que nuevas estructuras de apoyo desde abajo.

Entonces, esta reconfiguración cambia la lógica estadocentrista que guía las políticas de la recuperación posdesastre y las relaciones de poder por un modelo que parte desde las comunidades.

Al incluir a quienes experimentan la realidad objetiva de la necesidad en los procesos de definir, ponderar y responder a sus problemas, se produce una política social que revierte las dinámicas de poder existentes. Este cambio en la lógica estadocentrista propone una inclusión participativa de las comunidades, donde las "soluciones" a los problemas sociales surgen *"con* el pueblo y nunca *sobre* o simplemente *para él"* (Martínez Román 2012, 1046—énfasis añadido).

"Apoyo mutuo, esfuerzo propio" apunta hacia la interdependencia entre miembros de la comunidad a la vez que establece la responsabilidad de estos para con el colectivo. La incorporación de las comunidades marginadas en los procesos de recuperación involucra tanto un empoderamiento de estas así como cultivar el germen de la autogestión (Velázquez Reca 2007). Raquela y Marisel, de la Brigada Solidaria del Oeste y La Olla Común, respectivamente, definen el apoyo mutuo en práctica;

El lema que se ha estado utilizando desde las organizaciones comunitarias desde hace mucho tiempo es "apoyo mutuo, esfuerzo propio" [...] Que es, ¿qué te falta a ti para completar tu techo? ¿Tienes recursos? ... Yo Brigada te doy recursos, tu compromiso es en la próxima casa que nosotras vayamos a trabajar, tú tienes que ir allí a apoyar. Es un poco salir de esta mirada de "te doy y te doy" pero aquí tú tienes que dar a cambio el apoyo que estas recibiendo.

Modelar como una forma de romper un poco con el asistencialismo, en el sentido de que la gente se involucre a trabajar. Si tú consigues suministros, tú puedes donar algo, [o] tú puedes trabajar.

Los CAM empujan a que el individuo "se asuma", que reconozca su responsabilidad y autoridad sobre el proceso para afrontar los retos en su comunidad. Esto se fomenta a través de un ejercicio organizativo horizontal e inclusivo que se entiende que tiene un efecto estimulante sobre los colectivos, ya que "incrementa la autoestima, aumenta la solidaridad, crea perspectivas sociales y tiende a reducir la anomia" (Petras 2002).

El "apoyo mutuo, esfuerzo propio" se palpa en las prácticas cotidianas que nutren el funcionamiento de los CAM. En La Olla Común, un joven deambulante se da de voluntario a limpiar sus utensilios tras haber comido; en CAM-Las Carolinas, las señoras del barrio se turnan la ronda de entregas de comida; y en Bajadero, Lares, miembros de la comunidad asisten en construir un vivero y semillero junto a organizadores de CAM Jíbaro-Lares (Notas de campo). Rosario, de CAM Las Carolinas, describe el apoyo mutuo como un elemento de cohesión comunitaria:

[P]ara mí, lo importante en esta comunidad que quiero que sepa la gente es que estén unidos, como estaban nuestros abuelos, nuestros padres. [...] Tú necesitas, yo te doy, yo necesito, tú me das. [...] ellos levantaron esta comunidad y así me gustaría que esta comunidad se levantara. No esperar por nadie, que... que ellos mismo hagan sus labores.

Esta conjunción del participante/beneficiario, resuena con la descripción de Solnit (2009) sobre la ayuda mutua como un ejercicio recíproco, donde los participantes son tanto proveedores como receptores.

El apoyo mutuo es una vía alternativa a aquella provista por el Estado que se enfoca en soluciones individualizadas e informadas por tendencias del mercado. Por el contrario, el apoyo mutuo se sostiene tanto por redes de apoyo como por lazos afectivos entre los participantes (Molinari 2018). El documento fundacional de La Red de Apoyo Mutuo, proyecto que intentó abarcar a los CAM, expone la idea del apoyo mutuo y evidencia cuán central es dentro de la misión y visión de los CAM:

El apoyo mutuo es un valor que se refiere a la reciprocidad, ayuda, y colaboración entre personas o grupos para el beneficio mutuo. A diferencia de la caridad y las asistencias del gobierno, el apoyo mutuo no implica la superioridad de quien da sobre quien recibe, se fundamenta, en vez, en la solidaridad. Además, destaca la importancia del poder compartido, la participación directa de la gente, y la oposición a las jerarquías y la competencia. Para nosotrxs el apoyo mutuo, cuando se hace desde el corazón, es un valor integral y una herramienta de transformación desde las mismas comunidades (desde abajo) y desde lo emocional e interior (desde adentro).

Estos principios guían el discurso y la práctica de la autogestión en los CAM, a la vez que informan sus imaginarios y visiones de futuro para con Puerto Rico. Entonces, por medio del apoyo mutuo y el poder desde abajo, el CAM se convierte en vehículo de un proyecto colectivista cuyo objetivo es obtener cambio social profundo.

En nuestra observación del trabajo comunitario de los CAM para cultivar la autogestión, resaltan como denominadores comunes la educación como vía a la concienciación, la participación como fuente de empoderamiento y la autosuficiencia como germen de la autonomía comunitaria.

La autogestión como ejercicio organizativo

Según los CAM, el huracán María proveyó una coyuntura idónea para procurar y gestar un proyecto de transformación social de carácter profundo, ya que se revelaron las condiciones de desigualdad y precariedad preexistentes a la vez que ocurrió un alza en la solidaridad por parte de vecinos (Notas de campo). En nuestra observación del trabajo comunitario de los CAM para cultivar la autogestión, resaltan como denominadores comunes la educación como vía a la concienciación, la participación como fuente de empoderamiento y la autosuficiencia como germen de la autonomía comunitaria. Esta construcción de la autogestión es una a largo plazo, ya que los organizadores entienden el reto que representa en una sociedad que únicamente ha experimentado una versión asistencialista del poder y el desarrollo.

Educación y concienciación. Nuestro análisis refleja un patrón en el cual los CAM hacen uso amplio de talleres, ferias educativas y/o demostraciones como parte de los programas de apoyo comunitario. Desde talleres sobre huertos comunitarios, energía renovable, salud, y hasta filtración de agua, la educación resalta como elemento sobresaliente entre los CAM. Varios CAM describen sus intervenciones en comunidades como una bifurcada, ya que proveen algún tipo de recurso o servicio con un taller suplementario, promoviendo la consideración del suministro que reciben más allá de la situación actual.

Nosotros hicimos varias charlas de purificación de agua porque estábamos entregando filtros. No era como, aquí esta este filtro, lee las instrucciones y sigue caminando. Tú sabes, se organizaba la comunidad y se entregaban los filtros y se hacía un taller para educar sobre los distintos usos [del agua]. Y así siempre lo hemos hecho. Siempre traemos una base educativa. (Jorge – CAM-U)

De igual manera, sobresale la búsqueda de que el individuo cree conciencia sobre su participación en comunidad y sus metas como colectivo:

[P]arte también de lo que los Centros de Apoyo Mutuo buscan es crear una conciencia de clase, una conciencia de dónde estamos y de qué es lo que nos está afectando y que nosotros podemos ser entes históricos y entes de cambio. (María – CAM-U)

Podemos inferir que esta capacitación busca sustituir la visión de los individuos como simples beneficiarios de la ayuda a través de su incorporación en el proceso de recuperación. Estos espacios de aprendizaje sirven para cultivar una práctica didáctica sobre la identificación y solución de problemas, con el fin de producir una conciencia sobre la autogestión.

Tal como nos describe Carlos, exmiembro de la Brigada Solidaria del Oeste, esta dinámica de capacitación es fundamental para romper la dependencia:

...no podemos permitir el crear una cultura de asistencialismo dentro de las comunidades, porque a largo plazo lo que estamos haciendo es creando un problema [...] Tenemos que crear una cultura de cero dependencia. No, en vez de esperar de que ellos vengan y me traigan el agua, yo voy a conseguir una fuente de agua y yo voy a filtrarme mi agua, y yo voy a autogestionarme mi agua dentro de mi casa, para mí, mi familia, mi comunidad, mis vecinos...

Entonces, la educación se entiende como la inversión en el capital social de una comunidad para incrementar tanto la resiliencia como la efectividad de las comunidades para recuperarse de un desastre (Aldrich y Meyer 2015). El capital social toma un rol significativo en aquellas comunidades históricamente abandonadas por el gobierno o ignoradas en los procesos de respuesta y recuperación posdesastre (Harvey 2016).

La educación como elemento concienciador busca también la cristalización de otro tipo de relaciones sociales. Por ejemplo, ante el cuestionamiento de cómo gestar un aprendizaje a nivel comunitario, Omar, del CAM Bucarabones Unidos, reconoce las limitaciones de usar modelos tradicionalmente usados por activistas políticos:

No se puede hacer de la misma manera, no [es] que sea mejor o peor, pero es de otra manera. [...] ¿Cómo lo hacemos? Eso ha sido también el reto, cómo vamos implementando este método. [...] Porque esto es un asunto de observar, comprender, practicar, reflexionar, observar, comprender... y ese ciclo siempre nos conviene que esté ocurriendo.

Aquí se aprecia una educación liberadora que es solo posible cuando los individuos se involucran en una reflexión sobre su cotidianidad, problematizando las relaciones sociales que les rodean. Es en esa interacción donde ambos llegan a una conciencia sobre la realidad social y las inequidades que les rodean (Freire 1970).

Los procesos educativos que ocurren en los CAM toman una diversidad de formas y espacios, y asumen también que toda persona tiene el poder de educar. Nuestros datos reflejan cómo se busca potenciar el conocimiento en distintas áreas como la agricultura, la mecánica, el arte, la energía renovable y primeros auxilios, entre otros, maximizando en todo momento el uso del recurso humano existente en la comunidad:

Yo soy mecánico, electricista, carpintero, agricultor, de todo, de todo lo hago y eso lo comparto con los demás... si yo lo aprendí, que todos aprendan, porque estamos en la necesidad de que todos sepan defenderse. De momento, a alguien se le daña la guagua... pues que sepa defenderse, porque no en todos sitios vas a encontrar algún mecánico y tiene que saber desenvolverse uno. Pues hay que enseñarle lo que sea. (Jon – CAMBU)

Vemos cómo los CAM se convierten en un "sujeto educativo" de cuyas acciones y reflexiones emana una intencionalidad educativa. Bajo este modelo, todos los espacios, las acciones y las personas partícipes se convierten en entes pedagógicos que existen con la finalidad de transformar la comunidad a través de su propia transformación (Zibechi 2012).

Este proceso requiere que cada espacio e instante dentro de los CAM sea uno pedagógico y en el cual la reflexión y la autoevaluación siempre estén presentes. Pero esto requiere de una inversión humana que no todos los CAM poseen. Lourdes, de CAM Las Carolinas, nos habla sobre la necesidad de la educación popular como trabajo a tiempo completo y la falta de apoyo para esa gestión:

Yo creo que, si tuvieran la capacidad de que los organizadores trabajáramos a tiempo completo en la educación popular, sobre todo en la creación de actividades dinámicas en las comunidades, habría otros resultados. Pero los organizadores no estamos teniendo el apoyo para involucrar nuestra inteligencia y energía en esos procesos, porque para que esos procesos sucedan tienen que estar los seres humanos allí.

Las iniciativas de los CAM nos hacen ponderar el rol central de una educación popular como instrumento de concienciación de los individuos. En el contexto de los desastres, este capital social, aquí definido como el recurso humano entre los residentes, se entiende como determinante en la capacidad de recuperación de una comunidad. Entonces, el sujeto educado/educador es fundamental en el desarrollo comunitario hacia una recuperación desde la autogestión.

Participación y empoderamiento. Otro patrón que vemos surgir de nuestras observaciones es cómo se retan a los miembros de las comunidades a ser gestores de cambio por medio de su involucramiento en procesos de recuperación. Si miramos de cerca los proyectos establecidos por los CAM, vemos cómo estos reflejan prácticas de modelos de desarrollo social alternativos:

Pues no es que nosotros nos reunimos aparte a decidir qué va a pasar aquí [taller de salud]. Nos reunimos con ellos [comunidad La Granja] y aquí en una reunión con ellos hay una conversación de qué hacer. (Astrid – CAM-U)

Valiéndose de los recursos humanos disponibles en cada comunidad y otros voluntarios con destrezas, los CAM llaman a la movilización de la comunidad como el germen inicial hacia la recuperación.

Como medular estaba la intención de que [era] necesario que nuestro pueblo sepa o reconozca que tienen recursos a su haber, que somos capaces de... resolver nuestro propio... nuestras propias situaciones, apoderar la comunidad de sus herramientas verdad y de fomentar la autogestión. (Damary-BSO)

Una manifestación de este involucramiento lo podemos ver en los procesos de reconstrucción y en el diseño de iniciativas de interés colectivo. Por medio de procesos como los censos comunitarios, convocatorias de ideas o compromisos de apoyo mutuo, los CAM estimulan a reflexionar sobre sus necesidades, desarrollar soluciones y asumir responsabilidades. Por un lado, en una de nuestras visitas a comunidades impactadas por la Brigada Solidaria del Oeste, conocimos a una pareja que trabajó en la rehabilitación de su hogar y sirvió de voluntaria en varios de los hogares que la organización apoyó como parte de su iniciativa de reconstrucción. Por otro lado, ante la sugerencia de los jóvenes de crear un café teatro para generar ingresos y tener un espacio de intercambio cultural en su comunidad, la coordinadora de CAM Bartolo invitó a los jóvenes a asumir el diseño, asistir en la habilitación del espacio y operarlo (Notas de campo - junio 2018). El involucramiento de los beneficiarios en los procesos de recuperación, como se hace en BSO y CAM Bartolo, se puede entender como una implementación de participación implicativa. Estas acciones cohesionan la dimensión comunitaria, potencian el saber popular y produce un espacio donde los participantes son implicados en la dirección y profundidad de su recuperación (Vilaseca 2012).

De forma paralela vemos la introducción de otras prácticas sociales que invitan a producir cambios de índole social:

Aquí todo es horizontal. Si tu punto es válido y si todos los compañeros están de acuerdo pues... esto se hace así. Si hay un compañero que algo no le gusta, se vuelve atrás en la mesa, se trabaja, se eliminan los puntos que estén mal, se trabaja con los puntos que estén bien, y así logramos el mayor consenso... De que todas las decisiones [se toman] en colectivo, no hay una decisión que la toma una persona en particular. [...] Aquí nadie es más que otro, nadie menos. [...] (Carlos – BSO)

Similarmente, vemos el uso del lenguaje inclusivo entre los miembros de las organizaciones. Al preguntar sobre esta práctica en CAMBU, varios miembros hicieron referencia a la idea de lo común de usar "nosotros" cuando podrían utilizar igualmente "nosotras". Esta práctica también estuvo presente en los encuentros de los CAM donde se hizo referencia a "la corilla" en forma general e inclusivos como "nosotres" y "elles". Por medio de estructuras horizontales, toma de decisiones consensuales y la adopción de lenguaje inclusivo, los organizadores articulan una participación que promueve una ruptura de prácticas jerárquicas que reproducen relaciones de marginalización y exclusión.

Al poner en marcha formas organizativas solidarias cuyo fin ulterior es desmantelar la pasividad del ciudadano, se empoderan los individuos y se enfila la comunidad hacia la autogestión.

Entonces, con una participación implicativa se busca producir un compromiso hacia el colectivo que aprovecha el ímpetu de las prácticas solidarias que surgieron a raíz del huracán María. Tal como Bacallao-Pino (2016) advierte, la experimentación con modelos sociales diferentes a los vigentes es un vehículo importante para el empoderamiento. Estos nuevos modelos sociales buscan romper con y cuestionar las visiones de desarrollo que van de la mano con el individualismo, las jerarquías y la concentración del poder fuera de las comunidades que han producido una experiencia y respuesta desigual ante el desastre (Pérez-Lizasuain 2018). Al poner en marcha formas organizativas solidarias cuyo fin ulterior es desmantelar la pasividad del ciudadano, se empoderan los individuos y se enfila la comunidad hacia la autogestión.

Autosuficiencia y autonomía. En nuestro trabajo de campo, escuchamos de diversos integrantes de los CAM que el paso del huracán María "quitó el velo" que escondía la realidad social puertorriqueña. Esta revelación, entienden ellos, dio pie a cuestionar la enajenación del gobierno y el fallo de las instituciones en atenderla.

Yo entiendo que la gente sí se ha dado cuenta y desde mucho antes ya había una incomodidad. El huracán quita el velo y saca más afuera esa incomodidad y la posibilidad de la comunidad de autoorganizarse y responder a la inacción del gobierno. (María – CAM-U)

[El huracán ha sido u]n catalítico pa' muchas cosas, o por lo menos para observarlas. Quizás no para que se manifiesten, porque se están manifestando desde antes; no, pero sí para observarla. Eso de que se quitó el velo, yo creo que es una de las explicaciones, de que se quita el velo. No es que quizás provoca el surgimiento de un fenómeno, sino que lo visibiliza mejor. (Omar – CAMBU)

Dentro de esta apertura que crea el huracán, las prácticas solidarias y los procesos emergentes proveen un punto de contraste para que surjan visiones críticas a las respuestas al desastre desde el Estado.

Porque ellos están por ellos mismos, satisfaciendo lo que el sistema no les está dando y que cobren conciencia de eso. Que se den cuenta de que, mira... cómo fue una fortaleza tenerse como vecinos, salir todos juntos a hacer X o Y cosa. (Astrid - CAM-U)

Los CAM impulsan que las comunidades logren la mayor autosuficiencia posible de las estructuras institucionales con el fin de que experimenten cierta forma de autonomía comunitaria.

[Nos] falta ejercer esa [autonomía] y es la que vamos construyendo, porque la autonomía no se puede ejercer de manera individual. Es un proceso colectivo que tiene que ocurrir obligatoriamente y ese es el que estamos asumiendo ahorita como pueblo. (Pluma CAM JI-Lares)

La revelación para los puertorriqueños de las fisuras estructurales que aquejan la sociedad propició el comienzo de un diálogo sobre cómo mejor agenciar proyectos que potencien el empoderamiento y la autosuficiencia (Brown 2017; Maldonado-Torres 2018).

Cabe destacar que parte del proyecto neoliberal, que toma fuerza en la década de 1990 y que se manifiesta fuertemente en la respuesta del Estado a los desastres, busca cultivar la autogestión como una forma de liberar al

Estado de sus responsabilidades (Ortiz Gómez 2015; Pérez-Lizasuain 2018). Esto encubre la reticencia del gobierno a cumplir efectivamente con su función ministerial, y pone al descubierto las limitaciones de las comunidades para responder al desastre a través de la autogestión (Love 2016). Resulta imperativo que los proyectos o movimientos sociales con un enfoque en la autogestión o la autonomía no pierdan su lente crítico.

Por tal razón, los CAM entienden sus iniciativas de autogestión como una gesta que busca cultivar la autosuficiencia a la vez que producen una crítica al modelo actual de gobernanza. Por un lado, los miembros de CAM Jíbaro-Lares fomentan la autosuficiencia con la incubación de proyectos agrícolas que responden a la coyuntura de vulnerabilidad y precariedad alimentaria que se hizo patente en el contexto pos-María. En vías de promover una soberanía alimentaria, CAM Jíbaro-Lares está gestando un proyecto de vivero y semillero en la comunidad de Bajadero que proveería plántulas para el vecindario, en consorcio con una finca agroecológica del área. Por el otro lado, las iniciativas de autogestión producen una crítica del poder:

...mi visión es cómo construimos poder local, popular, en los espacios que estamos, que puedan realmente resistir ante la discapacidad del [gobierno]. [...] Veo este potencial en los CAM... de autogestión, ese potencial de construir, de poder y de resistencia. (Stephanie – La Olla Común)

Nosotros cuando hablamos de autogestión... nos vemos como facilitadores y facilitadoras de ayudar a derrumbar esa frontera [al poder], como esa pared que construye este sistema colonial, político, social... (Pluma – CAM JI-Lares)

La labor de construir autogestión cuestiona la vigencia de la relación que el Estado busca mantener para con los ciudadanos por medio del señalamiento de la negligencia que las comunidades confrontan. El énfasis es en integrar una práctica emancipadora junto a los principios filosóficos y las acciones autogestivas de los CAM.

Finalmente, el tema de la condición colonial de Puerto Rico es una presente y constante en las conversaciones de los organizadores, sea de forma individual en sus espacios de trabajo o en los encuentros de organizaciones (Notas de campo).

[Si] esta comunidad [Bucarabones] logra independizarse porque tienen luz solar, esta gente está viviendo la independencia. ¿Qué mayor fortaleza para predicar al resto del país la independencia que espacios que lo son de verdad? (Giovani - CAM Caguas)

La crítica al poder también busca la cultivación de una perspectiva descolonizadora entre las comunidades. La colonialidad se entiende como medular en la manera en que se han experimentado los desastres y la precariedad en la isla. Por lo tanto, auscultar experiencias de autonomía comunitaria se ve como una extensión de una experiencia descolonizadora.

La autogestión representa una expresión de descolonización donde las comunidades pueden atender sus necesidades sin depender exclusivamente del Estado, donde la dirección y forma del desarrollo son definidas por las comunidades y donde los individuos se reconocen como su mayor recurso. De igual manera en que se fomenta una visión crítica de las causas estructurales del desastre, se cultiva una experiencia de autonomía.

Conclusión

Ante el escenario de respuesta gubernamental tardía e ineficiente poshuracán María, los CAM asumieron una deconstrucción de lo que significa la asistencia en la respuesta y, con ello, cambiar las expectativas de los individuos sobre su rol dentro de esta. Miembros de distintos CAM interpretan la respuesta del Estado como una informada por políticas que buscan reproducir el orden social vigente y que desvinculan al individuo del proceso de toma de decisiones. Los CAM sugieren que la respuesta gubernamental al huracán inhibe un cuestionamiento sobre cómo las estructuras sociales han distribuido la manifestación del daño y produce una inercia de los sectores empobrecidos a depender de su asistencia. Tal como sugiere Maldonado-Torres, en los CAM vemos la creación de "actividades y ejecutorias que ayudan a generar personas que identifican y cuestionan" el desastre desde la acción y no tan solo la crítica (2018, 339).

Para poder lograr la asunción y el cuestionamiento por parte de las comunidades a los proyectos de respuesta y recuperación, los CAM pusieron en marcha un proceso de movilización que involucró la educación como vía a la concienciación, la participación como empoderamiento y la autosuficiencia como semilla para la autonomía comunitaria. Estos utilizan una variedad de plataformas y recursos humanos como mecanismos de educación popular, que buscan crear conciencia sobre la importancia de verse y trabajar como colectivo. Ante el desastre, se busca desarrollar el capital social de las comunidades a través de la capacitación, así como lograr que los miembros de las comunidades puedan identificar y agenciar las soluciones a sus problemas. Esta concientización lleva a los individuos a ver más allá de su propio bienestar, articulando otras relaciones sociales que prioriza al colectivo a través de la participación implicativa en proyectos comunitarios de respuesta y recuperación, que les encamina finalmente hacia la autosuficiencia.

En el proceso de respuesta y recuperación desde los CAM, vemos iniciativas ante el desastre que no son necesariamente únicas, pero sí innovadoras. Por un lado, la activación de la solidaridad como eje motivador se ha documentado en otros instantes de desastres, entendiéndose como parte de procesos emergentes. Lo innovador es la intención y búsqueda de una canalización de esta solidaridad como propulsor de otros procesos que atienden la precariedad y vulnerabilidad que antecede y excede el desastre. Contrario a asumir la solidaridad como algo de origen espontáneo y de impacto aleatorio, los organizadores entienden la solidaridad como una fuerza social que puede ser cultivada e intencionada. En los CAM vemos una lectura temprana del surgir de la solidaridad seguido por la articulación de una narrativa de cómo esta solidaridad nutre tanto un acercamiento "desde abajo", como una actitud empoderadora "desde adentro". Así, la solidaridad como producto emergente es canalizada y dirigida en vías a sostener las iniciativas y programas específicos de cada CAM.

Por otro lado, vemos la aplicación del apoyo mutuo, el cual se entiende como principio y método de desarrollo social-político. El apoyo mutuo ha tomado forma en otros escenarios de recuperación de desastres, pero es presentado como un mecanismo de uso individual, de viabilidad dentro de la temporalidad del desastre e impacto superficial. Contrario a la gestión de asistencia mutua que vemos descrita por Chamlee-Wright (2010) en Nueva Orléans y las iniciativas de autosuficiencia descritas por Kinder (2016) en Detroit, los CAM asumen una posición crítica-política, que intenciona una transformación radical de las dinámicas de poder y gobernanza. La misión empoderadora de los CAM asume la meta de alterar el orden de las relaciones de poder que existían antes del huracán, instaurando en las comunidades la asunción de sus responsabilidades y querencias. Entendemos que es este acercamiento de la crítica/acción donde reside la novedad y potencialidad del trabajo de los CAM hacia un cambio social profundo.

NOTAS

1 Los CAM de Vieques, Yabucoa y PAM Mariana (Humacao) ya no están en función. PAM Mariana se convirtió en Emerge Puerto Rico, una organización enfocada en temas de educación ambiental y liderazgo.

OBRAS CITADAS

Aldrich, Daniel P. y Michelle A. Meyer. 2015. Social Capital and Community Resilience. *American Behavioral Scientist* 59(2), 254–69.

Bacallao-Pino, Lázaro M. 2016. Agents for Change or Conflict? Social Movements, Democratic Dynamics, and Development in Latin America. *Voluntas* 27, 105–24. DOI 10.1007/s11266-015-9574-2.

Brown, Adrienne Maree. 2017. *Emergent Strategy*. Chico, CA: AK Press.

Cabán, Pedro. 2018. PROMESA, Puerto Rico and the American Empire. *Latino Studies Journal* 16, 161–84. DOI: 10.1057/s41276-018-0125-z.

Chamlee-Wright, Emily. 2010. *The Cultural and Political Economy of Recovery*. New York: Routledge.

Cotto Morales, Liliana. 2006. *Desalambrar: Orígenes de los rescates de terreno en Puerto Rico y su pertinencia en los movimientos sociales contemporáneos.* San Juan: Editorial Tal Cual.

Cutter, Susan. 2006. The Geography of Social Vulnerability: Race, Class and Catastrophe. *Items: Insights from the Social* Sciences 11 June. <https://items.ssrc.org/understanding-katrina/the-geography-of-social-vulnerability-race-class-and-catastrophe/>.

Drabek, Thomas E. 1986. *Human System Responses to Disasters: An Inventory of Sociological Findings*. New York: Springer-Verlag.

Drabek, Thomas E. y David A. McEntire. 2003. Emergent Phenomena and the Sociology of Disasters: Lessons, Trends and Opportunities from the Research Literature. *Disaster Prevention and Management* 12(2), 97–112.

Drury, John, Chris Cocking y Steve Reicher. 2009. Everyone for Themselves? A Comparative Study of Crowd Solidarity Among Emergency Survivors. *British Journal of Social Psychology* 48, 487–506.

Dynes, Russell. 1970. *Organized Behavior in Disaster*. Lexington, MA: Heath Lexington Books.

Dyson, Michael Eric. 2006. *Come Hell or High Water*. New York: Basic Books.

Freire, Paulo. 1970. *Pedagogía del oprimido*. Coyoacán, México: Siglo Veintiuno Ediciones.

Guardiola Ortiz, Dagmar. 2012. Los derechos humanos en Puerto Rico: pobreza, desigualdad y políticas sociales. En *Puerto Rico y los derechos humanos: una intersección plural*, eds. José Javier Colón Morera e Idsa E. Alegría Ortega. 221–43. San Juan: Ediciones Callejón.

Hartman, Chester y Gregory D. Squires, eds. 2006. *There Is No Such Thing as a Natural Disaster: Race, Class, and Hurricane Katrina*. New York: Routledge.

Harvey, Diana Cheyenne. 2016. The Discourse of the Ecological Precariat: Making Sense of Social Disruption in the Lower Ninth Ward in the Long-Term Aftermath of Hurricane Katrina. *Sociological Forum* 31(1), doi 10.1111/socf.12277.

Jon, Ihnji y Mark Purcell. 2018. Radical Resilience: Autonomous Self-management in Post-disaster Recovery Planning and Practice. *Planning Theory & Practice* 19(2), 235–51.

Kinder, Kimberley. 2016. *DIY Detroit: Making Do in a City Without Services*. Minneapolis: University of Minnesota Press.

Kleiner, Anna, John Green y Albert Nylander. 2007. A Community Study of Disaster Impacts and Redevelopment Issues Facing East Biloxi, Mississippi. En *The Sociology of Katrina: Perspectives on a Modern Catastrophe*, eds. D. Brunsma, D. Overfelt y S. Picou. 191–206. Lanham MD: Rowman & Littlefield.

Lavell, Allan. 2000. Desastres urbanos: una visión global. Seminario, El impacto de los desastres naturales en áreas urbanas y en la salud pública urbana en Centroamérica y el Caribe. ASIES Guatemala.

LeBrón, Marisol. 2016. People Before Debt: Puerto Ricans Confront the Island's Debt Crisis "From Below". *NACLA Report on the Americas* 48(2), 115–7.

Love, Bridget. 2016. Decentralizing Disasters: Civic Engagement and Stalled Reconstruction after Japan's 3/11. En *Contextualizing Disaster*, eds. Gregory V. Button y Mark Schuller. 112–33. New York: Berghahn.

Macías, Jesús Manuel. 1992. Significado de la vulnerabilidad social frente a los desastres. *Revista Mexicana de Sociología* 54(4), 3–10.

Maldonado-Torres, Nelson. 2018. Afterword: Critique and Decoloniality in the Face of Crisis, Disaster and Catastrophe. En *Aftershocks of Disaster*, eds. Yarimar Bonilla y Marisol LeBrón. 332–43. Chicago: Haymarket Books.

Martínez Martínez, Pedro Emilio. 2013. Impacto de los huracanes Gustav e Ike en las condiciones de pobreza de los habitantes del poblado Paso Real de San Diego. En *Pobreza, Ambiente y Cambio Climático*, ed. Guillermo Castro H. 139–56. Buenos Aires: CLASCO.

Martínez Román, Adi G. 2012. Lucha contra la pobreza en Puerto Rico y desarrollo sostenible: la participación ciudadana como herramienta para la consecución de los derechos fundamentales. *Revista Jurídica de la Universidad de Puerto Rico* 81, 1027–50.

Mileti, Dennis S., Thomas E. Drabek y J. Eugene Haas. 1975. *Human Systems in Extreme Environments*. Boulder: Institute of Behavioral Science, University of Colorado.

Molinari, Sarah. 2018. Authenticating Loss and Contesting Recovery: FEMA and the Politics of Colonial Disaster Management. En *Aftershocks of Disaster*, eds. Yarimar Bonilla y Marisol LeBrón. 285–97. Chicago: Haymarket Books.

Noboa-Ortega, Patricia. 2018. Psychoanalysis as a Political Act after María. En *Aftershocks of Disaster*, eds. Yarimar Bonilla y Marisol LeBrón. 271–84. Chicago: Haymarket Books.

Oliver-Smith, Anthony. 1994. Reconstrucción después del desastre: una visión general de secuelas y problemas. En *Al Norte del Río Grande: ciencias sociales y desastres: una perspectiva norteamericana*, ed. Allan Lavell 25-41, La Red de Estudios Sociales en Prevención de Desastres en América Latina. Accedido el 27 de noviembre de 2018. <http://www.desenredando.org/>.

Ortiz Gómez, María Guadalupe. 2015. Neoliberalismo, políticas públicas y cultura de autogestión para el desarrollo en México y Chile. *Revista Internacional de Ciencias Sociales y Humanidades* 25(2), 75–97.

Padilla-Elías, Nilsa D., Julieanne Miranda Bermúdez, Gabriela Algarín Zayas, Marisol Peña-Orellana, Ralph Rivera-Gutiérrez, Alejandro Nieves Santiago, Juan González Sánchez, Mónica Castellano Vega y Héctor Robles-García. 2016. Una mirada a las poblaciones vulnerables en Puerto Rico ante desastres. *Caribbean Studies* 44(1-2), 141–63.

Passerini, Eve. 2000. Disasters as Agents of Social Change in Recovery and Reconstruction. *Natural Hazards Review* 1(2), 67–72.

Pérez-Lizasuain, César. 2018. Entering the Contact Zone? Between Colonialism, Neoliberal Resilience and the Possibility of Emancipatory Politics in Puerto Rico's Post-María. *Alternautas* 5(2), 43–55.

Petras, James. 2002. Neoliberalism, Popular Resistance and Mental Health. *The James Petras Website*. Accedido el 15 de noviembre de 2019) <https://petras.lahaine.org/neo-liberalism-popular-resistance-and-mental-health/>.

Picou, J. Steven y Brent Marshall. 2007. Katrina as Paradigm Shift: Reflections on Disaster Research in the Twenty-First Century. En *The Sociology of Katrina*, eds. D. Brunsma, D. Overfelt y J.S. Picou. 1–20. Latham, MD: Rowman & Littlefield.

Primera Hora. 2018. Irma: a un año del preámbulo a la catástrofe de María. 6 de septiembre. <https://www.primerahora.com/noticias/puerto-rico/notas/irma-a-un-ano-del-preambulo-a-la-catastrofe-de-maria/>.

Rivera Quintero, Marcia y Bernardo Kliksberg. 2007. *El capital social movilizado contra la pobreza: la experiencia del Proyecto de Comunidades Especiales en Puerto Rico*. Buenos Aires: CLACSO.

Roberto, Giovanni. 2018. Community Kitchens: An Emerging Movement? En *Aftershocks of Disaster*, eds. Yarimar Bonilla y Marisol LeBrón. 309–18. Chicago: Haymarket Books.

Schneider, Saundra K. 2018. Governmental Response to Disasters: Key Attributes, Expectations, and Implications. En *Handbook of Disaster Research*, eds. Havidán Rodríguez, William Donner, y Joseph E. Trainor. Switzerland: Springer International.

Schuller, Mark. 2012. *Killing with Kindness: International Aid and NGO's*. New Brunswick, NJ: Rutgers University Press.

Schwartz, Stuart B. 2018. *Mar de tormentas: una historia de los huracanes en el Gran Caribe desde Colón hasta María*. San Juan: Ediciones Callejón.

Smith, Neil. 2006. There's No Such Thing as a Natural Disaster. *Items: Insights from the Social Sciences* 11 de junio. <https://items.ssrc.org/understanding-katrina/theres-no-such-thing-as-a-natural-disaster/>.

Solnit, Rebecca. 2009. *A Paradise Built in Hell*. New York: Penguin Books.

Sosa Pascual, Omaya y Patricia Mazzei. 2017. Huracán María: dónde falló el operativo de respuesta. *Miami Herald-Centro de Periodismo Investigativo*. 22 de octubre.

Stallings, Robert. 1978. The Structural Patterns of Four Types of Organizations in Disasters. En *Disasters: Theory and Research*, ed. E. L. Quarantelli. 83–103, Beverly Hills: Sage.

Stallings, Robert A. y E. L. Quarantelli. 1985. Emergent Citizen Groups and Emergency Management. *Public Administration Review* 45, 93–100.

Taylor-Gooby, Peter. 1981. The Empiricist Tradition in Social Administration. *Critical Social Policy* 1(2), 6–21.

Velázquez Reca, Annie. 2007. La autogestión: ¿Será posible apropiarnos de ella en función de un escenario educativo? *Revista Paideia Puertorriqueña* 2(2), 1–15.

Vélez-Vélez, Roberto y Jacqueline Villarrubia-Mendoza. 2018. Cambio desde abajo y desde adentro: Notes on Centros de Apoyo Mutuo in post-María Puerto Rico. *Latino Studies Journal* 16(4), 542–57.

Vilaseca, Marina. 2012. Desarrollo popular sostenible, autogestión e intervención comunitaria: apología a la cotidianidad. En *Autogestión*, eds. Javier Encina y María Ángeles Ávila. 208–15. Sevilla: Colectivo de ilusionistas sociales.

Wenger, Dennis. 1992. Emergent and volunteer behavior during disaster: research findings and planning implications. HRRC Publication 27P, Texas A&M University, Hazard Reduction Recovery Center.

Zibechi, Raúl. 2012. Los movimientos sociales como espacios educativos. En *Autogestión*, eds. Javier Encina y María Ángeles Ávila. 164–9. Sevilla: Colectivo de ilusionistas sociales.

VOLUME XXXII • NUMBER III • FALL 2020

Puerto Rico Housing and Community Development Industry's Capacity for Disaster Recovery

EDWIN MELÉNDEZ

ABSTRACT

My main goal with this case study of disaster policy implementation is to provide an assessment of the capacity of the nonprofit sector to become an active participant in the long-term economic recovery of Puerto Rico. And, more generally, I wish to examine barriers hindering nonprofit sector participation. The study is intended to take advantage of this window of opportunity to strengthen the housing and community development industry in the island. In the first section of the study I discuss the relative size and strength of the housing and community development industry in the context of the nonprofit sector in Puerto Rico. Puerto Rico has robust nonprofit and cooperatives sector but a smaller housing and community development sub-sector. In the second part of the study, I identified three significant barriers that have hindered the development of the housing community development industry in Puerto Rico: the exclusionary role of federal and local recovery funding policy; the relative weakness of the industry ecosystem; and, the relative scarcity of professionals with the understanding of reconstruction programs. The final section of the study presents conclusions, and policy and industry development strategies recommendations. I conclude that post-disaster federal funding for economic recovery offers Puerto Rico a unique window of opportunity to restore its economy and infrastructure in a more resilient fashion while strengthening the nonprofit sector capacity for community planning, housing and economic development, and neighborhood revitalization. However, such an opportunity is contingent on reforming public policy and implementing a comprehensive strategy to encourage and support nonprofit developers' participation in reconstruction programs, as well as building industry capacity by strengthening intermediaries and community development corporations, encouraging intra-industry partnerships and collaborations, and providing professional development for economic recovery. [Key words: Puerto Rico, housing, community development, nonprofit, economy recovery]

Introduction

Post-disaster planning and federal funding for economic recovery offer Puerto Rico a unique window of opportunity to restore its economy and infrastructure in a more resilient fashion. However, such an opportunity hinges on the capacity of the civic sector to join government efforts in planning and then executing a comprehensive reconstruction and recovery program. Many local and stateside foundations and other philanthropic efforts spearheaded initiatives in the aftermath of Hurricanes Irma and Maria to strengthen the nonprofit sector to serve the needs of the storms' victims, an effort that was renewed after the earthquakes damaged the island at the end of 2019. The Foundation Center estimates that these philanthropic efforts raised more than $375 million for relief and recovery from the storms, a substantial sixty-fold increase from prior years (Red de Fundaciones de Puerto Rico 2019). Yet these unprecedented philanthropic efforts pale in comparison to the federal funding assigned to the island in various recovery programs. My main goal with this mixed-methods case study of disaster policy implementation is to provide an assessment of the capacity of the nonprofit sector to become an active participant in the long-term economic recovery of Puerto Rico and, more generally, to take advantage of this window of opportunity to strengthen the housing and community development industry in Puerto Rico.

Shortly after the two 2017 storms, the government of Puerto Rico published two reports that jointly provide a framework for post-disaster planning for economic recovery for Puerto Rico: Transformation and Innovation in the Wake of Devastation: An Economic and Disaster Recovery Plan for Puerto Rico (Central Office of Recovery, Reconstruction and Resiliency 2018),[1] and Community Development Block Grant Disaster Recovery Action Plan (Puerto Rico Department of Housing 2018). Jointly, these two plans detail the estimated damages caused by Hurricanes Irma and Maria and offer an allocation plan for funding

The author (emele@hunter.cuny.edu) is a Professor of Urban Policy and Planning and the Director of the Center for Puerto Rican Studies at Hunter College, CUNY. In addition to numerous scientific papers and other publications, he is the author or editor of thirteen books including *State of Puerto Ricans* (Centro Press, 2017) and *Puerto Ricans at the Dawn of the New Millenium* (Centro Press, 2014), and served as guest editor of *CENTRO Journal*'s "Pathway to Economic Opportunity" (v.23 n.2, 2011) and "Puerto Rico Post-Hurricane Maria: Origins and Consequences of a Crisis" (v.30 n.3, 2018) issues.

and other resources received, assigned, or expected from the federal government for a total, estimated immediately after the storm, of $94 billion over the next decade (Rosselló 2017). In February 2020, the total disaster recovery funding appropriations to Puerto Rico were $44.5 billion.[2] In addition to the economic devastation of the 2017 storms, initial earthquake damages were assessed at about $3.1 billion (Center on Disaster Philanthropy 2020). Moreover, the impact of the COVID-19 pandemic has aggravated Puerto Rico's ongoing fiscal and financial crisis, rooted in an unpayable public debt of over $120 billion.

Following Smith and Wenger (2007, 237), I define disaster recovery as "the differential process of restoring, rebuilding, and reshaping the physical, social, economic, and natural environment through pre-event planning and post-event actions." The unique role of the nonprofit sector in disaster recovery and preparedness, by fostering community engagement and increased levels of disaster resilience and sustainable recovery, is well-established in the literature (Dyer 1999; Mileti 1999; Smith and Birkland 2012; Peacock, Morrow and Gladwin 1997; Scott and Murphy 2014; Welsh and Esnard 2009). Community engagement is defined along three dimensions: (a) decision-making, (b) relationship development, and (c) capacity-building (Butteriss 2020). The last five decades of studies on civic engagement in post-disaster scenarios have shown the importance of adequate community preparedness and how resilience to disasters requires enhancing existing social systems and structures to promote information flow and collaboration. Community preparedness requires increasing capacity and empowering local governments and communities to implement recovery actions and to foster coordination and collaboration across sectors and between federal and local governments (Johnson and Olshansky 2017; May and Williams 1985; McDonnell et al. 2019; Meyer and Hendricks 2018; Warren et al. 2015).

In short, federal policy and spending on community engagement processes and nonprofit sector participation, used to determine overall community recovery has been well established in the disaster recovery literature. Yet, as Garcia and Chandrasekhar (2020) found in a survey of nonprofit participation in Puerto Rico's reclamation, the nonprofit sector had a wide participation in the immediate emergency phase of the post-disaster recovery, a change primarily supported by private donations but with minimal support from the local or federal government. The nonprofit sector capacity to participate in the post-disaster economic recovery phase is constrained due to several factors. These factors are related to the various stages and capacity requirements for program participation, such as community planning for project development, competing for local and federal funding, and management and compliance of programs. There is limited experience in the nonprofit sector with federal housing and economic development and disaster mitigation programs, which constitute the focus of the post-disaster economic recovery phase. As Borges-Méndez (2020) has observed, even organizations with prior knowledge in community economic development have a limited capacity for real estate development, find it difficult to meet the NOFA requirements and be competitive for federal funding, and a significant barrier for the nonprofit sector participation in economic recovery is the lack of predevelopment funds.

It is not certain whether the nonprofit sector can become an active participant in the long-term economic recovery of Puerto Rico, nor do we know the barriers hindering or factors advancing such development. To answer these questions, I used a mixed method case study approach, which combined statistical data from various sources and reviewed public sector and other documents. In addition, I incorporate the findings from six major conferences and symposia, conducted by the Center for Puerto Rican Studies, on the impact of the hurricanes on the island and its reconstruction, and the technical and operational needs of non-profit organizations for participating in disaster recovery planning and program participation. The overall conclusion of the study is that whether the nonprofit sector can become an active participant in the long-term economic recovery of Puerto Rico is contingent on the implementation of a comprehensive strategy for reforming public policy to encourage and support nonprofit developers participation in reconstruction programs, building industry capacity by strengthening intermediaries and Community Development Corporations (CDCs), encouraging intra-industry partnerships and collaborations, and providing professional development for economic recovery.

In the first section of the study, I briefly explain the evolution of housing and community development in Puerto Rico and the historical policies and other factors that benefit or constrain the development of the industry. Federal policies are at the center of the evolution of the housing industry in Puerto Rico. When local and federal policy were combined to support local developers, as was the case when the American Recovery and Reinvestment Act (ARRA) of 2009 was enacted, nonprofit developers surpassed private sector units of housing through the Low-Income Housing Tax Credit (LI-HTC) program during the four years of ARRA funding.

In the second part of the study I identify three significant barriers to the development of housing and community development industry in Puerto Rico: the exclusionary role of federal and local recovery funding policy; the relative weakness of the industry ecosystem; and, the relative scarcity of professionals with economic development skills, especially professionals with the understanding of reconstruction programs. These barriers are associated with the relatively small number of CDCs in Puerto Rico and nonprofit sector capacity to participate effectively in federal economic recovery programs. I also report on the findings of a survey for the assessment of professional skills for the implementation of post-disaster planning for economic recovery for Puerto Rico. The results of the survey indicate a need for programs that offer systematic development of skills associated with the implementation of post-disaster planning for economic recovery for Puerto Rico.

The final section of the study is composed of conclusions, and recommendations for policy reform and industry development strategies. These recommendations include: the need to reform federal recovery funding policy to be more inclusive of nonprofit developers; development of a low cost, high risk predevelopment fund and promoting intra-industry partnerships to support CDCs; development of professional training for post-disaster economic recovery, possibly as continuing education targeting the nonprofit and municipal sectors; strengthening community development intermediaries to serve as financial intermediaries and as providers of technical assistance; and, improving access to interactive GIS maps for community planning visualizations and to provide empirical evidence for strategic planning and project development.

A Brief History of Housing and Community Development in Puerto Rico
The origins of Puerto Rico's housing and community development industry and its connection to federal policy can be traced back to the extension to Puerto Rico of the U.S. Housing Act (1937) and the federal mortgage program through the Federal Housing Administration (1938), or FHA. In response to this legislation, the local government created a public authority to

manage the implementation of these programs—the Autoridad de Hogares de Puerto Rico (1938). These programs were instrumental for the financing of new homeowners, and public and subsidized rental housing. In addition, the Legislature of Puerto Rico passed Law 26 (1941) for the creation of the Land Authority of Puerto Rico. This law distributed land to rural workers and launched a massive community planning effort that "developed more than 610 *parcela* communities, containing more than 185,000, in the 50-year period from 1941 to 1992" when "more than 35,000 houses were built under the Self-help and Mutual Aid Program" (Fuller-Marvel 2008).

In urban areas, the spread of squatters and informal housing became a significant problem in the early postwar years as workers transition from a declining agricultural production to manufacturing, government agencies and public enterprises, and service industries.

The post-war transition to labor-intensive manufacturing spearheaded under the Popular Democratic Party's Operation Bootstrap required and went in tandem to the expansion of urban development. In urban areas, the spread of squatters and informal housing became a significant problem in the early postwar years as workers transition from a declining agricultural production to manufacturing, government agencies and public enterprises, and service industries. Several federal legislations supported urban sprawl in Puerto Rico. The Serviceman's Readjustment Act (1944), also known as the GI Bill, fueled the expansion of urban housing developments, known as *urbanizaciones,* in Puerto Rico by providing veterans access to mortgage loans at reasonable terms guaranteed by the Veterans Administration (VA) or by the federally backed home mortgage companies Fannie Mae and Freddie Mac. By the same token, the Housing Act (1954) supported the expansion of public housing and homeownership through mortgage lending backed by the Federal Housing Administration (FHA). Following these federal programs, the Puerto Rico government created the Urban and Housing Renewal Administration (Administración de Renovación Urbana y Vivienda, 1958) and the Urban and Housing Development Administration (Corporación de Renovación Urbana y Vivienda CRUV, 1963) (Alameda-Lozada 2005).

The early postwar rural and urban housing programs succeeded in erad-icating slums and the most extreme forms of substandard housing. But, by the late 1960s and through the '70s, the squatters movement intensified and the lack of affordable housing in Puerto Rico was evident (Cotto 1993). In the United States, President Johnson's War on Poverty programs targeted housing segregation and discrimination and were seeking new models for urban renewal targeting areas with high concentration of the poor. With the support of the Ford Foundation, the community development corpora-tion (CDC) became the model for urban redevelopment (Sviridoff 2004). In unison with the Housing and Community Development Act of 1974 and the Community Reinvestment Act (CRA) of 1977, which provided mechanism to channel federal funding to nonprofit organizations, the Low-Income Hous-ing Tax Credit (LIHTC) was created as part of the Tax Reform Act of 1986 specifically to incentivize private equity investment in affordable housing. The LIHTC has played a critical role in the development of affordable hous-ing in the United States since its creation and has set the foundations for an increasing role for both the nonprofit and private sectors' participation in the housing and community development. In conjunction, the CRA's guide-lines to encourage banks and other financial institutions to reinvest in low income communities, in which they are chartered to do business. The LI-HTC provided the incentives and mechanisms for the present housing and community development industry to operate as an interdependent alliance of the private and nonprofit sector. Their joint efforts to date shape federal and local public policy for the industry.

Table 1 depicts the progression of the most important HUD-subsidized housing programs in Puerto Rico from 2000 to 2019. By far, public housing programs offer the largest number of subsidized units in the island, with 53,079 units in 2019. This number represents a small decline in the share of total units--from 65 percent in 2000 to 57 percent in 2019. The LIHTC is the second largest HUD-subsidized program, with 20,536 units or 22 percent of total units. This program also declined slightly from its peak in 2010 of 24,210 units or 23 percent of total units. Overall, the total number of HUD-subsidized units in Puerto Rico declined by ten thousand units, from 103,442 units in 2010 to 93,466 units. Section 8, the other significant HUD program, was the only program with a slight increase in its share of

Table 1. Total Units of HUD-Subsidized Rental Housing in Puerto Rico by Programs (2000, 2010, 2019)

Program	2000		2010		2019	
LIHTC	6,920	7.9%	24,210	23.4%	20,536	22.0%
Public Housing	56,888	64.9%	55,871	54.0%	53,079	56.8%
Section 8 NC/SR (a)	17,055	19.5%	15,466	15.0%	18,713	20.0%
Multi-Family/Other	6,746	7.7%	7,895	7.6%	1,138	1.2%
Total	87,609	100.0%	103,442	100.0%	93,466	100.0%

Source: HUD User Datasets. <https://www.huduser.gov/portal/pdrdatas_landing.html#dataset-title/>.
Notes: (a) Section 8 New Construction and Substantial Rehabilitation Program (S8 NC/SR).

units increasing from 15,466 units (15 percent of total) in 2010 to 18,713 (20 percent of total) in 2019.

In Puerto Rico the role and participation of CDCs in affordable housing and community development has been erratic, with tax credits largely favoring private over nonprofit developers. According to Ramos Bermúdez (2003), by 2002 there were eight established nonprofit Community Housing Development Organizations (CHDOs) in Puerto Rico. As depicted in Table 2, most of these organizations were incorporated in the mid-1990s. By 2002, CHDOs had built 28 projects for a total of 1,675 housing units. Most of these units (1,227) were for home ownership, and about one-fourth of the total (435) were affordable rental housing units. With 676 completed units, the Corporación para Desarrollo de Viviendas de Toa Baja, incorporated as a nonprofit development subsidiary of the municipality, built the largest share of units. The HOME program was the most significant federal program financing nonprofit organizations housing construction in the 1990s. Other federal programs subsidizing affordable housing construction and rehabilitation by nonprofits included the Community Development Block Grant (HUD CDBG), the Low Income Housing Tax Credit (LIHTC), Supportive Housing for People with Disabilities (HUD Sec. 811), and Housing Opportunities for People with Aids (HOPWA).

CDCs participation in affordable housing after the LIHTC program was instituted was minimal in Puerto Rico, whose HOME and CDBG programs subsidized most projects. Yet, as Figure 1 illustrates, nonprofit developers

Table 2. Puerto Rico Community Housing Development Organizations (CHDOs) Established by 2002

Organization (Incorporation Date)	Federal Programs	No. Proj.	New Const. Sale	New Const. Rent	Rehab Rent	Rehab Sale	Rehab Self-help	Total
CODEPCOVI – Corporación para el Desarrollo Económico Proyectos Comerciales y de Vivienda de Ponce (1995)	HOME, CDBG	8	187	65	14			266
Corporación para Desarrollo de Viviendas de Toa Baja, C.D.[1] (1995)	HOME, LIHTC	3	516	160				676
FUNDESCO – Fundación de Desarrollo Comunal de Puerto Rico (1996)	HOME, CDBG, Sec. 811	4		104				104
COCOPROVI – Comité Comunitario Pro Vivienda (1997)	HOME	1	24					24
La Fundita de Jesús (1985)	HOME, HOPWA,	2			11	25		36
Corporación Desarrolladora de Viviendas de las Barriadas de Israel y Bitumul (1996)	HOME, CDBG	1	109					109
Lucha Contra el SIDA (1994)	HOME	4	250	160		33		443
Apoyo Empresarial para la Peninsula de Cantera (1992)	HOME, LIHTC	5	270				13	283
Total		28	1169	424	11	58	13	1675

Source: Rolando Ramos Bermúdez, Las Primeras Historias Exitosas de los CHDOs en Puerto Rico. Fundacion Comunitaria de Puerto Rico. (2003).

Notes: [1] Corporacion Especial de Desarrollo Municipal Sin Fines de Lucro.

Abreviations:
HOME: HOME Investment Partnerships Program
CDBG: Community Development Block Grant
LIHTC: Low Income Housing Tax Credit
Sec. 811: Supportive Housing for People with Disabilities
HOPWA: Housing Opportunities for People with Aids»

played a significant role in affordable housing construction after the American Recovery and Reinvestment Act (ARRA) of 2009 was enacted. ARRA allocated over $206 million to HUD for Puerto Rico, with a significant portion of these funds specifically targeting "financing gaps caused by the reduction of equity investment in the Low-Income Housing Tax Credit (LIHTC) program" (Recovery Tracker 2020). Figure 1 depicts the overall impact of the stimulus funding on nonprofit developers. In 2009 and 2010, nonprofit developers built more affordable housing using federal tax credits than private developers who up to that point (and after the ARRA program ended) dominated the industry. During the four-year window provided by the ARRA funding, nonprofit developers built over 3,000 units of housing. This is a particularly important finding in the current context of post-disaster economic recovery and the use of CDBG-DR funding for housing rehabilitation, reconstruction, and new construction. Given an inclusive policy implementation, nonprofit developers were able to quickly respond to the challenge and developed as many units as the private sector, demonstrating a rapid

Figure 1. Total Units of LIHTC-Subsidized Housing Construction or Rehabilitation in Puerto Rico by Placed-in-Service Year and Sponsor

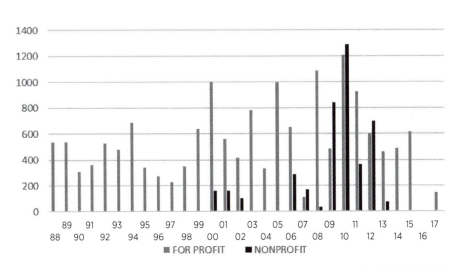

Source: HUD's Low-Income Housing Tax Credit Database. Data available for projects placed in service through 2017. Retrieved 4-22-20 from: <https://lihtc.huduser.gov/>.

deployment capability and surpassing private sector production in the initial years of the program.

Despite the significant role that CDCs played during the financial crisis of 2009-10, the available evidence indicates that the ARRA windfall did not lead to a sustainable expansion of the community development industry in Puerto Rico. The question is, Why? We have identified about a dozen currently active CHDOs and CDFIs operating in Puerto Rico, but there is almost no systematic data collection or tracking of these and other CBOs organizations, let alone information about the type of activities that they engage in their capacity to undertake economic development projects. In this context, one notable capacity assessment was conducted about a decade ago by Enterprise's Puerto Rico—the CHDO Technical Assistance project.[3] In an island-wide needs assessment of 24 CHDOs and CDCs in Puerto Rico completed in 2014, they found a general lack of capacity to undertake affordable housing development activities, poor interactions with government officials and lenders, and absence of accessible predevelopment funds. In response to these findings, Enterprise provided technical assistance for the submission of proposals to HOME funds and Low-Income Housing Tax Credits (LIHTC) and created a pre-development lending pool with HUD Section 4 dollars,[4] among other activities. Since the study was conducted, pre-development funding and CHDO participation in the LIHTC program disappeared for all practical purposes.

The findings from the aforementioned Borges (2020) and Enterprise studies are very telling—if these are the conditions of the "readiest" organizations to undertake social entrepreneurship projects using federal economic recovery funding, one can only imagine the existing capacity among other nonprofit organizations. Yet, literally, hundreds of nonprofit organizations and local governments are currently seeking potential projects to tap into federal recovery funding. In the next section, we address several factors that explain the weakening of nonprofit developers after ARRA in general, such as public policy and a weak industry ecosystem.

Barriers to Nonprofit Developers in the Community Development Industry in Puerto Rico

In our research and interviews with community leaders and other experts, we have identified three significant barriers to the development of the community development industry in Puerto Rico. These barriers are related to the key role of local implementation of federal policy, to the relatively small number and capacity of CDCs and financial intermediaries, and more generally to the nonprofit sector capacity to participate effectively in economic recovery and federal programs financing housing rehabilitation and reconstruction, urban and community development, and mitigation.

1. *Exclusionary federal and local recovery funding policy*
In contrast to the example of ARRA stimulus inclusionary funding, current recovery funding policy and implementation have resulted in the outright exclusion or minimal participation of nonprofit developers. Puerto Rico's policy for recovery funding is centralized into two agencies: the Puerto Rico Housing Finance Agency for the allocation of CDBG-DR funding, and the Central Office of Recovery, Reconstruction and Resiliency (COR3) for the management of FEMA funded programs. According to Torres-Cordero (2020), these two agencies function independently of each other and, in comparison to other U.S. jurisdictions, centralize decision-making and program implementation restricting municipal and nonprofit sector participation in publicly sponsored reconstruction projects. Though program authority remains within the federal oversight structure, the conventional practice in most states is to integrate reconstruction programs under one local agency and set up governance structures that promote interagency collaboration and are more inclusive of local governments and nonprofit organizations. Though the mechanisms for more inclusive participation vary under these types of governance and implementation arrangements, best practice examples include: subrecipient agreements to provide direct allocations to local governments (Louisiana, post-Hurricanes Gustav and Ike 2008); multiple local grantees including partnerships with nonprofit housing developers and community development corporations (South Carolina, post-Hurricane Joaquín 2015); regional differentiation through RFPs and joint ventures and partnerships between government agencies, for-profit and nonprofit organizations (Florida, post-Hurricane Irma, 2017); and, supplemental action planning and amendments to the action plan to redistribute resources from the state to county and city levels (Texas, post-Hurricane Harvey, 2017).

All funding for this program was contracted to the private sector, with 62 percent of the contracts awarded to foreign corporations.

The recent awards from the Puerto Rico Department of Housing Con-tracts to the Repair, Reconstruction, or Relocation Program (R3) program is the largest allocation of CDBG-DR funding to housing-related programs to date. Table 3 depicts the amount of funding for subcontractors to conduct housing rehabilitation, reconstruction or to facilitate relocation of disaster victims in Puerto Rico, and to other related programs. All funding for this program was contracted to the private sector, with 62 percent of the con-tracts awarded to foreign corporations. Though the nonprofit sector capac-ity to bid for these contracts was restricted given the specifications of the Notification of Funding Availability (NOFA) of the PRDOH as approved by HUD, other jurisdictions have implemented more inclusive policies to sup-port capacity building for municipalities and local nonprofit contractors.

Table 3. CDBG-DR Program Contracts Procured By the Puerto Rico Department of Housing (PRDOH), 2018 to 2020

Contractor Name	Total	
R3 Total	644,916,123	89.2%
R3 Foreign Corpoprations	414,916,123	57.4%
R3 Domestic Corpoprations	230,000,000	31.8%
Other Programs: Foreign Corpoprations	33,237,766	4.6%
Other Programs: Domestic Corpoprations	44,978,503	6.2%
Total	723,132,393	100.0%

Sources: Puerto Rico Department of Housing, CDBG-DR Program. Accessed from: <https://www.cdbg-dr.pr.gov/en/contracts/>. Puerto Rico Department of State, Registry of Corporations and Entities. Accessed from: <https://prcorpfiling.f1hst.com/CorporationSearch.aspx/>.

More recent PRDOH's CDBG-DR program allocations have earmarked Government of Puerto Rico agencies, municipalities, and nonprofit orga-nizations. Table 4 depicts data for Puerto Rico Department of Housing's Agreements with CDBG-DR Subrecipients from 2018 to 2020. Of the total $679 million in agreements, 84 percent was allocated to government agen-

Table 4. Agreements with CDBG-DR Subrecipients, 2018 to 2020, Puerto Rico Department of Housing (PRDOH)

Contractor Name	Total	
Agencies	555,975,628	81.8%
Central Office for Recovery, Reconstruction and Resiliency (COR3)	89,783,000	
Department of Economic Development and Commerce (DDEC)	85,000,000	
Economic Development Bank for Puerto Rico (EDBPR)	25,000,000	
Puerto Rico Housing Financing Authority (AFV)	356,192,628	
Municipalities	37,607,088	5.5%
(a) 5 Mun. Receiving $1m to $1.5m	9,391,398	
(b) 14 Mun. Receiving $1m to $1.5	18,072,645	
(c) 39 Mun. Receiving $283,045 to $164,400	8,994,645	
(d) 17 Mun. 69,600 to 34,800	1,148,400	
Government-Sponsored Nonprofit	13,755,000	2.0%
Discover Puerto Rico (e)	8,000,000	
Invest Puerto Rico (f)	5,755,000	
Nonprofit	86,096,619	12.7%
Foundation for Puerto Rico (FPR)	37,500,000	
Puerto Rico Science, Research And Technology Trust	30,472,000	
(g) 6 CDCs Receiving Housing Counciling Program Funding	4,369,619	
Total	679,679,335	100.0%

Notes:
(a) Ponce, Vieques, Aguadilla, Fajardo, Yabucoa.
(b) San Sebastian, Isabela, Naranjito, Coamo, Cidra, Gurabo, Villalba, Yauco, Orocovis, Aibonito, Camuy, Aguas Buenas, Maunabo, Luquillo.
(c) Ponce, Yauco, Villalba, Vega Alta, Toa Baja, San Lorenzo, San Germán, Sabana Grande, Rincón, Ponce, Patillas, Orocovis, Naranjito, Morovis, Maunabo, Manatí, Las Piedras, Las Marías, Lajas, Juncos, Juana Díaz, Jayuya, Isabela, Humacao, Culebra, Coamo, Cidra, Ciales, Cayey, Cataño, Canóvanas, Cabo Rojo, Barranquitas, Barceloneta, Arroyo, Arecibo, Aguada, Guayanilla, Dorado.
(d) Yabucoa, Vega Baja, Santa Isabel, Ponce, Naguabo, Las Marías, Las Piedra, Gurabo, Guaynabo, Fajardo, Comerío, Cataño, Camuy, Barranquitas, Añasco, Aguas Buenas, Guánica.
(e) Discover Puerto Rico is the official destination marketing organization (DMO) created by legislation in 2017.
(f) InvestPR is a nonprofit investment organization created by Act 13-2017.
(g) Pathstone Corporation, PueA25:D32rto Rico Neighborhood Housing Services Corp., Corporación Desarrollo Económico Vivienda y Salud (CODEVyS), Ponce Neighborhood Housing Services, INC., One Stop Career Center of Puerto Rico, Inc., Consumer Credit Counseling Services of Puerto Rico.
Sources: Puerto Rico Department of Housing, CDBG-DR Program. Accessed 10-6-20 from: <https://cdbg-dr.pr.gov/en/>.

cies and two newly created government-affiliated nonprofit organizations. With the sole exception of the six CDCs that participate in the Housing Counseling program, these funding allocations were made without following a conventional solicitation process. Municipalities are earmarked to re-

ceive 5.5 percent of the funding allocated through agreements, and nonprofits were allocated 12.7 percent of the funding to manage programs to benefit
municipalities and local communities. Most municipalities (56) received less
than $283,045. All in all, considering both contracts and agreements, non-
government-affiliated nonprofit organizations are earmarked to receive 6.1
percent of the $1.4 billion allocated so far from the CDBG-DR program, and
municipalities 2.7 percent. This is a sharp contrast to 51.5 percent of funds
allocated to the private sector, of which two-thirds are assigned to foreign
corporations, and 39.6 percent to government agencies.

 Despite the grim picture of CDBG-DR allocations supporting program
activities implemented by nonprofit organizations and municipalities, there
are a few factors to consider. For one, three years after Hurricane Maria land-
ed in Puerto Rico, the CDBG-DR and CDBG-MIT programs implementation
are in their initial phases. For example, the R3 program represent only 14 percent of the total $4.5 billion allocated to housing programs under CDBG-DR.
Typically, recovery programs will start about one year after HUDs approval
of the Action Plan. HUD's approval of the CDBG-DR Action Plan and first
authorization of $1.5 billion funding for Puerto Rico came on July 29, 2018.
Extended delays and inconsistencies in federal disaster responses and long-
term recovery funds in Puerto Rico are partly related to local factors such as
local government capacity and preparedness, but also to endemic problems
of federal policy implementation. According to Martin (2018, 4), in a review
of CDBG-DR funding allocations from 2005–15, multiple factors contribute
to the quality, speed, and costs of CDBG-DR implementation. Among these
factors are those related to the specific disaster such as "the disaster severity
and type and magnitude of damage, the preexisting state of housing quality and land use planning, and the quality of immediate relief and response
efforts before longer-term recovery activity." These problems seem to be affecting disaster recovery across the board. Federal Disaster Spending data
for all disasters declared in 2017 indicate that from the total Congressional
allocation to HUD of $35.4 billion, as of July of 2020 less than one billion has
been outlayed.[5] In Puerto Rico a similar pattern is seen—only a small fraction
($96 million) has been outlayed to date from the total $19.9 billion allocated
to CDBG-DR and CDBG-MIT programs. A final point is that the NOFAs issued in fiscal year 2019-2020 were affected by the pandemic. Many of these

solicitations (the acronym NOFA stands for Notice of Funding Availability) were solely for nonprofits or municipalities, and more recent solicitations included less restrictive qualifications for nonprofit organizations than prior solicitations. Yet since vendors for these programs have not been selected to date, it is an open question to what extent future implementation of CDBG-DR and CDBG-MIT programs will be more inclusive of nonprofit organizations, and for that matter municipalities.

In sum, Puerto Rico's housing and community development has been intricately connected to federal policy and to how local authorities have implemented such policies, from the extension of federal mortgage programs to Puerto Rico to the more recent allocation of CDBG-DR funding. Federal programs have subsidized over one hundred thousand public and affordable housing units. But, in contrast to the stateside experience, nonprofit developers have been relatively a small component of the housing and community development industry where private developers and the central government have played the dominant role. A critical exemption to this general assessment was during the financial crisis of 2009, when ARRA funding and the local implementation of federal policy was inclusive of nonprofit developers. In this context, it is important to understand how public policy and other factors have led to critical barriers to the role nonprofit developers play in the housing and community development industry in Puerto Rico, and how these policies curtail their potential contribution to economic reconstruction.

2. Weak Community Development Ecosystem

The economic crisis in Puerto Rico and the ongoing responses to the devastation of Hurricane Maria have heightened the need for and stimulate the advancement of community development intermediaries. Puerto Rico's community development and social enterprises ecosystem is developing through the growth of networks that support CDCs and other CBOs specifically for social entrepreneurship. If these trends continue, they could play a vital role in forging a national advocacy coalition for capacity building and for the advancement of the industry in the era of economic reconstruction. In this section we summarize the most salient existing and evolving community development intermediaries.

The community development and social enterprises ecosystem is integrated by CDCs, CDFIs and other financial intermediaries (such as capacity building and training vendors, often subsidiaries or affiliated with financial intermediaries), and other sector-specific networks that play a key role as regional and national advocacy coalitions for the advancement of the industry.[6] In the housing and community development industry in the U.S., this business ecosystem has vested interests in building organizational capacity, expanding the industry, lobbying for supportive policies to insure sustainability, organizing timely forums to discuss new directions, best practices, and funding availability, training professionals to adapt to new regulations and funding, as well as other capacity building initiatives. Because stateside federal policy and reconstruction funding are extended to Puerto Rico, island-based organizations potentially could take advantage of all the benefits that these network organizations offer to their members.

Puerto Rico has no significant local financial intermediaries, with the notable exception of Banco Popular, which holds a significant portfolio of community development investments, but this portfolio is seemingly more modest in terms of support to nonprofit developers than comparable stateside financial institutions. However, some established stateside-based developers and intermediaries have developed or currently develop affordable housing projects in Puerto Rico. Among these are private developers, such as McCormack, Baron, Salazar, and the Richman Group, and nonprofit intermediaries, such as Acacia Network, Enterprise Community Partners, Habitat for Humanity, Neighborhood Reinvestment Corporation (NeighborWorks America), PathStone, Hogar Hispano, and the Local Initiative Corporation (LISC). Despite such an explicit interest in expanding operations in Puerto Rico, too few CDCs with significant operational capacity are a tangible barrier to the potential expansion of financial intermediaries, as CDCs typically maintain a steady pipeline of local development projects for the volume required for syndication and reasonable returns on the investment of financial intermediaries' organizational resources.

The most significant constraint for community development intermediaries to expand their presence in Puerto Rico is the thin infrastructure of CDCs and other nonprofit organizations that could generate and develop social purpose economic development projects.

Based on the findings of four recent events in Puerto Rico co-sponsored by the Center for Puerto Rican Studies (Centro) with a focus on social entrepreneurship and reconstruction,[7] community-based organizations and non-profits alluded to a vicious cycle that might be contributing to the industry's underdevelopment. The most significant constraint for community development intermediaries to expand their presence in Puerto Rico is the thin infrastructure of CDCs and other nonprofit organizations that could generate and develop social purpose economic development projects. The complexity of undertaking recovery projects using federal funding in the context of insufficient trained or experienced professionals and the scarcity of potential CDCs partners constitute a significant constraint for the expansion of social purpose or economic recovery projects undertaken by established or emerging local financial intermediaries.

The weak business ecosystem in Puerto Rico's community development industry results in a scattered industry strategy for reconstruction. Few netting organizations with a focus on social entrepreneurship and community development provide the mechanisms for systemic learning about environmental changes affecting the local industry. Furthermore, the scant number of intersectoral alliances and leading development intermediaries constitute a significant challenge for the island's incipient housing and community development industry. Typically, an ecosystem of industry associations in alliances with large financial intermediaries takes the lead in understanding policy changes and funding opportunities in the industry. Because financial intermediaries are involved in most transactions in the industry, often partnering with CDCs and other local private developers, they lead in developing the legal and financial mechanisms intended to take advantage of new funding opportunities. This is particularly evident in key reconstruction areas such as infrastructure (energy, water systems, land fields, and waste disposal systems, etc.), agriculture, and repurposing public buildings, to name a few.

Besides the LIHTC, the community development industry in the United States is financed through multiple federal programs, and often these programs are combined to finance different aspects of a project. Besides LIHTC subsidization of affordable housing and CDFIs low interest lending, other popular programs broadly utilized in the industry include New Market Tax Credits (NMTC), CDBG and HOME, USDA programs for rural development, EDA programs for economic development programs, SBA small business support programs, and many others. These federal programs often are paired with state and local subsidies. Yet, in Puerto Rico, many federal social purpose programs are grossly underutilized.

According to the Congressional Task Force for the Economic Development of Puerto Rico, the island has the lowest HUBZone utilization of all jurisdictions, and non-residents receive six of every ten federal dollars allocated to the island in contracts. Though the "9 percent" LIHTC program is very competitive, and local authorities receive numerous proposals exceeding the capacity they have to support projects, the "4 percent" tax credit for affordable housing has been largely underutilized.[8] The current window of great opportunity for the island is provided by the availability of reconstruction funding and of other underutilized non-disaster related federal programs. In Louisiana after Hurricane Katrina, for example, LIHTC 4 percent funding was combined with CDBG-DR for leveraging $1.1 billion for the development of 8,448 units, of which 63 percent were affordable (Severino 2018). In addition, the current CDBG-DR program allocates $413 million to the LIHTHC-Gap program to provide gap funding for financing affordable rental housing units.

In addition to the window of opportunity opened by the CDBG-DR, FEMA and all other federal disaster funding, we need to consider the potential impact of non-disaster funding from Opportunity Zones, USDA, SBA, EDA and other federal agencies that potentially can be combined for financ-

Table 5. Puerto Rico's Existing and Emerging Community Development Intermediaries

Organization	Revenues ($)	Assets ($)	Grants 2017 (e) ($)
Puerto Rico Community Foundation (a)	9,132,268	37,819,101	3,271,315
Foundation for Puerto Rico (b)	6,149,360	6,990,888	2,638,490
Puerto Rico Science Technology and Research Trust (c)	22,996,445	115,682,560	NA
Para La Naturaleza (d)	16,271,811	7,855,342	665,000

Sources:
a. IRS Form 990Tax Filings for 2018.
b. IRS Form 990Tax Filings for 2018.
c. IRS Form 990Tax Filings for 2018.
d. IRS Form 990Tax Filings for 2017. Para la Naturaleza is a subsidiary of the Puerto Rico Conservation Trust with income of $28,770,630 and$459,093,965 in Assets in 2018.
e. Foundation Center, 2019.

ing projects. These programs offer a window of opportunity for the island to attract capital investment, especially potential investments in the housing and community development industry. All these programs are applied in different ways to economic development and target different types of populations. CDCs and financial intermediaries specialize in certain sectors of the community development industry. For example, there are CDCs and financial intermediaries that focus on affordable housing; some even specialize further in the use of 4 percent financing. Other pursue the construction of schools and other commercial facilities using NMTC. In other words, industry strategies are often developed targeting specific sectors.

There are two nonprofit organizations that were created to serve as community development intermediaries with programs to support nonprofit and private organizations. Founded in 1984, the Puerto Rico Community Foundation (PRCF) is perhaps the oldest organization with an established program to support organizations' community-based economic development and social entrepreneurship, and to a far less extent, affordable housing. In 2018, PRCF had $9 million in revenue and $38 million in assets (Table 5). Besides a conventional community foundation giving program, recently the PRCF created the Community Investment Fund to help capitalize community economic development through loans up to $250,000. Post disaster, besides relief assistance to nonprofit organizations, they have renewed their efforts to support core infrastructure projects in housing, energy, and water. This fund can be potentially used to cover housing, commercial, and other real estate transactions. In addition, PRCF in partnership with Enterprise Community Partners (Enterprise) and NeighborWorks America launched the Puerto Rico Nonprofit Capacity Building Network. This recent initiative provides six local CDCs a $35,000 operational grant, technical assistance, and one-to-one staff mentoring in addition to providing a structured peer-to-peer component for capacity building.

Founded in 2011, Foundation for Puerto Rico (FPR) is a nonprofit organization implementing an economic development initiative based on destination tourism in partnership with local governments and nonprofits organizations. These partnerships are known in the literature as Comprehensive Community Initiatives (Stagner and Duran 1997), in this case with a focus on the development of regional tourism. Currently, in 2018, FPR has revenues of $6 million and $7 million in assets (Table 5). Beginning in 2019, FPR received $37.5 million CDBG-DR funding from the Puerto Rico Department of Housing to lead the coordination of the Whole Community Resilience Planning Program (Foundation for Puerto Rico 2019). According to the Foundation Center, in 2019, FPR and PRCF received six million dollars in grants to support community organizations (Table 5).

Besides the FCPR and the FPR, there are two other important organizations that are initiating or renewing efforts for community development programs and potentially can have great impact on fostering social entrepreneurship in Puerto Rico. Two of the most important emerging community development intermediaries are established as public trusts. The Puerto Rico Science, Technology & Research Trust (PRSTRT) has undertaken several social ventures and developed specific business development models that serve as capacity-building and financial intermediaries especially for technology companies. In 2018, the PRSTRT was the largest intermediary in Puerto Rico worth $23 million in revenues and $116 million in assests (Table 5). Two of PRSTRT signature programs, Parallel18 and Colmena 66, focus on business development--the first as an incubator and accelerator, while the second support the entrepreneurship ecosystem. Though these programs focus on innovation and scaling up private businesses, this infrastructure could be extended to support social purpose enterprises and the nonprofit sector. The PRDOH recently allocated $92.5 million from the CDBG-DR program to the PRSTRT for the implementation of the Re-grow Puerto Rico Urban-Rural Agriculture Program.

Para la Naturaleza (PLN) is a nonprofit subsidiary of the Conservation Trust of Puerto Rico that oversees 42 natural areas throughout the island that are managed as social ventures, and implement fundraising, educational and volunteerism initiatives. Though their focus is environmental conservation and ecotourism, they increased their community development activities and partnerships after Hurricane Maria. They have significant organizational capacity, and their programs are already promoting sustainable development and conservation and impacting partnering communities. In 2018, PLN had $16 million in revenues and $8 million in assets (Table 5). These two public trusts have played a prominent role in reconstruction, implemented numerous programs with local community organizations, and have the revenues and assets capacity to evolve into the anchors of the community development industry.

In sum, PRCF, FPR, PRTRT and PLN are intermediaries that play or have the potential capacity to play a leadership role in the community development industry, and for fostering understanding among nonprofit organizations of how federal reconstruction funding can support social entrepreneurship and the development of the housing and community development industry in Puerto Rico. An evident gap in the emergent industry eco-system is a specialized intermediary supporting, financing and underwriting affordable housing development.

3. *Too few professionals with experience in federal economic recovery programs*
The development of CDCs and by implication the housing and community development industry in Puerto Rico is largely a workforce development challenge. In Puerto Rico, there is a wealth and abundant supply of well-trained, talented, and experienced nonprofit and business professionals. However, there are not enough professionals with social entrepreneurship and community economic development skills in the industry, especially professionals with the understanding of reconstruction programs and other federal programs supporting the housing and community development industry. The root cause of this barrier for community development is the actual abandonment of CDCs support through public policy though there are other impinging factors such as the availability of capacity building programs in the industry and the scarcity of specialized professional development training.

No academic or training organization has implemented a systematic program for the typical skills development required in the field.

The scarcity of professionals who have experience in community development, housing and commercial real estate development, and social entrepreneurship (i.e., the use and management of federal and local government funding programs for a social purpose program) is compounded by the lack of training and workforce development programs for the development of industry professionals. No academic or training organization has implemented a systematic program for the typical skills development required in the field. This is not to say that, for example, there are no for-credit or continuing education courses on real estate investment offered in Puerto Rico or on proposals preparation. The point is that few continuing education courses, workshops, and other forms of training and capacity building are offered with a focus on the skill sets and specific content required for economic recovery programs or the development and rehabilitation of affordable housing using federal programs such as the Low-Income Housing Tax Credit (LIHTC) and HOME, or the New Market Tax Credits (NMTC) for commercial development, or other similar programs devoted to this type of specialized financing. Practitioners who have acquired these skills had prior stateside experience or learned through local experiences with a relatively steep learning curve. On the whole, the available pool of experienced professionals in the social entrepreneurship field in Puerto Rico is limited, insufficient for the challenge of reconstruction, and constitute a real impediment for the expansion of the industry.

Though there are very capable community planners and social entrepreneurs in Puerto Rico, they are insufficient for the present challenges posed by recovery and reconstruction, and they are unevenly distributed across the island. Furthermore, even among those with expertise in social entrepreneurship, every active professional in the field is facing a new and challenging context (*e.g.,* the advent of CDGB-DR and mitigation funding) that requires a deeper understanding of the environment in which municipal and community programs currently operate. A first step is to recognize the need to adapt and, in many cases, introduce, concepts and practices of community development, disaster recovery planning, and social entrepreneurship in Puerto Rico to face the new challenges posed by post-disaster recovery.

We decided to ascertain the training needs of community development professionals for the implementation of post-disaster planning for economic recovery for Puerto Rico based on a social entrepreneurship approach. To accomplish our goal, we conducted a survey for the assessment of professional skills. The survey was distributed to professionals directly involved or overseeing programs that are part of or align with the economic and disaster recovery plans for Puerto Rico. The study was voluntary, and the respondents had the option of not answering any question. Eighty-seven (87) professionals participated in the study. The survey was conducted as a convenience sample and directed to all organizations identified as part of the housing and community development industry. We asked participants questions regarding work objectives, educational attainment, modalities for courses, preferential options for learning the competencies, and municipalities in which they worked in.

A core finding from the survey of professional skills is that, even though self-selection of survey respondents biased results toward the most educated and experienced, there are significant gaps in knowledge to undertake effectively planning and economic development projects in the context of federal programs devoted to reconstruction. Survey participants were highly educated, reflecting a bias toward organizational leaders. Nearly half of the participants had a master's degree (45.5 percent), followed by a bachelor's degree (29.9 percent), and Ph.D. (18.2 percent). Overall, two-thirds of the participants had a graduate level education. In other words, survey respondents were community leaders most likely to show advanced community planning in economic development skills. The survey also indicates that there is great interest among community leaders across all fields for professional training that targets professional skills gaps in the community development industry and among nonprofit organizations in general. Professionals in the field seem to prefer online continuing education courses to traditional academic formats.

Regarding objectives for professional work and social impact, participants were asked to choose from the following: Affordable Housing, Community Development, Education, Economic Development, Infrastructure, Civic Engagement, Food and Agriculture, and/or Health and other. Community Development was the area with the largest group of participants' objectives with 30.4 percent. The following objective was Education (15.8 percent), then Economic Development (12.3 percent), Infrastructure (11.7 percent), Health and other (9.4 percent), Affordable Housing (8.8 percent), Food and Agriculture (6.4 percent), and lastly Civic Engagement (5.3 percent). Whether these general findings from a self-selected group of practitioners could be extrapolated more generally to the overall staff of nonprofit organizations, let alone to community leaders, remains an open question. Yet, the findings from the survey offer the only available evidence regarding how professionals immerse in reconstruction efforts perceive their own skills to implement these programs.

The survey asked respondents to assess their level of knowledge in a range of competencies that were categorized into four areas encompassing corresponding competencies: Community Planning, Social Entrepreneurship and Economic Reconstruction, Municipal and Regional Economic Development, and Community and Municipality Master Plans. We asked survey respondents to indicate their level of proficiency for each of the competencies. They were offer the following description of the various levels of proficiency:

[ ] Minimal or none.

[ ] Basic. Familiarity with the competency. You may have a general understanding of the concepts and methods associated with the competency.

[ ] Intermediate. In addition to basic, you have some practical experience on the subject. You may have applied the competency in a community or municipal context under the supervision of someone more experienced in the field.

[ ] Advanced. In addition to intermediate, you have worked extensively in the field applying the competency, possibly supervising others in a community or municipal work context. If there are new circumstances or methods required, you feel confident to be able to learn those on your own, with little or no support from others.

Within the Community Planning category, we listed eight (8) different competencies such as conducting risk analysis or community engagement. In reference to Table 6, most respondents had basic knowledge of the eight planning competencies listed. Basic knowledge was the most selected level of knowledge from six out of the eight competencies listed followed by Minimal or none. The competencies participants determined they had the most knowledge of were in Establishing community priorities and Conducting community engagement. However, most participants within these competencies still had basic knowledge of them. On the other hand, the competency participants selected they had the lowest level of knowledge was Risks assessment and background research. Overall, the participants had basic to minimal or no knowledge within the Community Planning competency category.

Table 6. Community Planning

	Minimal/none	Basic	Intermediate	Advanced
Principles Planning Econ. Recovery	28.7%	36.8%	16.1%	18.4%
Risk Assessment and Background Research	42.4%	32.9%	16.5%	8.2%
Conducting Soc/Environ/Econ Impact Analysis	33.3%	44.8%	10.3%	11.5%
Identify potential strategic initiatives	25.3%	34.5%	23.0%	17.2%
Restructuring municipal governments	38.4%	33.7%	17.4%	10.5%
Establishing community priorities	24.1%	29.9%	25.3%	20.7%
Conducting community engagement	22.1%	38.4%	18.6%	20.9%
Conducting community events	9.8%	35.3%	27.5%	27.5%

Table 7 summarizes the results for the set of six (6) competencies associated with Social Entrepreneurship and Economic Reconstruction. Like the Community Planning category, most respondents selected either having basic or minimal to no knowledge across the Social entrepreneurship and Economic reconstruction competencies. "Minimal to none" was the most selected level of knowledge followed by basic knowledge, and an equal number of participants having intermediate and advanced knowledge of economic reconstruction competencies. The competency that participants had the most knowledge on was Identification of community development assets. However, nearly half of the participants within this competency still had basic knowledge of it. On the other hand, the competency participants selected they had the lowest level of knowledge was the Developing affordable housing projects and Developing commercial real estate syndication opportunities. In general, survey respondents had basic to minimal or no knowledge of competency in the Economic Reconstruction category.

Regarding the Municipal and Regional Economic Development category, depicted in Table 8, participants selected having minimal to no knowledge the most--in five of the six competencies listed. Nearly half of the participants selected were recorded as having Minimal to no knowledge followed by basic, intermediate, and, lastly, advanced. In reference to all the categories, Municipal and Regional Economic Development has the least number of participants with advanced knowledge across all the competencies listed. The competency that participants selected they had the least amount of knowledge was Development of strategies to stabilize neighborhoods. On the other hand, the com-

Table 7. Social Entrepreneurship and Social Reconstruction

	Minimal/none	Basic	Intermediate	Advanced
Identification of community development assets	21.4%	40.5%	15.5%	22.6%
Identification of social entrepreneurship options	21.2%	44.7%	18.8%	15.3%
Developing affordable housing projects	52.9%	27.1%	10.6%	9.4%
Developing syndication opportunities	62.4%	27.1%	5.9%	4.7%
Developing commercial and/or mixed-used project	50.0%	36.6%	6.1%	7.3%
Developing social enterprise options	27.4%	46.4%	14.3%	11.9%

Table 8. Municipal and Regional Economic Development

	Minimal/none	Basic	Intermediate	Advanced
Developing municipal circular economy	37.0%	42.0%	14.8%	6.2%
Developing municipal solar coops	50.0%	32.1%	11.9%	6.0%
Developing neighborhood stabilization strategies	54.1%	30.6%	9.4%	5.9%
Developing visitor-based economic development	44.7%	41.2%	9.4%	4.7%
Promoting recycling ordinances and executive orders	50.6%	32.9%	11.8%	4.7%
Creating a regional workforce development plan	48.8%	38.4%	7.0%	5.8%

Table 9. Community and Municipal Master Plans

	Minimal/none	Basic	Intermediate	Advanced
Developing a municipal or community master plan	41.2%	29.4%	18.8%	10.6%
Using community visioning	24.4%	37.8%	15.9%	22.0%
Developing market analysis and policy scenarios	30.2%	44.2%	17.4%	8.1%
Developing an action and implementation plan	25.9%	31.8%	25.9%	16.5%
Preparing a final report of a municipal master plan	40.0%	28.0%	16.0%	16.0%
Integrating the regions	42.0%	34.0%	18.0%	6.0%
Presentation of the municipal master plan to stakeholders	38.0%	20.0%	26.0%	16.0%

petency listed that had the highest amount of knowledge was Development of the municipal circular economy. However, most participants within this competency still expressed basic knowledge. All in all, throughout the competencies listed in this category, the participants had minimal to no knowledge of developing municipal or regional economies.

Table 9 summarizes findings for the Community and Municipal Master Plans competencies category. Most survey respondents either had basic knowledge or minimal to no knowledge of these competencies. Most respondents selected having intermediate knowledge of competencies in this area of expertise when compared to the prior two categories discussed. Like the Community Planning category, there was a greater range between the levels of knowledge within this group of competencies related to the development of municipal master plans. Both basic knowledge and minimal to none accounted for about 60 percent of respondents or above. The succeeding level of knowledge was intermediate, followed by advanced. The competencies that participants selected they had the least amount of knowledge of were Integration of the regions and Development of market analysis and political scenarios. On the other hand, the competency they had the highest amount of knowledge was the Use of community vision. However, like all other categories discussed, most of the participants had minimal to no knowledge of community and municipality master plans.

In addition to examining competencies proficiency, we participants were asked to identify preferences for course delivery. We asked them to choose from the following: an Online Course, Regular Course, Summer Course, Seminar and/or Over the Weekend. The majority of participants preferred the competencies to be taught as an Online Course (37.2 percent), followed by in a Seminar (32.1 percent), Over the Weekend (25.5 percent), and the least preferred options were the Summer Course (2.6 percent) and the Regular Course (2.6 percent). Participants were also asked to select in which modality they would like the courses: Continuing Education, For Credit: postgraduate, For Credit: current grade, or a Non-academic Certificate. More than half of the participants selected Continuing Education for their preferred course mode (55.8 percent), followed by a Non-academic Certificate (28.6 percent), For Credit: postgraduate (10.4 percent), and For Credit: undergraduate (5.2 percent).

Based on the results of the survey, I conclude that respondents revealed a need for a continuing education online courses that covers all competencies associated with economic and disaster recovery plans for Puerto Rico, particularly those focusing on community economic development and planning. Professionals in the field are interested in the systematic development of skills associated with the implementation of post-disaster planning for economic recovery for Puerto Rico and on social entrepreneurship. Even among those most educated and actively engaged in the industry there is a recognition for the need for the development of professional skills in the industry moving forward. Findings from the survey provide a clear picture of the professional skills gap and a pathway to close it.

Conclusions and Recommendations

In this study I review the evidence and assess the capacity of the nonprofit sector to become an active participant in the economic recovery of Puerto Rico. Specifically, I sought to answer the question whether the nonprofit sector would be able to take advantage of this window of opportunity to contribute to the economic recovery of Puerto Rico while inducing a much broader community participation and strengthening the community development industry of the island. I also examined the factors that may contribute to the advancement or stand as barriers to nonprofit and municipal participation in recovery programs. The evidence presented in this report based on an empirical examination of the field leads us to the following conclusions when examining such critical questions.

In contrast, CDCs and nonprofit developers demonstrated that, when given the opportunity during the ARRA program, they were able to build more than 3,000 units of housing using the LIHTC program and surpassed the number of housing units built by the profit sector.

First, to date, federal recovery programs implementation, and more specifically recovery funding policy, have resulted in the outright exclusion or minimal participation of nonprofit developers in publicly sponsored reconstruction projects. The recent awards for housing rehabilitation and reconstruction, the largest funding allocated to date for housing, was solely awarded to the private sector, with 62 percent of the contracts awarded to foreign corporations. In contrast, CDCs and nonprofit developers demonstrated that, when given the opportunity during the ARRA program, they were able to build more than 3,000 units of housing using the LIHTC program and surpassed the number of housing units built by the profit sector. Yet, the ARRA experiment led only to short-term gains. A study conducted shortly after demonstrated that a reversal of public policy led directly to the exclusion of nonprofit developers from the LIHTC and other programs.

Second, the nonprofit sector capacity to participate in the post-disaster economic recovery phase is limited. In part the lack of capacity is attributed to their focus on education, community development, and health programs prior to the disaster, and that only a fraction of nonprofit organizations implemented housing and economic development programs that constitute the focus of the post-disaster economic recovery phase. Yet there are other reasons for the lack of capacity in economic recovery in general; more specifically, these reasons affect the use of federal funding. Among others, organizations reported on the need to have better access to information, predevelopment funds, staff training in recovery issues, and technical assistance for projects and submission of proposals as key areas for organizational development in the era of reconstruction.

Third, a close examination of CDCs in Puerto Rico revealed that there are too few nonprofit organizations devoted to affordable housing rehabilitation and construction, and to other community economic development projects. Though these organizations exhibit a wide range of capacity to implement development projects, they have a limited operational and financial capacity for real estate development and only a few have undertaken housing counseling or rehabilitation but no other recovery-related economic development project. In general, the nonprofit sector participation in economic recovery is also limited by the number of professional staff with social entrepreneurship and community development skills, especially professionals with the understanding of reconstruction programs and other federal programs available or to become available to Puerto Rico in the near future.

Fourth, one of the critical barriers for the development of the community development industry in Puerto Rico is the lack of professionals with the skills to implement federal economic recovery programs, housing and economic development, and community planning. The first step in the development of professional training for the community development industry involves understanding the Governor's Action Plan, which governs the allocation of funding for economic recovery. An assessment of the tasks and competencies associated with the implementation of the Action Plan calls for the development of economic recovery and community planning training that is interdisciplinary, empowers participant to collect and analyze data relevant for the implementation of recovery projects, and an understanding of regions, municipal reconstruction, and the policy context in which these programs operate.

These general findings from the study serve as a foundation for the following recommendations:

Policy

1. Inclusionary policy reforms to support nonprofit developers and CDCs. The evidence indicates the need to set up governance structures that promote policies that are more inclusive of local governments and nonprofit organizations. Examples of best practices inclusionary policies from other states include subrecipient agreements to provide direct allocations to municipalities, promoting partnerships with nonprofit housing developers and community development corporations, regional differentiation through RFPs and joint ventures and partnerships between government agencies, for-profit and nonprofit organizations, and supplemental action planning and amendments to the action plan to redistribute resources from the state to county and city levels.

CDC capacity building

2. Development of a low-cost, high-risk predevelopment fund for CDCs. Capacity building among nonprofit organizations require targeted strategies. For the existing CDCs with some experience in housing and other community development activities, organizational capacity building requires subsidization of predevelopment costs and technical support for submissions of competitive proposals for FEMA, CDBG-DR, and other economic recovery targeted funding, as well as for the combination of such funds with other traditional community development programs such as housing tax credits, new market tax credits, USDA programs, and the understanding of newer programs such as Opportunity Zones. Predevelopment costs are a critical barrier in Puerto Rico since the few financing programs for these types of projects that exist are not designed to serve high-risk projects and often require CDCs to comply to terms like those offered by the commercial banking industry.

3. Promoting intra-industry partnerships. Economic recovery in Puerto Rico is beginning, with only a fraction of funding allocated to programs. For effective nonprofit participation in recovery programs it is urgent to accelerate project development capacity. A proven strategy to improve capacity in the short term to develop housing rehabilitation and construction projects is for established CDCs to partner with nonprofit organizations that would like to implement community development projects in their neighborhoods. Effective project development requires not just financial means and real estate or economic development expertise, but also local organizing and public sector support for the project. Nonprofit organizations can generate local support in partnership with experience developers. Nonprofits lacking CDC-type capacity will probably require partnerships with established CDCs or other intermediaries with development capacity and understanding of disaster recovery funding when implementing the first generation of projects.

4. Development of support for nonprofits to become CDCs. Though creating a predevelopment fund could be a relevant strategy for capacity building among nonprofit organizations that are seeking ways to engage in economic recovery, for the typical nonprofit organization lacking any experience in housing, real estate and economic development participating in such activities is a more challenging task. For these organizations to participate in programs financed through federal programs for post disaster economic recovery, professional development for current staff on housing and community economic development and the understanding of federal funding is imperative. In addition, nonprofit organizations involved in economic recovery will benefit from organizational assessments and strategic planning processes in close connection and engagement of the communities they serve. In this transition to community economic development it is common for nonprofit organizations to revamp their board of directors to include more professionals with business expertise and to promote residents' participation in community planning.

Professional training

5. Development of professional training for post-disaster economic recovery. Professional development is at the core of the expansion of housing and economic development projects and programs in the nonprofit sector. The experience of CDCs and other nonprofit organizations with training in Puerto Rico is mixed. Common barriers involve the lack of funding targeting these programs and the time commitment of their staff, given that these organizations have limited staff and financial resources. In addition, most of the training in Puerto Rico is offered as workshops targeting specific topics. CBO leadership expressed frustration with the abundant and fragmented supply of disconnected and abstract workshops with little value-added to contribute to their operations. By comparison, in the business capacity development field there are well-structured programs with a comprehensive curriculum, an embedded technical assistant, and a support ecosystem. The findings from the survey on the preparedness of professionals in the field indicate that professionals in the community development field prefer comprehensive courses offered as continuing education, and online course offerings or structured as seminars.

Industry ecosystem

6. Strengthening community development intermediaries. The development of intermediaries requires the scaling up of capacity to serve as a financial intermediary and to provide technical assistance to members of the network of nonprofit developers. Puerto Rico does not yet have a specialized Community Development Financial Institution (CDFI) for housing financing and development, with underwriting capabilities, and only Banco Popular is a Community Development Entity (CDE). Of all the actors in the industry, the cooperative sector with a substantial financial assets base is in the best position to strengthen existing credit unions that operate CDFIs to build up capacity for housing development and underwriting. These financial intermediaries are important for both understanding the plethora of federal programs available to nonprofit developers, including complex transactions involving syndication and the combination of funding required for most housing and commercial development projects, and the complexity of bidding, managing, and complying with federal recovery programs. Ultimately, the establishment of these institutions depend on a steady stream of viable projects, which in turn rely on capacity building of nonprofit developers.

7. Creation of a hub for the exchange of information and networking. An urgent need in the industry is to create communication mechanisms and shared knowledge of effective practices for community and economic development in the era of reconstruction. This could be achieved through forums and conferences, publications, newsletters, web seminars, and other means of dissemination of effective community practices; the provision of community services; the analysis of policies; and the exchange of ideas for the well-being of residents and communities. These communication mechanisms also promote the dissemination of integral and sustainable community development research. In addition, such a hub could make available basic information for networking and community building such as a directory of individuals and organizations, a calendar of activities, and opportunities for volunteerism and collaborations.

8. Creation of a data hub. The research presented in this report indicates the need for a hub to easily access data, ideally as interactive GIS maps available for each community and municipality in the island, and to construct visualizations for community planning and contribute to crowdsourcing data efforts. Data collection is also important for tracking progress in overcoming the barriers to the growth of the community development industry and social entrepreneurship. Ideally, there would be an ongoing directory of individuals and organizations, an easily accessible repository of grants available and funded projects, and an industry communication platform. Besides the obvious direct benefit of this type of data collection on understanding the industry and the needs of professionals and organizations, data collection and analysis would be beneficial for formulating business and sector strategies. Centro's RebuildPR digital platform is one step in that direction. This platform currently contains a comprehensive set of layers available to the public. Next steps involve the training of community groups for the use of the platform for community planning and development. Training in the use of this data hub will serve as a complement to professional training for post-disaster economic recovery.

In conclusion, post-disaster federal funding for economic recovery offers Puerto Rico a unique window of opportunity to restore its economy and infrastructure in a more resilient fashion while strengthening the nonprofit sector capacity for community planning, housing development, and neighborhood revitalization. However, such an opportunity is contingent on reforming local public policy and implementing a comprehensive sector strategy to encourage and support nonprofit developers participation in reconstruction programs, building industry capacity by strengthening intermediaries, and CDCs, encouraging intra-industry partnerships and collaborations, and providing professional development for economic recovery.

ACKNOWLEDGEMENTS

I am indebted to the anonymous reviewers of the original manuscript for providing insightful comments and providing directions for the additional work that has resulted in this paper. I would like to thank Damayra Figueroa-Lazu for her support retrieving and organizing the data for tables and graphics. This study would not have been possible without the support and willingness of the leadership and staff of the various community-based organizations who contributed to this research. I would like to extent my gratitude to: Reverendo Heriberto Martínez, Presidente, La Sociedad Bíblica de Puerto Rico, who provided our researchers with office space and other support infrastructure; to Centro's Staff Alejandra Del Monte Medina, Diana Ramos, and Elisa Sánchez Torres for support during various conferences on the topic and with general coordination for the research projects; to the research assistants who conducted case studies and compiled other data, including José Luis Colón, Yamil Corvalán, Miriam Morales Suárez, and Katsyris Rivera Kientz; to Professor Ivis García Zambrana from the University of Utah, who coordinated the skills project Institutional Review Board compliance and provided valuable feedback on the manuscript; and to Professors Ramón Borges-Méndez and Ariam Torres for reading an early version of the manuscript. Finally, I want to thank members of the Grupo Académico de IDEAComún for their valuable input and support: Marinés Aponte; Antonio J. Fernós Sagebien; Federico Del Monte; Nilsa Medina Piña; Omayra Rivera Crespo; Luisa Seijó; and Rafael A. Torrech San Inocencio.

NOTES

[1] This plan was prepared by the Homeland Security Operational Analysis Center (HSOAC), a federally funded research and development center (FFRDC) that RAND operates for the Department of Homeland Security (DHS).

[2] With the Department of Housing and Urban Development recent release of $9.7 billion in Community Development Block Grant Disaster Recovery funding, a total of $22 billion has been obligated from the total of $44 billion across 14 agencies to disasters in Puerto Rico (Office of Management and Budget 2020).

[3] Enterprise's technical assistance to the Puerto Rico Housing Finance Authority and Department of Housing was recommended by the President's Task Force on Puerto Rico in March 2011 and concluded with the approval of an updated State Housing Plan by the Puerto Rico Housing Policy and Implementation Committee on 24 October 2014. The updated plan included a concrete action plan and implementation schedule, and a "better targeting resources to meet community needs and improving the quality of program delivery" (see <https://www.enterprisecommunity.org/solutions-and-innovation/technical-assistance-and-consulting/direct-ta-and-capacity-building/>.

[4] The Section 4 Capacity Building for Community Development and Affordable Housing (Section 4) program strengthens low-income communities across the nation by providing critical support to local nonprofit organizations that develop affordable housing, finance small businesses, revitalize commercial corridors, and help address local healthcare, childcare, education, and safety needs. Enterprise is one of four organizations eligible for the program.

[5] Source: FEMA's Spending Explorer, Data as of 1 September 2020.

[6] A business ecosystem is the network of organizations — including suppliers, distributors, customers, competitors, government agencies, and so on — involved in the delivery of a specific product or service through both competition and cooperation (Hays 2019).

[7] Resiliencia y Solidaridad: Encuentro con la Diáspora Conference, San Juan, Puerto Rico, June 2018; Empresarismo Social y Reconstrucción, 5 October 2018, at Universidad de Puerto Rico, and 6 October 2018, Industriales de Puerto Rico. Simposio de Empresarismo Social y Reconstrucción Económica, Universidad Interamericana, Recinto Metropolitano, San Juan, Puerto Rico, 7 August 2019; Simposio Vivienda y Desarrollo Económico Comunitario en Puerto Rico, 5 February 2020, Colegio de Abogados, Miramar, Puerto Rico.

[8] The Non-Competitive (4 percent) Housing Tax Credit program is coupled with the Multifamily Bond Program when the bonds finance at least 50 percent of the cost of the land and buildings in the development.

REFERENCES

Alameda-Lozada, José I. and Carlos Alberto Rivera Galindo. 2005. La Vivienda de Interés Social en Puerto Rico. San Juan: Departamento de la Vivienda, Estado Libre Asociado de Puerto Rico.

Borges-Méndez, Ramón. 2020. Community Development Corporations and Reconstruction Policy in Puerto Rico. Unpublished manuscript.

Butteriss, Crispin. 2020. What is community engagement, exactly Accessed 31 August 2020. <https://www.bangthetable.com/blog/defining-community-engagement/>.

Center on Disaster Philanthropy. 2020. Puerto Rico Earthquakes. 9 March. Accessed 31 August 2020. <https://disasterphilanthropy.org/disaster/puerto-rico-earthquakes/>.

Central Office of Recovery, Reconstruction and Resiliency. 2018. Transformation and Innovation in the Wake of Devastation: An Economic and Disaster Recovery Plan for Puerto Rico. 8 August.

COSSEC, Corporación Pública para Supervisión y Seguro de Cooperativas de Puerto Rico. 2018. Total de Activos, Número de Socios y de Empleados, Por Cooperativa 30 junio. Accessed 30 August 2020. <http://www.cossec.com/cossec_new/est/Junio18/Anejo_9_Total_de_Activos,_Socios_y_Empleados_Tiempo_Completo_Por_Cooperativa_jun_2018.pdf/>.

Cotto, Liliana. 1993. The Rescate Movement. In Colonial Dilemma: Critical Perspectives on Contemporary Puerto Rico, eds. Edwin Meléndez and Edgardo Meléndez. Boston: South End Press.

Dyer, Christopher L. 1999. The Phoenix Effect in Post-Disaster Recovery: An Analysis of the Economic Development Administration's Culture of Response after Hurricane Andrew. In The Angry Earth: Disaster in Sociological Perspective, eds. Anthony Oliver-Smith and Susana Hoffman. New York: Routledge.

Eller, Warren, Brian J. Gerber and Lauren E. Branch. 2015. Voluntary Nonprofit Organizations and Disaster Management: Identifying the Nature of Inter-Sector Coordination and Collaboration in Disaster Service Assistance Provision. Risk, Hazards & Crisis in Public Policy 6(2), 223–38.

Foundation for Puerto Rico. 2019. Foundation for Puerto Rico Begins Phase One Of Whole Community Resilience Program. 15 January. Accessed 31 August 2020. <https://static1.squarespace.com/static/59e4cf35a8b2b019331ce112/t/5c3e08c203ce640330cd5e0e/1547569347160/FOUNDATION+FOR+PUERTO+RICO+BEGINS+PHASE+ONE_ENGLISH_01-15-19-converted.pdf/>.

Fuller-Marvel, Lucilla. 2008. Building a Just, Integrated and Sustainable Planning and Housing System: The Puerto Rican Experience. Paper presented at the 52nd IFHP World Congress on Housing and Planning Housing Beyond Its Walls: Planning for an Affordable and Sustainable Housing, San Juan, Puerto Rico. Accessed 31 August 2020. <http://spp-pr.org/oct2012/old/images/documents/ifhp/plenarias/Construyendo%20un%20sistema%20de%20Planificacion%20...%20Lucilla%20Fuller%20Marvel.pdf/>.

García, Ivis and Divya Chandrasekhar. 2020. Impact of Hurricane María to the Civic Sector: A Profile of Nonprofits in Puerto Rico. *CENTRO: Journal of the Center for Puerto Rican Studies* 32(3), 67–88.

Hayes, Adam. 2019. Social Entrepreneur. Investopedia. Updated 13 August 2019. Accessed 31 August 2020. <https://www.investopedia.com/terms/s/social-entrepreneur.asp/>.

Hoffman, Alexander von. 2013. The past, present, and future of community development: The changing face of achieving equity in health, education, and housing in the United States. *Shelterforce* 17 July. Accessed 31 August 2020. <https://shelterforce.org/2013/07/17/the_past_present_and_future_of_community_development/>.

Johnson, Laurie, and Robert Olshansky. 2017. *After Great Disasters: An In-Depth Analysis of How Six Countries Managed Community Recovery*. Cambridge, MA: Lincoln Institute of Land Policy.

Martín, Carlos. 2018. The Evidence Based on how CDBG-DR Works for State and Local Stakeholders. Statement of Carlos Martín, Senior Fellow, Urban Institute, before the Subcommittee on Oversight and Investigations, Committee on Financial Services, United States House of Representatives. 17 May 2018.

May, Peter J. and Walter Williams. 1986. *Disaster Policy Implementation: Managing Programs under Shared Governance*. New York: Springer.

McDonnell, Simon, Pooya Ghorbani, Courtney Wolf, Maria Jessa Cruz, David M. Burgy, Swati Desai, Daniel Berkovits and Renata Silberblatt. 2019. A Managed-Participatory Approach to Community Resilience: The Case of the New York Rising Community Reconstruction Program. *The American Review of Public Administration* 49(3), 309–24.

Meléndez, Edwin and Lisa J. Servon. 2007. Reassessing the Role of Housing in Community-Based Urban Development. *Housing Policy Debate* 18(4), 751–83.

Mileti, Dennis S. 1999. *Disasters by Design: A Reassessment of Natural Hazards in the United States*. Washington, DC: Joseph Henry Press.

Office of Management and Budget. 2020) Statement of Administration Policy. 5 February. Accessed 31 August 2020. <https://www.whitehouse.gov/wp-content/uploads/2020/02/SAP_HR-5687.pdf/>.

Peacock, Walter Gillis, Betty Hearn Morrow and Hugh Gladwin. 1997. *Hurricane Andrew: Ethnicity, Gender, and the Sociology of Disasters*. New York: Routledge.

Puerto Rico Department of Housing. 2018. Puerto Rico Disaster Recovery Action Plan, approved by the U.S. Department of Housing and Urban Development (HUD) on 29 July 2018. Accessed 31 August 2020. <https://www.cdbg-dr.pr.gov/en/action-plan/>.

Rosselló, Ricardo. 2020. Build Back Better. Puerto Rico. Request for Federal Assistance for Disaster Recovery. 13 November 2017. Accessed 31 August 2020. <https://media.noticel.com/o2com-noti-media-us-east-1/document_dev/2017/11/13/Build%20back%20better%20Puerto%20Rico_1510595877623_9313474_ver1.0.pdf/>.

Ramos-Bermúdez, Rolando. 2003. Las primeras historias Eexitosas de los CHDOs en Puerto Rico. Fundacion Comunitaria de Puerto Rico. Unpublished Manuscript.

Recovery Tracker, Funds by Department of Housing and Urban Development, San Juan, P.R. *ProPublica*. Accessed 10 March 2020. <https://projects.propublica.org/recovery/locale/puerto-rico/san-juan/dept/8600/>.

Red de Fundaciones de Puerto Rico. 2019. Philanthropy and Puerto Rico After Hurricane Maria: How a Natural Disaster Put Puerto Rico on the Philanthropic Map and Implications for the Future. 1 March. Accessed 31 August 2020. <https://philanthropynewsdigest.org/news/hurricane-relief-put-puerto-rico-on-philanthropic-map-study-finds/>.

Robinson, Scott and E. Haley Murphy. 2014. Frontiers for the Study of Nonprofit Organizations in Disasters. *Risk, Hazards & Crisis in Public Policy* 4(2), 128–34.

Severino, Kathya. 2018. Rebuild Puerto Rico: A Guide to Federal Policy and Advocacy. New York: Center for Puerto Rican Studies. <https://centropr.hunter.cuny.edu/sites/default/files/data_briefs/CENTRO_POLICYGUIDE_PB2018-02.pdf/>.

Social Enterprise. 2020. What is Social Enterprise? Accessed 31 August 2020. <https://socialenterprise.us/about/social-enterprise/>.

Stagner, Matthew W. and M. Ángela Durán. 1997. Comprehensive Community Initiatives: Principles, Practice, and Lessons Learned. *The Future of Children* 7(2), 132–40.

Smith ,Gavin P. and Dennis Wenger. 2007. Sustainable Disaster Recovery: Operationalizing An Existing Agenda. In *Handbook of Disaster Research*, eds. Havidan Rodriguez, Enrico L. Quarantelli and Russell Dynes. New York: Springer Science & Business Media.

Smith, Gavin and Thomas Birkland. 2012. Building a Theory of Recovery: Institutional Dimensions. *Journal of Mass Emergencies and Disasters* 30(2), 147–70.

Sviridoff, Mitchell, ed. 2004. Inventing Community Renewal: The Trials and Errors that Shaped the Modern Community. New York: Community Development Research Center, Milano Graduate School, New School University.

Torres-Cordero, Ariam L. 2020. What is possible? Disaster Policy Options for Long-term Recovery in Puerto Rico. *CENTRO: Journal of the Center for Puerto Rican Studies* 32(3), 199–223.

Welsh, Mark G. and Ann-Margaret Esnard. 2009. Closing Gaps in Local Housing Recovery Planning for Disadvantaged Displaced Households. *Cityscape: A Journal of Policy Development and Research* 11(2), 195–212.

Community Development Corporations and Reconstruction Policy in Puerto Rico

RAMÓN BORGES-MÉNDEZ

ABSTRACT

After the destruction caused by hurricanes Irma and Maria in 2017, and the earthquakes of January 2020, community-based organizations (CBOs) in Puerto Rico (PR) intensified their activity in accessing economic and capacity-building resources allocated by the federal government. This investigation of twelve case studies of Puerto Rican community development corporations (PRCDCs) addresses several critical questions relevant to the reconstruction of the island. First, why should policy makers explicitly involve PRCDCs in the short-term and long-term reconstruction of communities in the island? Second, what are PRCDCs currently doing in Puerto Rican communities, and what can we learn from them? Third, what are the challenges faced by PRCDCs in participating effectively in the future recovery and reconstruction at local, municipal, and regional levels? Our findings indicate that the prevailing narrative of centralized post-disaster planning and government recovery policy underestimates the PRCDCs' experience and capabilities. While PRCDCs might have limited experience with specific federal funding and programs, they have accumulated legitimate experience in implementing projects with state and federal agencies. PRCDCs have the entrepreneurial drive, and the professional, community-based talent, to participate directly in the reconstruction of communities and municipalities. PRCDCs' collective experience represents a strong foundation from which it is possible to "scale-up from the bottom-up" the processes of reconstruction and resilience-building. [Key words: Community Development Corporations, Puerto Rico, Disasters, Reconstruction, Housing]

Introduction

In the United States, community development corporations (CDCs) have almost sixty years of history creating housing solutions, promoting equity policies for the inclusion of vulnerable populations, and harnessing resources to address social and economic disadvantage in cities and rural areas. CDCs are perhaps the most common non-profit entity involved in community planning in the United States. They engage in housing and economic development, but also participate in workforce development, asset-building, community organizing, health and food system planning, and education, among other activities. In addition, CDCs acting as community development finance institutions (CDFI) and community housing development organizations (CHDO) leverage capital resources from financial intermediaries and markets to satisfy social and economic needs in disadvantaged communities.[1]

After the destruction caused by hurricanes Irma and Maria in 2017, and more recently after the earthquakes of January 2020, community-based organizations (CBOs) in Puerto Rico (PR) intensified their activity in trying to access economic and capacity-building resources allocated by the federal government. In the process, CBOs have turned to social entrepreneurial strategies to "bundle" public, private, philanthropic, and market resources to finance projects and assure financial sustainability. Among such CBOs, I have focused this investigation on twelve Puerto Rican community development corporations (PRCDCs) to address several critical questions that are relevant to the reconstruction and resilience-building efforts of the island. First, why should policy makers in Puerto Rico and the US, especially in the federal government and the government of the Commonwealth of Puerto Rico, explicitly involve PRCDCs in the short-term and long-term reconstruction of communities in the island? Recent processes of allocation of Community Development Grants-Disaster Reconstruction (CDBG-DR)

The author (RBorgesMendez@clark.edu) was born in Puerto Rico, and has worked in the U.S., Latin America, and Asia. He is an Associate Professor of Urban Planning at the International Development, Community, and Environment Department at Clark University (Worcester, MA). He holds a PhD and an MCP in Urban and Regional Planning from MIT. Prof. Borges-Méndez is co-founder of Fundación Bucarabón in Maricao, PR. His work has appeared in *CENTRO Journal, Economic Development Quarterly,* and *Local Environment.*

funds seem explicitly interested in reaching Puerto Rican organizations, yet so far PRCDCs have been sidelined by the state government from the substantial reconstruction and mitigation funding outlays reaching the island. PRCDCs stand to remain disconnected from such funding streams without explicit policy measures to support their inclusion. Second, what are PRCDCs currently doing in Puerto Rican communities, and what can we learn from them? The case studies suggest that a more decentralized, placed-based, and collaborative governance of post-disaster planning and recovery in Puerto Rican communities and municipalities is in fact feasible and desirable from a public policy standpoint. The evidence suggests that prevailing practices of centralized post-disaster planning and recovery among the policy makers designated by the government of the Commonwealth of Puerto Rico, in the Department of Housing and the Central Office for Recovery, Reconstruction and Resiliency (COR3) ignore the PRCDCs' experience and capabilities.

The devastating impact of the natural hazards on the island (and of the ongoing debt and political crisis) has opened up a wide array of community-based and institutional efforts to support communities.

Third, what are the challenges faced by PRCDCs in participating effectively in future recovery and reconstruction, at the local, municipal, and regional levels? PRCDCs unfold their activity and projects in a rather hostile, politicized, and complex policy ecosystem, while resourcing from highly "imperfect" input markets (of land, capital, construction materials, and expertise). In addition, PRCDCs work, by all kinds of metrics, in highly disadvantaged communities, while complying with cumbersome local, state, and federal regulatory systems. Beyond their conventional functions, PRCDCs were at the frontline of meeting basic community needs during the post-Maria emergency, and currently remain fulfilling such roles during the recovery stage. After the earthquakes of January 2020, their job has become even more complex and burdensome, as they get involved in assessing the damage, demolishing, and future reconstruction of destroyed housing and other critical infrastructure. Finally, in what strategic areas of reconstruction and resilience-building activity do PRCDCs have important comparative advantages?

In Section I, I draw from the community development and housing, and post-disaster recovery research and policy literatures to make a general conceptual, practical, and policy case for involving PRCDCs in the recovery and housing development process in Puerto Rico. In this section, I briefly characterize the historical context and structural forces influencing PRCDCs as well. Section II details the comparative case-study methodological approach and the value of the case studies for long-term "learning" in the local community development ecosystem of the island. In Section III, I describe the organizational characteristics of the twelve PRCDCs and discuss their past and present housing development, and more recent activity including reconstruction projects. The core objective of this section is to demonstrate the organizational and operational suitability of PRDCs for the current tasks of community recovery and reconstruction. Some of the PRCDCs are specialized on housing development, while others implement "housing plus" models, which combine housing and other social and community-based services.[2] The devastating impact of the natural hazards on the island (and of the ongoing debt and political crisis) has opened up a wide array of community-based and institutional efforts to support communities. In such an environment, PRCDCs can provide important lessons about housing development, social entrepreneurship, and service delivery to communities and citizens.[3] Section IV focuses on the leadership, social entrepreneurship, and the challenges which PRCDCs face to achieve meaningful participation in housing and economic development at various geographic levels. Most critically, for example, several PRCDCs emphasized the absence of institutions and funding to pay for housing pre-development costs, and to accelerate project planning, including land acquisition, feasibility studies, and to meet specialized staffing needs. In Section V, as a conclusion, I discuss critical supports that PRCDCs may require to meet the needs of vulnerable populations and achieve equitable representation for the community development sector in policy making and in the housing reconstruction ecosystem.

I. The Policy Case for the Inclusion of Community Development Corporations in Community Post-Disaster Planning and Recovery.

1.1 *CDCs in the United States: From Bricks and Mortars to Disaster Recovery*

Multiple experts in the academic and policy world have documented the positive contribution of community development corporations in the US to housing and economic development in disadvantaged communities and urban areas since their formation during the mid-1960s (Anglin 2004, 2011; Meléndez and Servon 2007; Schwartz 2015). CDCs exists in multiple urban and rural contexts, and they vary in staff size and the scope of activities performed beyond housing and economic development, such as workforce development (Borges-Méndez 2011; Meléndez et al. 2015). Since their inception in the late 1960s until the present, four generations of CDCs have created a complex landscape of community activity, and significant organizational diversity (Stoutland, 1999). NACEDA estimates that by 2006 approximately 4,600 CDCs operated in the US, although the number might have decreased due to the decline of public and private sector resources for affordable housing construction, and the impact of the 2008-2012 recession (NACEDA-Website).[4] Nonetheless, they have evolved to be a strong force in community development, having developed and rehabilitated thousands of housing units (Meléndez and Servon 2007; Schwartz 2015), and they continue to innovate in community planning and development (NeighborWorks 2016). However, it is important to emphasize that CDCs' level of success must be tempered by the fact that their socioeconomic impact has been limited relative to the challenges they face in the communities they work, such as persistent poverty, resilient racial segregation, and disempowerment (Halpern 1995; Stoutland 1999). Further, as Stoutland states about the research on the impact of CDCs: "For the most part the story of CDCs is told from the point of view of the 'CDC greats.' A few of these organizations have been studied over and over again, while there continues to be very little information about smaller, younger, struggling and failed organizations" (1999, 201).

CDCs, in addition to "brick and mortar" activity concerned with housing construction and rehabilitation, have opened participatory spaces for communities in the policy making environments of cities, and have supported equity advocacy for disenfranchised communities (Krumholz and Hexter 2018; Marwell 2010; McQuarrie 2010; Stoutland 1999). Neighborhood stabilization work can take decades and may imply significant modifications to the built-environment and socio-economic circumstances of communities (Curry, Durban and Page 2014; US Department of Housing and Development 2015). Research has shown that organizing activity by CDCs reinforces the capacity to survive political cycles, activate communities against unbridled urban renewal, gentrification, mega-infrastructure construction, and large real estate development projects, and identifies local leadership, lending continuity to CDCs' neighborhood stabilization work (Krumholz and Hexter 2018; Stoutland1999). CDCs, notwithstanding their accomplishments and despite 50 years of existence, continue to evolve and to adapt to large-scale environmental changes, which create strategic tensions between their mission to solve pressuring housing and social problems, and the need to overcome chronic difficulties, such as undercapitalization, limited technical capacity, complex financing mechanisms, and weak support systems of capital intermediation (Stoutland 1999). Actually, some scholars argue that many CDCs in their evolutionary pathway have strayed from their social mission, coopted by their participation within the "non-profit industrial complex," which has encouraged social movements to model themselves after capitalist structures rather than to challenge them, and to compete for government funding (Samimi, 2010).[5] By contrast, other scholars and CDC advocates argue that CDCs have become increasingly savvy organizations with the ability to deliver decentralized, low-cost services, and can become "network learners," banding together to achieve strategic objectives in the face of state retrenchment, government devolution, and outsourcing (Harrison and Weiss 1998).

More specifically, CDCs perform several critical functions in underserved neighborhoods:

1. Build affordable housing with multiple sources of capital;
2. Attract investment capital for business and economic development; offer homeownership and civil rights education to disadvantaged communities;
3. Serve as advocates and community organizers to protect communities against discrimination (red lining), fast gentrification, displacement, abandonment and blight;
4. Serve as catalysts for community stabilization, which goes hand-in-hand with reducing violence, incorporating newcomers and immigrants to the community, and reducing youth social disconnectedness;
6. Orchestrate bottom-up community planning processes, which tend

to be inclusive of community residents and expand local leadership;
7. Collectively participate in legislative, banking, and policy making reforms in favor of disadvantaged communities.

During the most recent economic and mortgage crisis in 2008, CDCs experienced significant distress, yet they proved their ability to protect disadvantaged communities from the risky lending practices of predatory lenders (Curry, Durban and Page, 2014; US Department of Housing and Development, 2015). CDCs' educational and legal work prevented low- and middle-income homeowners from being evicted or foreclosed during the crisis (Bledsoe and McHale 2014; Silberman 2013). After the crisis, many CDCs, especially small ones, were forced to revise their "business models" by becoming more active and better equipped at fundraising, especially through the use of "tax-credits" and financial instruments in mainstream or subsidized capital markets (Bledsoe and McHale 2014). Currently, CDCs are creatively engaged in broad-based urban redevelopment efforts and "whole street/community" revitalization to revive gateway cities affected by the long-term sequels of deindustrialization and depopulation in states such as Massachusetts, Connecticut, Rhode Island, and Vermont (Bendersakya and Dawicki 2017). CDCs are becoming players in the restructuring of food systems and in the creation of "maker spaces" as well (Levers and Wolf-Powers 2016; Low et al. 2015; Wolf-Powers et al. 2017).

More relevant to the context of recovery and reconstruction in the island, CDCs in the US are actively engaged during natural disasters and their recovery stages. However, the paucity of research on the role of CDCs in post-disaster reconstruction and how disasters impact CDC operations is noticeable in the disaster research literature. Conceptually, the role of CDCs in disaster and post-disaster scenarios and their activity would have to be understood within the "emergency shelter-permanent housing continuum" (Peacock, Dash and Zhang 2007), in the context of communities coping with pre-existing vulnerabilities (housing insecurity, informality, precariousness), existing social inequalities (race, gender, class, ethnicity), and addressing environmental and spatial dislocations caused or exacerbated by disasters (Bolin 2007; Peacock, Dash and Zhang 2007; Quarantelli 1982). Considering FEMA's emphasis on federal emergency management "whole community" strategy, it makes operational sense to visualize CDC's within that strategic framework (Koch, et al. 2016). Further strategic reframing of CDC activity will need to take place in order to balance the allocation of low-income housing tax credits (LIHTC) after disasters, which so far has been uneven due to the inability of state and local authorities to incorporate them in the disaster mitigation, preparedness, or recovery provisions of the "qualified allocation plans" (QAP) (Mehta, Brennan and Steil 2020).[6]

As per the impact of natural disasters on CDCs, existing research touches, at best, indirectly on the subject. Evidence about the impact of disasters on the broader category of CBOs suggests that, during the emergency and early recovery stages, CBOs experience some "mission dispersion" away from long-term housing development with a focus into immediate community relief and advocacy to access resources, especially to address the needs of homeless populations (Wyczalkoski, Esnard, Lai and van Horn 2019). Research also emphasizes two types of organizational adaptive responses. On the one hand, resulting from perceived heightened organizational risk after disasters, CBOs increase their entrepreneurial activity to maximize funding opportunities after disasters (Alesch et al. 2001). On the other hand, CBOs and housing recovery organizations (CDCs included) adopt defensive strategies to address economic exclusion from reconstruction efforts or to make known the practices of developers seeking a profit opportunity in the depressed values created by damage from natural hazard events (Bolin et al. 1999; Wyczalkoski, Esnard, Lai and van Horn 2019).

The federal government was slow in supporting community recovery and recognizing the importance of local efforts in recovery after natural disasters (Olshansky and Johnson 2014). However, in 2006 Congress passed the Post-Katrina Emergency Management Reform Act (PKEMRA), which directed the Federal Emergency Management Agency (FEMA), the lead agency during disasters, to develop a National Disaster Recovery Framework (NDRF). According to Olshansky and Johnson: "Through NDRF, the federal government takes a bold step in emphasizing that recovery must be led by local communities to be successful" (2004, 301). Federal bureaucracies, such as HUD, FEMA, SBA, and EDA, were slow to respond to the mandate. Yet the new framework has led them to reconsider the efficiency and effectiveness of centralized recovery governance, both at the federal and state levels. Such agencies are also recognizing that CDCs and other community actors can be critical partners in solving coordination and implementation problems during the recovery and reconstruction period following disasters (Chamlee-Wright et al. 2017; Olshansky and Johnson 2014; Pho 2019).

In spite of the new policy framework, research on recovery and reconstruction after Hurricanes Katrina and Sandy has demonstrated that severe inequities in the distribution of resources and exclusionary policies were perpetuated by large federal agencies and reproduced by state agencies (Bolin 2007; Gotham 2014a). Likewise, the laissez-faire, market-driven approach to permanent housing recovery has reproduced pre-existing patterns of inequality and economic exclusion (Bolin 2007; Peacock, Dash and Zhang 2007). According to Peacock and associates, the market-based logic of housing recovery in the United States is problematic in that "private insurance is the primary source of most private funding for repairing and rebuilding homes" (2007, 266). The "mosaic of coverage patterns" (Peacock, Dash and Zhang, 2007), which emerges from applying such an approach, has generated vastly uneven opportunities and prospects of housing recovery for households and communities. The Federal government policy for housing recovery tries to fill the funding recovery gap for some disadvantaged populations and communities, yet falling short most of the time, as has been observed in the recovery efforts after hurricanes and earthquakes during the last few years (Peacock, Dash and Zhang 2007). The reality is that little is known about the agency and sustainability of CDCs in recovery scenarios, and about the impact of disasters on CDCs' operations. But as I discuss below, the collective action of local actors, including CDCs, seems mostly bounded by contesting the unfairness of market-driven outcomes in applying insurance coverage and compensation rules, by pushing for adaptations to Federal policy approaches to permanent housing recovery, by responding to the immediate emergency, and intervening in operations of post-disaster housing and community recovery on behalf of their communities.

In Louisiana, CDCs, in liaison with other affordable housing advocates through litigation, have forced modifications to local allocation funding formulas in Louisiana's Road HOME Program to reimburse African-American homeowners in New Orleans (Gotham 2014b). In addition, new CDCs have been created to support community development. For example, shortly after

Hurricane Katrina a new CDC in the Vietnamese community of New Orleans East spearheaded a multiracial campaign of churches and environmental groups to address environmental justice issues related to the management of storm-debris dumps. The new Vietnamese CDC also turned a trashed trailer park into an elderly housing facility and inaugurated a pediatric clinic for underserved neighborhoods (Sánchez 2009). In NYC, after the Sandy super-storm, CDCs in coalition with other social justice organizations exercised political pressure to "turn the tide" against "top-down approaches to recovery and redevelopment that were established in the wake of 9/11 and Katrina" (Graham 2020; Greenberg 2014, 45) and attracted resources for reconstruc-tion for public housing tenants (Graham 2020; Gotham and Greenberg 2008).

Most recently, policy experts and organizations such as National Low-Income Housing Coalition (NLIHC), have identified strong barriers imposed upon local organizations by HUD and FEMA in the post-disaster housing reconstruction programs (Michelson et al. 2019). The NLIHC strongly empha-sizes the inclusion of local housing actors as a way to address weak inter-agency coordination, inequitable distribution of funding and contracts, and discrimina-tion, and to enhance continuous capacity-building for disaster preparedness (Mickelson et al. 2019). Further, policy experts suggest that HUD grantees under the CDBG-DR program can contribute to address weaknesses and "blind spots" created by supplemental statutory authority of CDBG-DR appropriations (Martín 2018). CDCs' knowledge of the local landscape can reduce duplication in documentation, reconcile and implement waiver issuances, assist more cen-tralized agents with data collection and estimates of damages, and prepare the required FEMA-Action Plans (Martín 2018; Pinke et al. 2017).

Undeniably, the lack of experience of local actors with CDBG-DR fund-ing impedes their participation in recovery efforts, although the research literature on disaster recovery and reconstruction indicates that their learning curve has been improving after every event (Martín 2018). Policy practitio-ners emphasize that every disaster is very much "context bounded" regarding institutional preparedness and impacts, and that specific disasters generate their own "politics of recovery planning and coordination" (Olshansky and Johnson 2014). Through collective action, local CDBG-DR grantees have responded with efficacy to advocate for modifications to the centralized styles of jurisdiction and coordination accompanying CDBG-DR funding.

In sum, given the opportunity, CDCs have accumulated significant experience and expertise in local planning, and not just in housing development. Through collective action and engagement they have expanded their role in underprivileged communities, serving as catalysts to attract resources looking into long-term neighborhood stabilization by making investments in workforce development, health, and education as well. During the last two decades, they have also stepped into disaster recovery, representing underprivileged communities in federal and state bureaucracies and advancing modifications to recovery programs, and have been involved in direct reconstruction of housing and critical infrastructure. PRCDCs, as we document below, are poised to do the same in rather adverse circumstances, constrained by the fiscal crisis and the political and bureaucratic pressures of recovery and reconstruction.

1.2 *The Embeddedness of Puerto Rican Community Development Corporations*[7]

PRCDCs are working embedded within the historic forces that shape their origin and the current context of crisis. During the 1980s, the community development movement in the island expanded, in both urban and rural areas (Ayala and Bernabe 2007; Pizarro-Claudio 2012). Communities coalesced to satisfy unmet social needs, exclusion, or destruction of the environment around place-based community development, grassroots collective action, and faith-based organizing, (Cotto-Morales 2011; García-López et al. 2018; Llanes-Santos 2001; Massol-González 2019; Meléndez and Medina 1999; Pizarro-Claudio 2012). Relative to the organizations born in the 1960s and 1970s, these newer organizations were more complex, their leadership was more professionalized, and they used community-driven financing mechanisms with a strong emphasis on self-help, sustainability, and partisan independence (Algoed et al. 2018; Fuller-Marvel 2018; García-López et al. 2018; Meléndez and Medina 1999; Pizarro-Claudio 2012). Specifically, a small group of nonprofits and more traditional social service organizations received support in housing and economic development from the government and newly created intermediaries, such as the Community Foundation of Puerto Rico (Fundación Comunitaria de Puerto Rico), formed in 1985 (Kliksberg and Rivera 2007). The foundation, a first in Puerto Rico, also attracted resources from bigger foundations and nonprofits in the US mainland (Estudios Técnicos 2015; Fundación Comunitaria n.d.).

The 1990s, however, vastly changed the context of the urban and eco-nomic development of the island (Guilbe 2009; Martinuzzi et al. 2007). In 1996, the US Congress and the government of the Commonwealth of Puerto Rico began a ten-year phasing out of Section 936 of the Internal Revenue Code (IRS), which offered tax exemption to American corporations for opera-tions within the island (Baver 2000; Meléndez 2018). The change in the devel-opment model triggered a fiscal and economic crisis from which the island is yet to recover. In 2017, in the midst of the fiscal crisis, back-to-back hurricanes Irma and Maria devastated the island with losses reaching $90 billion, on top of the existing $90 billion-debt (Meléndez and Venator-Santiago 2018), which exacerbated the housing crisis caused by the 2008–12 Great Recession (Hinojosa and Meléndez 2017).[8] Overall, Hurricane Maria affected about 23 percent of the housing stock of the island (Hinojosa and Meléndez 2018). The response of Ricardo Rosselló's administration (2017–19) to the disaster, just like the federal government's, has been widely criticized for its lack of effec-tiveness and preparedness, post-disaster funding scandals, misinformation, and delays in aid provision (Centro de Periodismo Investigativo 2020).

In the summer of 2019, Ricardo Rosselló was forced to resign.[9] His resignation triggered a succession crisis adjudicated by the Supreme Court of Puerto Rico by appointing Secretary of Justice Wanda Vázquez Garced as governor. Her administration was responsible for responding to the earthquakes in January 2020.[10] The initial damage estimate was $3.1 billion. President Trump signed a Major Disaster Declaration on January 16, 2020 (Center on Disaster Philanthropy 2020). His administration's response to the new crisis was also plagued by more institutional neglect, recovery and reconstruction scandals, and a high rotation of public officials (Pagán 2020). The government of Puerto Rico and federal agencies (especially FEMA) have been unable to organize a coherent process of recovery (García 2020; US Department of Homeland Security 2020; Wyss 2020).

In Puerto Rico, there is a window of opportunity to capitalize on federal reconstruction funding to support the development of a more robust community development ecosystem. However, PRCDCs currently face the severe austerity of the policy landscape imposed by the fiscal and economic crisis, the downsiz-ing of the Puerto Rican government, shifting federal policies (Caraballo-Cueto and Lara 2018; Meléndez and Venator 2018), and the natural hazards, which have accelerated immigration to the mainland, income inequality, and further deterioration of housing markets and shelter security (Ayala 2020; Hinojosa and Meléndez 2018; Meléndez, Román and Hinojosa 2018).[11] The agenda for PRCDCs is long, since many residents in disadvantaged communities still lack regularized land property titles, and they have experienced a wave of claim denials by FEMA, and still live in places highly vulnerable to flooding and other natural disasters (Fuller-Marvel 2018; García 2020; Ocasio 2018; Vélez and Villarrubia 2018). In the midst of the most unfavorable conditions, PRCDCs are using their accumulated operational and adaptive experience, which they gained while "struggling through" the complex web of municipal, state, federal policy regulation and legislation to obtain resources, while also building bridges into the growing philanthropic sector of the island, the US, and internationally (Estudios Técnicos 2015; Suárez 2018).

II. Research Methods

In this study I used the comparative case study method for investigating the organizational and project development history of PRCDCs (Ragin 1987; Yin 1984). The main objective of the research was to assess the organizational capacity and accumulated operational expertise of PRCDCs to tackle post-disaster community and housing reconstruction. Contrary to a prevalent narrative by the Puerto Rican (and federal) government which currently supports central control of resources as the optimal strategy for local (housing) reconstruction, I argue that PRCDCs have the experience to serve as stewards in local community and housing development, and creatively use federal resources to improve reconstruction in disadvantaged communities. In addition, the current research searches for evidence of social entrepreneurialism by PRCDCs by using a blend of public, private and non-profits resources. The comparative strategy served to extract lessons from the various approaches of PRCDCs to community development and housing construction, and to detect nuances in the quality of their social entrepreneurial activity.[12]

I selected the 12 organizations in discussions with academics, practitioners, planners, and other professionals involved in community development in Puerto Rico. Recognizably, the "convenience sampling" was biased toward a small slice of the diverse universe of organizations currently at work in the island, especially after the natural disasters. However, a side-by-side comparison of this cluster of twelve organizations has been useful in uncovering evidence of strategic adaptation to environmental challenges. During their lifetime, these organizations have cruised through the island's political cycles, survived the economic swings of the island's economy, and have absorbed changes in federal policies, all while supporting their communities. Thus, in such regard we can draw lessons and learn from them, while looking into the future stage of reconstruction.

My primary source of data includes in-depth interviews with the executive directors and other senior staff from twelve community development corporations spread throughout the island. A list of such organizations and their basic characteristics are detailed in Appendix I.[13] The research team complemented the interviews with site visits to the headquarters of the organizations, and in most cases, to their main housing construction and community development projects. In addition, the research team gathered online information about the organizations, as well as other relevant printed material provided by the organizations. The interviews were conducted by teams of two investigators, often accompanied by the principal investigator, during the summer of 2019. The interviews lasted between 45–60 minutes and were all audio recorded, and subsequently transcribed. The interview protocols complied with Institutional Review Board requirements. As per the interview protocol, it was prepared by the principal investigator and was vetted by the Academic Working Group of IDEAComun. The protocol covered three main areas of activity: (1) Characteristics of the Organization, Governance, and Areas of Operational Activity; (2) Past and Current Projects; (3) Obstacles and Challenges of Development.

III. The Puerto Rican Community Development Corporations

3.1 *Origin and Organizational Characteristics of PRCDCs*

Except for one of the twelve organizations in our study, which was founded in 1966, the rest were founded between 1983 and 2005, and are dispersed throughout the island.[14] These organizations were (See further detail in Appendix 1):

I. Asociación Mayagüezana de Personas con Impedimentos (AMPI)-Mayagüez.

2 Corporación para el Desarrollo Económico de Trujillo Alto (CDETA)-Trujillo Alto.

3. Corporación para el Desarrollo Económico de Ceiba (wCDEC)-Ceiba.
4. Corporación para el Desarrollo Económico,Vivienda y Salud (CODEVyS)-Arecibo.
5. Corporación para el Desarrollo de la Vivienda de Toa Baja (CDVTB)-Toa Baja.
6. Corporación Desarrolladora de Vivienda de Israel y Bitumul (CDVI& B)-San Juan.
7. Lucha Contra el SIDA, Inc.[15] (LUCHA)-San Juan
8. Ponce Neighborhood Housing Services (PNHS)-Ponce.
9. Programa de Educación Comunal de Entrega y Servicio (PECES)-Humacao.
10. Sabana Grande Community and Economic Development Corporation (SACED).
11. Fundación de Desarrollo Comunal (FUNDESCO)-Caguas.
12. Instituto para el Desarrollo Socioeconómico y de Vivienda de Puerto Rico, Inc. (INDESOVI)-Mayagüez

It is hard to measure the historical and organizational record of PRCDCs with the same yardstick. First, the origin of PRCDCs' collective action and activity is not all related to housing development challenges. They evolve through various streams of action, including housing, such as: youth development, health and human services, education, and poverty alleviation. In that regard, some of these organizations were created exclusively to produce and develop housing, while others were not. As a result, several of the CDCs currently support "housing plus" programming, while others simply focus on housing development. Second, the geography of activity of PRCDCs is quite diverse. Altogether they work in over fifty municipalities, including the downtowns of urban municipalities, informal or peripheral settlements, peri-urban areas away from urban cores, and *barrios*[16] edging coastal and inland rural areas. This geographic diversity represents a tremendous technical and operational challenge, especially in formulating projects and complying with the various legal, environmental, and planning codes regulating such different geographies. Third, all the PRCDCs are incorporated as 501-3c organizations under the local and federal codes, ten out of the twelve currently are or were, certified CHDOs, and three out of the total are certified CDFIs. These certifications allow them to participate in federal programs of various kinds. Fourth, their operating budgets range between $200K and $12 million, which fluctuate according to the characteristics of projects under execution. They have drawn funding from a broad range of public, private, and non-profit sources, which includes federal and state public agencies, foundations, corporations, and individual donors. The mix of sources demonstrates great ability to bundle resources to finance operations and projects. Further down, we provide greater detail about the specific housing development projects executed by these organizations.

3.2 Housing Development and Community Development Activity

During the last twenty years, PRCDCs have received significant funding from HUD, mainly from the conventional CDBG and housing counseling programs, yet currently they have been sidelined from the CDBG-DR funding streams. The Puerto Rico Housing Finance Authority, through the Repair, Reconstruction, or Relocation Program (R3) Program, according to their website, has awarded fifty-five CDBG-DR contracts to local and mainland companies as of October 2020, amounting to approximately $723,132,393. Sixteen of such projects are for $15 million or more, and they represent 90.3 percent of the total amount of dollars awarded in contracts. Only five Puerto Rican companies are in the "$15 Million Plus" cluster, and they represent 25 percent of the total awarded, and 28 percent of the amount awarded to projects for more than $15 million. So far,

Figure 1

Map created by Francisco Borges-Rivera

no contracts in the current allocation have been awarded to non-profit housing developers.[17] This landscape stands in stark contrast with the situation a decade ago (2009–10), when non-profit developers, including the PRCDCs, using funding from the American Recovery and Reinvestment Act (ARRA-2009), built more affordable housing using federal tax credits than private developers, who up to that point dominated the industry. During the four-year window provided by the ARRA funding, non-profit developers built more than 3,000 units of housing (Meléndez 2020). Below, we provide previous evidence of the participation and effectiveness of the PRCDC in the housing development and other social and economic programming (See Appendix II).

Several organizations have a record primarily building and reconstructing housing, while others combine further community development activity in their portfolio. INDESOVI, CDVTB, CDVI & B, CDEC, CDTA, and CDEC are all certified as CHDOs, with CDEC certified as a CDFI as well. These six organizations all primarily specialize in housing development. INDESOVI, headquartered in the west coast city of Mayagüez, invested approximately $23.4 million in reconstructing and building single and multifamily housing units, and commercial space during 2005–2017. This investment translated into 453 housing units. Subsequently, between 2017–19, after Hurricanes Irma and Maria, INDESOVI extended its portfolio to build ninety-two units more and has planned for the construction of 440 additional units. In that two-year period, in addition, they have generated about 150 direct jobs and approximately 300 indirect jobs. INDESOVI's funding strategy combines the use of LIHTC with funding from HUD (HOME; CDBG; CDBG-DR), private banks, municipalities, and foundations.

CDVTB, headquartered in the north coast municipality of Toa Baja, since 1995 has built approximately 1,016 units in various construction projects totaling about $83.2 Million in investments, and generating $6 Million in resources for the organization. Unlike INDESOVI and the other organizations, CDVTB remains a municipal corporation (and has a 501-3c status as well). Their projects were also financed by combining LIHTC, municipal funds, and a partnership with private investors. For example, their elderly housing construction project, Proyecto Elderly-Golden Age Tower, a six-story and 160-unit building, cost $12.3 million, which was mostly financed with the sale of LIHTC ($9.5 million).

CDVI & B was organized by community residents at the heart of one San Juan's poorest neighborhoods, Israel and Bitumul. During their early stage of development, they received significant help from the Municipality of San Juan, the Office of Special Communities (Oficina de Comunidades Especiales), as well as from the Mita Congregation, a Christian denomination church.[18] Subsequently, they obtained funding from HUD (CDBG; HOME; Section 811), and Fundación Comunitaria de Puerto Rico and Fundación Ángel Ramos, and sought several loans from private banks. Their landmark project, Proyecto Villas del Paraíso I (1999–2002), was built at a cost of $10 million (including land acquisition), yielding 109 units and serving to stabilize other housing units in the vicinity.

CDTA, located in the Municipality of Trujillo Alto in the greater San Juan Metro Area, used LIHTC to finance affordable housing for senior citizens, and commercial real estate development to revitalize the downtown district of Trujillo Alto. For instance, the Égida Aires del Manantial, at a total cost of $18 million, is a ten-story tower with 120 units of high-quality rental housing for senior citizens. Goldman Sachs has been buying the tax credits from CDTA.

Finally, located on the eastern part of the island in the coastal Municipality of Ceiba is CDEC. Originally a municipal corporation, it became an independent non-profit organization and primarily builds housing, but it is also involved in microenterprise development, and some disaster relief activity. CDEC's main housing project was Portal de CEIBA, a complex of fifty townhouses for low-income households with eight units reserved for people with disabilities. The project was built at a cost of $7 million with HUD funding (HOME program) and private banking sources.

Entering the 2000s, the winds of change brought shifts in federal policy, compression of the local banking industry, crowding-out from private contractors, and the gradual phasing out of the Office of Special Communities. Such changes significantly slowed down the activity of the CHDOs in the island. INDESOVI, CDTA, and CDEC have remained active, while CDVTB and CDVI & B still exist but have not undertaken any further projects. These organizations belonged to a time during the 1990s, when HUD and the Office of Special Communities and the local philanthropic sector, especially the Fundación Comunitaria de Puerto Rico, strongly promoted local community development efforts.

In contrast to the previous subgroup of PRCDCs, another subgroup, composed of FUNDESCO, PECES, AMPI, CODEVyS, LUCHA, PNHS, and SACED, incorporates other community development activities (housing plus social programming) in addition to housing development and reconstruction in their portfolio. While they may produce relatively lesser numbers of housing units, they are active in health, education, youth development, substance abuse and rehabilitation, violence prevention, and small business development, and produce housing for challenged and highly disadvantaged populations such as homeless people, cognitively challenged people, victims of domestic violence, and poor elderly.

Their housing portfolio has been building up gradually while creating a grid of various social and economic supports to reconnect deambulantes (severely disconnected homeless) diagnosed with HIV to meaningful employment, healthy living, and physical/mental well-being.

FUNDESCO, the oldest organization in our study (1966), is grounded in the Municipality of Caguas, which has increasingly become part of the extended San Juan Metro Region. Housing development for vulnerable populations has been at the core of FUNDESCO's mission for at least thirty years. Their housing portfolio has been building up gradually while creating a grid of various social and economic supports to reconnect *deambulantes* (severely disconnected homeless) diagnosed with HIV to meaningful employment, healthy living, and physical/mental well-being. The support infrastructure includes a microenterprise managed by the residents of group homes. The microenterprise contracts with the municipality and the private sector for building and landscape maintenance. At the same time, some of their housing rehabilitation projects have been strategically positioned to revive and repopulate the municipality's deteriorated downtown (*casco del pueblo*). For example, prototypical of FUNDESCO's housing project is Villas del Peregrino. It is a permanent, mixed income three-story housing complex with fifty-four apartments, some occupied by previous homeless individuals who have returned to full civilian life and can afford to pay for rent or a modest mortgage. The project was financed at a cost of $2.4 million with HUD funding (CDBG, HOME Programs) and an additional amount from the Municipality of Caguas.

PECES, headquartered in the eastern Municipality of Humacao, has been active in housing reconstruction after Hurricane Maria. They have developed an integrated housing rehabilitation program through the Centro de Sostenibilidad Comunitaria, which already has rebuilt around 100 homes in Punta Santiago, Humacao. Their housing rehabilitation and reconstruction approach involves connecting affected residents to a social support system involving social workers, which reduces "downtime" for contractors and minimizes disruption and displacement of vulnerable families. In addition, PECES has a robust strong youth leadership and development program, which is anchored at a 300-student public school for youth-at-risk. Further, PECES maintains an incubation program for small businesses to support emerging entrepreneurs. PECES supports its programs with resources from a long list of funders, including the PR Departments of Education and Justice, Fundación Comunitaria de Puerto Rico, FEMA, United Way, Global Giving, and Fundación Banco Popular, among others.

AMPI, operating in Mayaguez, has renovated three subsidized independent-living houses, Casa Juni, Inc., Casa AMPI, Inc., and Casa Doña Here, Inc., for eighteen low-income people with cognitive disabilities. All three houses operate as separate corporations, which then receive social and human services from AMPI. AMPI provides services through two semi-therapeutic facilities, the Centro de Mejoramiento de Calidad de Vida (CEMECAV), and the Centro de Estimulación Basal y Recreación Pasiva para Adultos con Impedimentos Significativos (CEBRAIS). The three residential projects, at an approximate cost of $2 million, were funded by HUD and were the first assisted-living facilities of their kind in the island. Renters contribute 30 percent of their income toward rent, which is matched by AMPI with federal funding for maintenance costs. AMPI also has a legal services program to assist in housing titling and reconstruction, AMPI Pa' Puerto Rico, which has assisted about 500 families with housing stabilization since Hurricanes Irma and Maria. At a smaller scale, AMPI is growing a sustainable community economic development project—Proyecto de Comunidad La Chorra—which includes a bio-digestor, a community food garden, and, eventually, a solar energy hub. The project is a collaboration with the Municipality of Yauco, and partially supported by the Hispanic Federation ($30K).

CODEVyS is headquartered in the northern coastal Municipality of Arecibo. The organization has significant expertise in housing counseling and rehabilitation, qualifying homeowners for subsidized mortgages, and providing integrated health, social and human services to vulnerable populations like the elderly, victims of violence, and HIV/AIDS-positive individuals. Shortly after Hurricane Maria, with funding from FEMA, CODEVys ran the VALOR project, which provides construction materials and connects survivors of natural disasters with voluntary construction agencies. CODEVyS is a FEMA-denominated Community Resource Center, and it is a certified CHDO. With more recent funding from HUD/PR Dept of Housing, CODEVyS finances housing counseling and first-time homebuyers' programs, which include access to subsidized mortgages. Their integrated services grid is anchored in various community development projects. For example, CAPERNUM I, II, and III are multi-municipality projects operating with about $1.1 million from the Health and Human Services Administration (HHSA) to support HIV/AIDs patients, generally marginalized from general social service providers. Likewise, the Iniciativa Comunitaria de Arecibo is a community economic development project that provides childcare services for working parents. CODeVyS supports a microenterprise incubation program funded by Puerto Rico's Trade and Export Company as well.

LUCHA's headquarters are in one of the most disadvantaged district quadrants of San Juan PNHS, edging the barrios of Cantera and Israel. However, LUCHA has eleven projects in San Juan, Carolina, Gurabo, Caguas y Ponce. Five of those are permanent housing projects, and the others are transitional housing and assisted adult care projects, and an urban greenhouse for medicinal plants. Their "housing plus" community stabilization strategy connects housing development and construction to a grid of integrated services and supports to improve the quality of life and education of vulnerable populations, such as HIV/AIDS-positive homeless men, female survivors of domestic violence, people with chemical dependencies, people with disabilities, poor elderly, at-risk youth, and low-income families. For example, the Renacer de Vida housing development provides transitional housing and clinical supports for HIV/AIDS-positive homeless men. The Nuevo Horizonte housing development provides transitional housing and support for female survivors of domestic abuse and violence. To deliver such support LUCHA has service agreements with federal, state, and municipal governments and memorandums of understanding with thirty-four organizations. Because of their programmatic innovations in this "housing plus" model, the University of Puerto Rico-Rio Piedras, School of Social Work, and its School of Medical Sciences have chosen LUCHA as a training site for various undergraduate and graduate academic programs. LUCHA attracts resources from HUD (CoC; CDBG; CDBG-DR), the PR Department of Housing, PR Dept of Health, the island's philanthropic and charitable sector, the Municipality of San Juan, and the private sector. Altogether, LUCHA has constructed around 485 units, many of which are still managed by the organization, for a total amount of approximately $45 million in investments.

PNHS and SACED, in the southern Municipalities of Ponce and Sabana Grande (respectively), are the smaller organizations in our sample. PNHS is a certified CDFI, and the only NeighborWorks America affiliate in PR.[19] The organization is headquartered in the *casco urbano* (downtown) of Ponce. Since Hurricane Maria in 2017, they have been active in housing counseling, reconstruction, and rehabilitation. They have rehabilitated fifty-eight units with financing ($700K) from Unidos por Puerto Rico and Fundación Comunitaria de Puerto Rico. As a CDFI, PNHS created a housing reconstruction lending program, lending homeowners up to $7,000 to reconstruct their homes. PNHS has lent about $2.4 million through this program, which includes financial education and community organizing activity. The program has a relatively low delinquency rate (7 percent). In the future, PNHS is seeking to intensify its redevelopment activity in Ponce's Historic District, which greatly suffered during the earthquakes in early 2020, and to expand its community economic development activity with faith-based organizations in other communities of Ponce. SACED, the youngest organization in our sample set of cases, started mainly as a drug prevention program, which has been increasingly venturing into housing reconstruction, education, and small business incubation. The COMPASS drug prevention program is a five-year grant in collaboration with the Office of National Drug Control Policy of the White House and FEMA's Drug-Free Communities Program. The small business incubation program receives funding mostly from local foundations and the Puerto Rico Legislative Fund. They are currently seeking funding from USDA and SBA.

3.3 *Gender, Organizational and Community Training, Social Entrepreneurship, and Challenges*

Women play a central role in the leadership and senior staff of the PRCDCs. In six of the cases (CDTA, CDEC, PNHS, CODEVyS, AMPI, and FUNDESCO), women were Executive Directors and senior staff. Even though this fact might not be representative of the universe of Puerto Rican CBOs, gender diversity contributes toward inclusiveness and equity in CBO and community development management. Professionally, they come from different backgrounds such as teaching, health and human services, business, marketing, finance, and government. Such diverse professional expertise is central to the development of their "housing plus" models (AMPI & CODEVyS). Their "gendered approach" is also influential in the special attention several PRCDCs pay to the development of services to address the needs of highly vulnerable populations like victims of domestic violence, and single female heads of households.

The organizations objected to the proliferation of a saturated market of workshops, seminars, and conferences offered by people with little or no applied expertise in a multitude of topics.

In the interviews, the senior staff of the PRCDCs highlighted the capacity-building challenges for accessing more (federal, state, and philanthropic) funding, and for assuring organizational and programmatic continuity. First, they mentioned that leadership and professional development in their organizations would benefit from a pedagogic and training approach that relies on peer-to-peer learning. For example, one interviewee commented: "I think that peer-to-peer is going to be very important because often you [*are*] sitting at a table in a group or in an interactive and dynamic setting helps organizations to see themselves rather than having people who stand in front and talk and talk...the organizations do not visualize themselves nor learn about themselves." The organizations objected to the proliferation of a saturated market of workshops, seminars, and conferences offered by people with little or no applied expertise in a multitude of topics. One interviewee commented: "In terms of the creation of workshops, it is important that they are effective, efficient, and assertive...We think that the topics are very interesting but the pedagogy, how to prepare the workshop and how to carry the message maintains a classroom style, and that's it... And there is no continuity to know whether or not the organizations managed to learn or implement what was discussed in the workshops".

Second, all organizations stressed the importance of applied training for their staff, boards of directors, community stakeholders, and politicians in project development, planning, and evaluation. As a request for that kind of staff training, one senior staff CDC staff stated: "For example, workshops for housing construction, workshops for proposal preparation... the technical part...how do I answer a question for a federal agency in a funding request, and how I should answer it in order to get the money." Training and content should be relevant for the actual task and job at hand. Outside the organization, the interviewees also expressed the importance of education and training for citizens and politicians, who often request ad hoc changes to projects, or make demands about their planned trajectory, without understanding the potential impact of those requests and modifications. Reducing such "dissonance" between the organizations and the external actors will be critical in the upcoming years. For example, access to FEMA funding, and planning and implementing mitigation programs, will have to take place within a "whole community" planning framework,[20] which requires significant citizen input and alignment of stakeholders around common goals. The implication is that much education is needed to formulate strategic plans and modify attitudes about community development. PRCDCs stressed that community-development should not be approached as an opportunistic and improvised endeavor.

An import objective of the research was to assess the qualities of the social entrepreneurship of PRCDCs. Among the PRCDCs, some were CHDO- and CDFI-certified, as well as having accreditation from specific entities that are critical to operate in key policy areas, such as vocational education, special education, and housing counseling. Practically all the organizations in our sample showed experience blending a variety of financial mechanisms, some of them quite complex, including market mechanisms to co-finance their projects. Although the collective experience with federal funding is uneven, some specific organizations, such as FUNDESCO, LUCHA, and INDESOVI, demonstrate an in-depth understanding of acquiring and managing federal funding and leveraging resources for housing development. CDVTB, CDVI & B showed expertise in leveraging private banking resources (and federal sources). AMPI has demonstrated singular managerial expertise creating a sustainable "business model" to support its group homes. Among half of the organizations, the use of LIHTC and borrowing from private banks are relatively well-understood mechanisms for finding resources for housing development. However, the PRCDCs were emphatic about the stern and lengthy compliance requirements of selling and using tax credits, and the need to grow significant expertise on real estate, taxation, financial intermediation, and economic development. Two of the PRCDCs related stories about the dearth and unreliability of local financial consultants with expertise on affordable housing development. In addition, they commented on the cumbersome procedures to access CRA funding, and the use of economic development incentives available through Opportunity and Promise Zones.

PRCDCs were forthcoming in outlining the challenges they face in project community planning, housing development, and management.

- First, while PRCDCs have mainly collaborative relations with municipalities, we also heard stories about the politics of local/municipal/state patronage, gatekeeping by political parties, corruption, and policy centralization. In their remarks, leadership from the organizations were particularly critical of the traffic of influence at the municipal level, which thwarts the flow of information, local action, and fosters an opportunistic environment in the search for state and federal funding. Most organizations expressed a desire to achieve greater autonomy from the island's electoral cycles.

- Second, for the most part PRCDCs are able to reply to requests for proposals (RFP) from federal agencies, such as HUD and FEMA, although their capacity to prepare complex, multi-year projects for CDBG-DR is hindered by the bureaucratic complexity of federal funding applications. The history of poor central and local government accountability in contract allocation does not help either. It is always present in the mind of PRCDCs and their decision-making and planning.

- Third, PRCDCs suffer from the limited project-management and compliance expertise within their own staff, since every funding stream comes with its own reporting requirements, and demands strong English language skills. For example, reconstruction work requires obtaining significant permits from authorities, and dealings with environmental agencies such as EPA, US Corps of Engineers, and Department of Natural Resources of Puerto Rico.
- Fourth, PRCDCs expressed clear dissatisfaction with the management of the Centro de Recaudación de Ingresos Municipales (CRIM), and the instability and inefficiency of the local permit offices and the application of planning codes. The result of such instability are project delays, increased overhead costs, and overextension of project development phases.
- Fifth, PRCDCs mentioned the lack of resources to include communities and other potential stakeholders in strategic planning, which is increasingly a salient requirement of federal applications.
- Sixth, they remarked on the lack of data and applied research to document community needs, elaborate project justifications, and for project monitoring and evaluation.
- Finally, and not least important, PRCDCs mentioned the lack of pre-development finance to plan projects, land/property acquisition, site preparation, and architectural and engineering studies. In the island, unlike other locations of the mainland, there is no institution or financial intermediary to meet such pre-development finance needs. PRCDCs also discussed the impact that the contraction in the banking sector of the island, which has reduced the availability of finance capital.

IV. Conclusions: Critical Strategic Areas

This research has identified several organizational trends within PRCDCs, requiring strategic attention in the near future. First, six of the PRCDCs have extensive geographic target/service delivery areas, sometimes comprising between 10 to 15 (or more) municipalities, often geographically non-contiguous ones, with differences in road access, and spread over coastal or hilly topographies. Although the dispersion might be justified by the types of programs under implementation, it may also indicate that these organizations are "spreading to thin." The senior staff of the organizations said that this represents a relatively easy form of organizational survival. However, such distension may compromise the effectiveness of program impact. Second, all the PRCDCs are led by committed professionals and staff. Stability in leadership is a fundamental asset of these organizations. However, a new cadre of community development professionals and talent will be needed for the long-term process of redevelopment. It will take time to train them, and to gain the trust of communities. Rebuilding and reconstruction, and accessing funding, is an exercise in accountability, as is trust- and legitimacy-building, all currently severely eroded in the public life of the island. PRCDCs can be trusted partners in reconstruction and assuring that the equity prevails as the desired outcome of policy implementation.

As shown by the cases of PRCDCs, there is no single "path" to social entrepreneurship. PRCDCs have accumulated significant organizational capital to seed further projects, and they stand ready to learn about new avenues to finance and develop projects. Their collective experience can be the basis to expand the pool of organizations capable of managing substantive public funding and harnessing markets to enhance their long-term sustainability, fundamentally required to meet the challenges of reconstruction. The leadership of PRCDCs are an untapped pool of talent to fuel "cross-fertilization" among organizations in the island, and between the island and the US mainland, and globally. The learning process will require new organizational and "hard" investments to achieve the following:

1. **Education and Capacity-Building for PRCDCs.** It seems critical to create an affordable and open-source education platform with grounded and applied content that could be delivered by practitioners who have navigated the pathways of social entrepreneurship, and have completed projects in the complex "funding ecology" of the island and the mainland. The leadership of PRCDCs expressed some frustration with the abundant and fragmented supply of disconnected and abstract workshops with little value added to contribute to their operations. This is also a message to funders and training organizations to refine their "training products".

2. **Education Opportunities for Non-CDC actors.** Within the complex ecology of funding, social entrepreneurship implies interacting and establishing partnerships with various stakeholders, communities, and the public, non-profit, and private sectors. These stakeholders will also require training and education about their roles and responsibilities. The sole weight of community development cannot simply fall upon CBOs "subcontracted" by for-profit corporations or the government.

3. **Stronger Intermediaries.** The ecology of housing development, especially during periods of reconstruction, requires the creation of island-based intermediaries in various policy sectors which in tandem with CDCs could attract federal funding. Otherwise, the windfalls of planning and implementation will not be maximized by CDCs, but by companies and firms driven mostly by the profit motive. In this regard, for example, the creation of a pre-development finance revolving loan fund could significantly accelerate the housing and economic development of PRCDCs.

4. **Inclusion.** Safeguarding the inclusion of disadvantaged populations, and of the organizations created to work on their behalf, must be a clear objective of equity planning, which also takes into consideration the local context of communities.

5. **Maximize Comparative Advantage.** Through their social entrepreneurship, PRCDCs have managed to harness substantial funding from diverse sources to attend not just housing needs but to satisfy other unmet social and economic needs in their communities. In the process, they have not only used "brick and mortar" strategies to advance downtown redevelopment (*renovación de los cascos de pueblos*), neighborhood stabilization, but also have consolidated "housing plus" approaches to attend the needs of highly vulnerable populations. The expertise they have in this regard could be better utilized to continue in the long road of reconstruction in disadvantaged communities.

6. **Voice in Policy Making.** PRCDCs do not have a collective organization to represent their interests vis-à-vis the government and the private sector. In many cities and states of the US, CDCs are grouped in associations or other cooperative formats. These organizations facilitate training, negotiate policymaking, and represent CDCs in legislative

processes. In addition, they work on quality control issues in the community development industry.

The string of natural hazards and disasters that hit the island during the last three years (hurricanes, earthquakes, the COVID-19 pandemic), and the sustained fiscal and political crises of the island cannot be resolved easily. Climate change, for instance, will continue to expose communities to further shocks, and deplete our fragile natural resources. The burden of an unsustainable debt, and institutional fragmentation and policy centralization will exacerbate the scarcity of resources in communities. In such an environment, PRCDCs are potentially an important resource to prevent further exclusion and marginalization in disadvantaged communities.

ACKNOWLEDGEMENTS
First, we want to acknowledge the support and willingness of the leadership and staff of the various community development corporations and community organizations who participated in the research. Second, we want to thank La Sociedad Bíblica de Puerto Rico, who provided our researchers with office space and other support infrastructure, and the Center for Puerto Rican Studies (Centro) staff for support during conferences and with general coordination. Third, we want to thank Prof. Ivis García Zambrana from the University of Utah for her support with the research's Institutional Review Board compliance, and other community-development and planning professionals such as Rafael Torrech and Rolando Ramos for their insights about the non-profit sector in Puerto Rico. Valuable research assistance was provided by José Luis Colón, Yamil Corvalán, Miriam Morales-Suárez, and Katsyris Rivera-Kientz. Alejandra Del Monte-Medina, Elisa Sánchez-Torres, and Diana Ramos from IDEAComún, and Rosa Cruz-Cordero from Centro, provided important logistical coordination in the project. Sincere gratitude to all of them. Also, we want to thank the Grupo Académico IDEAComún: Prof. Marinés Aponte, Prof. Federico Del Monte, Prof. Luisa Seijó, Prof. Ivis García Zambrana, Rev. Heriberto Martínez, and Prof. Edwin Meléndez. Finally, I would like to acknowledge the anonymous reviewers who contributed to help improve the manuscript.

NOTES

[1] Many CDCs are certified as community development finance institutions (CDFI) and as community housing development organizations (CHDO). CDFIs can be banks, credit unions, loan funds, microloan funds, or venture capital providers. CDFIs are helping families finance their first homes, supporting community residents starting businesses, and investing in local health centers, schools, or community centers. CDFIs are certified by the Department of the Treasury, which opens the door for certified organizations to leverage, access, and manage capital to be invested in communities. A CHDO is a private nonprofit, community-based organization that has staff with the capacity to develop affordable housing for the community it serves. In order to qualify for CHDO designation, the organization must meet certain requirements pertaining to their legal status, organizational structure, and capacity and experience. CHDOs are certified by the Housing and Urban Development Dept (HUD).

[2] "Housing Plus Services" is an umbrella term coined by the National Low-Income Housing Coalition to capture the phenomenon of combined housing and service initiatives. Housing Plus Services refers to permanent affordable housing that incorporates various levels of services with housing, with services provided, preferably, by trained staff for whom service delivery, not property management, is their primary responsibility" (<https://nlihc.org/explore-issues/other/hps/>).

[3] In this paper I adopt the social entrepreneurship definition proposed by Martin and Osberg (2007). They state: "Unlike the [conventional] entrepreneurial value proposition that assumes a market that can pay for the innovation, and may even provide substantial upside for investors, the social entrepreneur's value proposition targets an underserved, neglected, or highly disadvantaged population that lacks the financial means or political clout to achieve the transformative benefit on its own".

4 The National Alliance of Community Economic Development Associations (NACEDA): <https://www.naceda.org/index.php?option=com_dailyplanetblog&view=entry&category=bright-ideas&id=25%3Awhat-is-a-community-development-corporation-&Itemid=171/>.

5 Samimi defines the non-profit industrial complex as: a "system [which] forces nonprofits to professionalize, wherein they must focus on maintaining their funding sources rather than fulfilling their mission" (2020, 17).

6 The federal LHITC program requires each state agency and some localities that allocate tax credits to have a Qualified Allocation Plan (QAP). The QAP sets out the state's eligibility priorities and criteria for awarding federal tax credits to housing properties (Leung 2015).

7 Regarding the meaning of "embeddedness," Polanyi's *The Great Transformation* analyzed the performance of economic systems as "submerged in social relations" and of markets as an "accessory feature of an institutional setting" (1944, 67).

8 Prior to Hurricane Maria, out of 449,377 Puerto Rican homeowners with a mortgage, 48.5 percent spent more than 30 percent of their income on mortgage costs, while 38 percent of the population as a whole paid more than 30 percent on housing. A variety of other indicators of housing and economic distress reaffirm the depth of the housing crisis. Median home values declined from $117,860 in 2016 to $110,000 in 2018, a difference of $7,860. In some municipalities the decline between 2016 and 2018 was more dramatic, reaching almost $31,006. Further, the price per square foot, building permits, employment in the construction industry, cement sales/prices, and the economic activity index (Government Development Bank for Puerto Rico) depict a profoundly depressed housing market (Hinojosa and Meléndez 2018).

9 Rosselló resigned as a result of the "Chatgate," a political scandal that began on July 8, 2019, with the leak of hundreds of pages of a group chat between Rosselló and members of his staff (Weissestein and Colón 2019).

10 There were 2,455 earthquakes (since December 22, 2019) in southern Puerto Rico. This includes 571 earthquakes in the three weeks leading up to February 17, 2020 (Center on Disaster Philanthropy 2020).

11 In addition, the political and economic colonial relationship between PR and the United States, and the limited sovereignty of the island, often introduces serious distortions on the request, allocation, management, and implementation of federal programs in the island—in practically any area of public policy.

12 See footnote 5 for the definition of social entrepreneurship used in this paper.

13 Logistical obstacles prevented a fully structured interview with Lucha Contra el Sida, Inc.

14 Each of the eleven stars represents the headquarters of the organizations, with the "star" in San Juan representing two organizations.

15 Síndrome de Inmunodeficiencia Adquirida (SIDA).

16 Barrios are the primary legal divisions of the seventy-eight municipalities of Puerto Rico. Barrios are also recognized as geographic units by US Bureau of the Census. Barrios can be rural or urban.

17 Computations by the author. At the time of drafting the final version of this paper, the information on new contracts and potential agreements that may include Puerto Rican non-profit housing developers is unavailable.

[18] The Mita Congregation (Spanish: Congregación Mita) is a Christian denomination headquartered in Puerto Rico with a presence in other countries of Latin America.
[19] NeighborWorks America (NWA) is one of the country's largest affordable housing and community development organizations. NWA delivers its community-focused programs through the national NeighborWorks network—over 240 independent, community-based non-profit organizations serving more than 4,500 communities nationwide (http://neighborworksbrv.org/about-nwbrv/our-national-networks/>).
[20] FEMA defines the whole community approach as: "a means by which residents, emergency management practitioners, organizational and community leaders, and government officials can collectively understand and assess the needs of their respective communities and determine the best ways to organize and strengthen their assets, capacities, and interests. By doing so, a more effective path to societal security and resilience is built. In a sense, Whole Community is a philosophical approach on how to think about conducting emergency management" (FEMA 2011, 3).

REFERENCES
Alesch, D.J., J.N. Holly, E. Mittler and R. Nagy. 2001. What Happens When Small Businesses and Not-for-Profits Encounter Natural Disasters. Public Entity Risk Institute. Fairfax: VA. Accessed on 18 November 2020. <http://www.chamberofecocommerce.com/images/Organizations_at_Risk.pdf/>.
Algoed, L., M.E. Hernandez-Torrales and L. Rodriguez-Del Valle. 2018. El Fideicomiso de la Tierra del Caño Martín Peña: Instrumento Notable de Regularizacion de Suelo en Asentamientos Informales. Documento de Trabajo (Working Paper) WP18LA1SP. Lincoln Institute of Land Policy. Massachusetts: Cambridge.
Anglin, R.V., ed. 2004. Building the Organizations that Build Communities: Strengthening the Capacity of Faith-Based and Community-Based Organizations. Washington, DC: Office of Policy Development and Research. Accessed on 14 October 2020. <https://www.huduser.gov/Publications/pdf/buldOr00gCommunities.pdf/>.
Anglin, R.V. 2011. Promoting Sustainable Local and Community Economic Development. Boca Raton, FL: CRC Press, Taylor & Francis Group.
Ayala, C. 2020. La desigualdad regional de ingresos en Puerto Rico. 80Grados 11 September. Accessed on 14 October 2020. <https://www.80grados.net/la-desigualdad-regional-de-ingresos-en-puerto-rico/>.
Ayala, C. and R. Bernabe. 2007. Puerto Rico in the American Century: A History Since 1898. Chapel Hill: The University of North Carolina Press.
Baver, S. 2000. The Rise and Fall of Section 936: The Historical Context and Possible Consequences of Migration. CENTRO: Journal of the Center for Puerto Rican Studies 9(2), 44–55.
Benderskaya, K. and C. Dawicki. 2017. Sparking Change in New England's Smaller Cities: Lessons from Early Rounds of the Working Cities Challenge. Community Development Investment Review 1, 35–42.
Bledsoe, T. and B. McHale. 2013. Innovative Strategies for Mitigating the Foreclosure Crisis and Stabilizing Communities. Community Development Investment Review 2, 5–6.

Bolin, B. 2007. Race, Class, Ethnicity, and Disaster Vulnerability. In *The Handbook of Disaster Research*, eds. H. Rodríguez, E.L. Quarantelli and R.R. Dynes. New York: Springer.

Bolin R. and L. Stanford. 1998. The Northridge Earthquake: Community-based Approaches to Unmet Recovery Needs. *Disasters* 22(1), 21–38.

Borges-Méndez, R. 2011. Stateside Puerto Ricans and the Public Workforce Development System: New York City, Hartford, Springfield/Holyoke. *CENTRO Journal: Journal of the Center for Puerto Rican Studies* 23(2): 64–93.

Brookfield, S. and L. Fitzgerald. 2018. Homelessness and Natural Disasters: The Role of Community Service Organisations. *Australian Journal of Emergency Management* 33(4), 62–8.

Caraballo-Cueto, J. and J. Lara. 2017. Deindustrialization and Unsustainable Debt in Middle-Income Countries: The Case of Puerto Rico. *Journal of Globalization and Development* 8(2), 1–11.

Center on Disaster Philanthropy. 2020. Puerto Rico Earthquakes. 16 March. Accessed on 14 October 2020. <https://disasterphilanthropy.org/disaster/puerto-rico-earthquakes/>.

Centro de Periodismo Investigativo. 2020. Federal Warnings Cause Further Delay in Post-Maria Recovery Process. Centro de Periodismo Investigativo. San Juan. Accessed on 14 October 2020. <https://periodismoinvestigativo.com/2020/08/federal-warnings-cause-further-delays-in-the-post-maria-recovery-process-in-puerto-rico/>.

Chamlee-Wright, E., E. Haeffele-Balch and V. Henry-Storr. 2017. How Robust Community Rebound Necessarily Comes from the Bottom Up. In The Future of Disaster Management in the US.: Rethinking Legislation, Policy and Finance, ed. A. LePore. 87–102. New York: Routledge.

Cotto-Morales, L. 2011. *Desalambrar: orígenes de los rescates de terreno en Puerto Rico y su pertinencia a los movimientos sociales contemporáneos*. 2da edición. San Juan: Editorial Tal Cual.

Curry, R., K.M. Durban and S. Page. 2014. Targeted Neighborhood Stabilization: Lessons in Resilience in Weak Market Cities. *Community Development Innovation Review*. Accessed on 14 October 2020. <https://www.frbsf.org/community-development/publications/community-development-investment-review/2014/february/neighborhood-stabilization-resilience-weak-markets/>.

Edwards, M. 2008. Just another emperor? The Myths and Realities of Philanthrocapitalism. New York: Demos & The Young Foundation. Accessed on 17 November 2020. <https://www.futurepositive.org/edwards_WEB.pdf/>.

Estudios Técnicos, Inc. 2015. Estudio de las Organizaciones Sin Fines de Lucro en Puerto Rico. Informe Final. Mayo. Accessed on 14 October 2020. <https://www.fundacionbancopopular.org/sin-categoria-es-es/estudio-de-las-organizaciones-sin-animo-de-lucro-en-puerto-rico/>.

Federal Emergency Management Agency. 2011. A Whole Community Approach to Emergency Management: Principles, Themes, and Pathways for Action. FDOC 104-008-1/December 2011. Accessed on 18 November 2020. <https://www.fema.gov/media-library-data/20130726-1813-25045 0649/whole_community_dec2011_2_.pdf/>.

Fuller-Marvel, L. 2018. La planificacion participativa y su rol en la recuperación de desastres: la experiencia de Mameyes. *Polimorfo* 5, 14–25.

Fundación Comunitaria de Puerto Rico. n.d.. Las primeras experiencias de los CHDOs en Puerto Rico. Mimeo. Accessed on 14 October 2020. <https://fdocuments.net/document/las-primeras-historias-exitosas-de-los-chdos-en-puerto-rico-autnomos-de-puerto.html/>.

García. I. 2020. The Lack of Proof of Ownership in PR is Crippling Repairs in the Aftermath of Hurricane Maria. *Human Rights* 44(2). Accessed on 14 October 2020. <https://www.americanbar.org/groups/crsj/publications/human_rights_magazine_home/vol--44--no-2--housing/the-lack-of-proof-of-ownership-in-puerto-rico-is-crippling-repai/>.

García-Colón, I. 2009. *Land Reform in Puerto Rico: Modernizing de Colonial State. 1941-1969.* Gainesville: University Press of Florida.

García-López, Gustavo A., A. Torres-Abreu and C.M. Concepción-Rodríguez. 2018. Introducción: hacia un análisis de las experiencias de gestión ambiental comunitaria en Puerto Rico. In *Ambiente y Democracia*, eds. G.A. García-López, A. Torres-Abreu and C.M. Concepción-Rodríguez. Rio Piedras. Editorial de la Universidad de Puerto Rico.

Gin, J., Kranke, D., R. Saia and A. Dobalian. 2016. Disaster Preparedness in Homeless Residential Organizations in Los Angeles County: Identifying Needs, Assessing Gaps. *Natural Hazards Review* 17. Accessed on 13 November 2020. <https://ascelibrary.org/doi/full/10.1061/%28ASCE%29 NH.1527-6996.0000208/>.

Gotham, K.F. 2014a. Reinforcing Inequalities: The Impact of the CDBG Program on Post-Katrina Rebuilding. *Housing Policy Debate* 24(1), 192–212.

_____. 2014b. Racialization and Rescaling: Post-Katrina Rebuilding and Louisiana Road Home Program. *International Journal of Urban and Regional Research.* 38(3), 773–90.

Gotham, K.F. and M. Greenberg. 2008. From 9/11 to 8/29: Post-Disaster Recovery and Rebuilding in New York and New Orleans. *Social Forces* 87(2), 1039–62.

Graham, L. 2020. Public Housing Participation in Superstorm Sandy Recovery: Living in a Differentiated State in Rockaway, Queens. *Urban Affairs Review* 56(1), 289–324.

Greenberg, M. 2014. The Disaster inside the Disaster: Hurricane Sandy and Post-Crisis Redevelopment. *New Labor Forum* 23(1), 44–52.

Guilbe, C.J. 2009. Big Boxes, Mega Stores, and Category Killers Overseas: The Emerging Geography of North American Chain Stores (NACS) in Puerto Rico. *Southeastern Geographer* 49(4), 326–39.

Halpern, R. 1995. Rebuilding the Inner City: *A History of Neighborhood Initiatives to Address Poverty in the United States.* New York: Columbia University Press.

Harrison, B. and M. Weiss. 1998. *Workforce Development Networks: Community Organizations and Regional Alliances.* Thousand Oaks, CA: Sage Publications.

Hinojosa, J. and E. Meléndez. 2018. The Housing Crisis in Puerto Rico and the Impact of Hurricane Maria. Center for Puerto Rican Studies. CENTRO RB2018-04. June. Accessed on 14 October 2020. <https://centropr.hunter.

cuny.edu/research/data-center/research-briefs/housing-crisis-puerto-rico-and-impact-hurricane-maria/>.

Kliksberg, B. and M. Rivera. 2007. *El capital social movilizado contra la pobreza: la experiencia del proyecto de Comunidades Especiales en Puerto Rico.* Buenos Aires: CLACSO/UNESCO.

Koch, H., Z.E. Franco, T. O'Sullivan, M.C. DeFino and C. Ahmed. 2016. Community Views of the Federal Emergency Management Agency's "Whole Community" Strategy in a Complex US City: Re-envisioning Societal Resilience. *Technological Forecasting & Social Change* 121, 31–8.

Krumholz, N. and K. Hexter. 2018. Conclusion: The Future of Equity Planning Practice. In *Advancing Equity Planning Now,* eds. N. Krumholz and K. Hexter. 263–82. Ithaca: Cornell University Press.

Levers, A. and L. Wolf Powers. 2016. Planning, Social Infrastructure, and the Maker Movement in New York City. Accessed on 14 October 2020. <https://doi.org/10.17615/d6s6-m951/>.

Leung, R. 2015. A Primer on Qualified Allocation Plans: Linking Public Health & Affordable Housing. ChangeLabs Solutions. Accessed on 18 November 2020. <https://www.changelabsolutions.org/sites/default/files/QAP-Primer_Public-Health_Affordable-Housing_FINAL_20150305.pdf/>.

Llanes-Santos, J. 2001. *Desafiando el poder: las invasiones de terreno en Puerto Rico.* San Juan: Ediciones Huracán.

Low, S.A., A. Aaron, E. Beaulieu, N. Key, S. Martinez, A. Melton, A. Perez, K, Ralston, H. Stewart, S. Suttles, S. Vogel and B. Jablonski. 2015. Trends in U.S. Local and Regional Food Systems. AP-068, U.S. Department of Agriculture, Economic Research Service, January. Accessed on 14 October 2020. <https://www.ers.usda.gov/publications/pub-details/?pubid=42807/>.

Martin, C. 2018. The Evidence Base on How CDBG-DR Works for State and Local Stakeholders. Testimony before the Subcommittee on Oversight and Investigations, Committee on Financial Services. US House of Representatives. 17 May. Urban Institute. Washington DC. Accessed on 14 October 2020. <https://www.urban.org/research/publication/evidence-base-how-cdbg-dr-works-state-and-local-stakeholders/>.

Martinez, S. et al. 2010. Local Food Systems: Concepts, Impacts, and Issues. ERR 97, U.S. Department of Agriculture, Economic Research Service, May. Accessed on 14 October 2020. <https://www.ers.usda.gov/webdocs/publications/46393/7054_err97_1_.pdf?v=0/>.

Martin, R.L. and S. Osberg. 2007. Social Entrepreneurship: A Case for Definition. *Stanford Social Innovation Review* Spring. Accessed on 17 November 2020. <https://ssir.org/articles/entry/social_entrepreneurship_the_case_for_definition/>.

Martinuzzi, S., W.A. Gould and O.M. Ramos-Gonzalez. 2007. Land Development, Land Use, and Urban Sprawl in Puerto Rico Integrating Remote Sensing and Population Census Data. *Landscape and Urban Planning* 79, 288–97.

Marwell, N.P. 2010. Privatizing the Welfare State: Nonprofit Community-Based Organizations as Political Actors. In *Politics + Partnerships: The Role of Voluntary Associations in America's Political Past and Present*, eds. E.S.

Clemens and D. Guthrie. Chicago: The University of Chicago Press.

Massol-González, A. 2019. *Casa Pueblo cultiva esperanzas: proyecto de autogestión comunitaria*. Adjuntas, PR: Casa Pueblo Editorial.

McQuarrie, M. 2010. Nonprofits and Reconstruction in Urban Governance: Housing Production and Community Development in Cleveland, 1975-2005. In *Politics + Partnerships: The Role of Voluntary Associations in America's Political Past and Present*, eds. E.S. Clemens and D. Guthrie. Chicago: The University of Chicago Press.

Mehta, A., M. Brennan and J. Steil. 2020. Affordable Housing, Disasters, and Social Equity: LIHTC as a Tool for Preparedness and Recovery. *Journal of the American Planning Association* 86(1), 75–88.

Meléndez, E. 2018. The Economics of PROMESA. *CENTRO: Journal of the Center for Puerto Rican Studies* 30(3), 72–103.

Meléndez, E. and N. Medina. 1999. *Desarrollo económico comunitario: casos exitosos en Puerto Rico*. San Juan: Editorial Nueva Aurora.

Meléndez, E. and L. Servon. 2007. Reassessing the Role of Housing in Urban Community Development. *Housing and Policy Debate* 18(4), 751–83.

Meléndez, E., R. Borges-Méndez, M.A. Visser and A. Rosofsky. 2015. The Restructured Landscape of Economic Development: Challenges and Opportunities for Regional Workforce Development Collaborations. *Economic Development Quarterly* 29, 150–66.

Meléndez, E. and C. Venator. 2018. Introduction to Puerto Rico Post-Maria: Origins and Consequences of a Crisis. *CENTRO: Journal of the Center for Puerto Rican Studies* 30 (3), 5–29.

Meléndez, E., N. Román and J. Hinojosa. 2018. Puerto Rican Post-Maria Relocation by States. Centro Research Brief. Centro RB 2018-03. Accessed on 14 October 2020. <https://centropr.hunter.cuny.edu/sites/default/files/PDF/Schoolenroll-v4-27-2018.pdf/>.

Mickelson, S.S. et al. 2019. Fixing America's Disaster Housing Recovery System. Part 1: Barriers to a Complete and Equitable Recovery. National Low-Income Housing Coalition. Washington, DC. Accessed on 14 October 2020. <https://nlihc.org/sites/default/files/Fixing-Americas-Broken-Disaster-Housing-Recovery-System_P1.pdf/>.

NeighborWorks. 2016. Practical Solutions from America's Community Development Network. Washington, DC: NeighborWorks America.

Ocasio, J. 2018. La titularidad propietaria: su formalidad opresiva en un Puerto Rico post-María. *Revista Jurídica de la Universidad de Puerto Rico* 87(3), 1021–46. 2018.

Olshansky, R and L.A. Johnson. 2014. The Evolution of the Federal Role in Supporting Community Recovery after US Disasters. *Journal of the American Planning Association* 80(4), 293–302.

Pagán, J.K. 2020. Funcionarios que ya no están bajo la administración de Wanda Vázquez. *El Vocero* 11.

Peacock, W.L., N. Dash and Y. Zhang. 2007. Sheltering and Housing Recovery Following Disaster. In *The Handbook of Disaster Research*, eds. H. Rodríguez, L.E. Enrico and R.R. Dynes. New York: Springer.

Pho, S. 2019. Totally Familiar Yet Completely New: Opportunities for and Challenges to Integrating Disaster Risk Management in Community Development. Joint Center for Housing Studies & NeighborWorks. Gramlich Fellowship Paper. April.

Pinke M., S. Mann and E. Todak. 2017. Assisting Individual with Access and Functional Needs: The Intersection of Disabilities, Planning and Disaster Policy. In *The Future of Disaster Management in the US.: Rethinking Legislation, Policy and Finance*, ed. A. LePore. New York: Routledge.

Pizarro-Claudio, D. 2012. Construcción de ciudadanía desde las luchas comunitarias en Puerto Rico: su dimensión política-transformadora y la cuestión social. In *Trabajo comunitario y descolonización*, eds. A. Cotté-Morales, M. Orfila-Barreto, D. Pizarro-Claudio, W. Quiñones-Sierra, R.M. Seda-Rodríguez and L.A. Vega-Rodríguez. San Juan: Impresión Independiente.

Quarantelli, E.L. 1982. General and Particular Observations on Sheltering and Housing in American Disasters. *Disasters* 6, 277–81.

Ragin, C.C. 1987. *The Comparative Method: Moving Beyond Qualitative and Quantitative Strategies*. Oakland: The University of California Press.

Samimi, J.C. 2010. Funding America's Nonprofits: The Non-Profit Industrial Complex's Hold on Social Justice. *Columbia Social Work Review* 1, 17–25.

Sanchez, C. 2009. Communities rebuild in the aftermath of Hurricanes Katrina, Rita and Ike. www. Prospect. Org. March. Accessed on 14 October 2020. <https://issuu.com/americanprospect/docs/katrinareport_may2009/>.

Schwartz, A. F. 2015 *Housing Policy in the United States*. New York: Routledge.

Silberman, A. 2013. *Community Development Corporations and Academic Partnerships*. Boston: Mel King Institute.

Stoutland, S.E. 1999. Community Development Corporations: Mission, Strategy, and Accomplishments. In *Urban Problems and Community Development*, eds. R.F. Ferguson and W.T. Dickens. Washington, DC: Brooking Institution Press.

Suárez, C. 2018. Two Philanthropic Approaches to Strengthening Puerto Rico. *Nonprofit Quarterly* 13 February. Accessed on 14 October 2020. <https://nonprofitquarterly.org/strengthening-puerto-rico-nonprofits-two-philanthropic-approaches/>.

US Department of Housing and Urban Development. 2015. The Evaluation of the Neighborhood Stabilization Policy. Office of Policy Development and Research. Washington, DC.

US Department of Homeland Security. 2020. FEMA Mismanaged the Commodity Distribution Process in Response to Hurricanes Maria and Irma. Office of the Inspector General. 25 September. OIG-20-76.

Vélez-Vélez, R. and J. Villarrubia-Mendoza. 2018. Cambio desde abajo y desde adentro: Notes on Centros de Apoyo Mutuo in post-María Puerto Rico. *Latin American Studies* 16, 542–7 .

Vickery, Jamie. 2015. Compounded Vulnerability: Homeless Service Organizations During Disaster. Master's thesis, University of Colorado, Boulder.

Weissenstein. M. and J. Colón. 2019. 'Chatgate' scandal throws Puerto Rico's governor into crisis. Associated Press 16 July.

Wolf-Powers L, M. Doussard, G. Schrock, C. Heying, M. Eisenburger and S. Marotta.

2017. The Maker Movement and Urban Economic Development. *Journal of the American PlanningAssociation* 83(4), 365–76.

Wyczalkowski, C., A. Esnard, B. Lai and E.J. van Holm. 2019. Uneven Neighborhood Recovery: Hurricane Damage and Neighborhood Change in the Houston–Galveston Region Since 1970. *City & Community* 18(2), 689–709.

Wyss, J. 2020. Anger Grows in Puerto Rico Over Hidden Emergency Aid, Government Corruption. *Miami Herald* 21 January. Accessed on 14 October 2020. <https://www.miamiherald.com/news/nation-world/world/americas/article239469148.html/>.

Yin, R. 1984. *Case-Study Research: Design and Methods.* Thousand Oaks, CA: Sage Publications.

APPENDIX 1

Characteristics of Puerto Rican Community Development Corporations

Names and Acronyms for Organizations

- Asociación Mayagüezana de Personas con Impedimentos (AMPI)-Mayagüez.
- Corporación para el Desarrollo Económico de Trujillo Alto (CDETA)-Trujillo Alto.
- Corporación para el Desarrollo Económico de Ceiba (CDEC)-Ceiba.
- Corporación para el Desarrollo Económico,Vivienda y Salud (CODEVyS)-Arecibo.
- Corporación para el Desarrollo de la Vivienda de Toa Baja (CDVTB)-Toa Baja.
- Corporación Desarrolladora de Vivienda de Israel y Bitumul (CDVI& B)-San Juan.
- Lucha Contra el SIDA, Inc.[1] (LUCHA)-San Juan
- Ponce Neighborhood Housing Services (PNHS)-Ponce.
- Programa de Educación Comunal de Entrega y Servicio (PECES)-Humacao.
- Sabana Grande Community and Economic Development Corporation (SACED).
- Fundación de Desarrollo Comunal (FUNDESCO)-Caguas.
- Instituto para el Desarrollo Socioeconómico y de Vivienda de Puerto Rico, Inc. (INDESOVI)-Mayagüez

1. **Asociación Mayagüezana de Personas con Impedimentos (AMPI)-Mayagüez.** AMPI, founded in 1983 and currently with about thirty employees, implements housing solutions and reconstruction, and offers support services for the disabled, cognitively challenged, elderly and vulnerable populations in the western municipalities of the island. AMPI draws funding from public, private and non-profit sources such as FEMA, HUD, the Angel Ramos Foundation, and the Popular Bank Foundation.

2. **Corporación para el Desarrollo Económico de Trujillo Alto (CDETA)-Trujillo Alto.** CDETA, originally founded in 1986 as a municipal corporation (currently an independent 501-3c), builds affordable housing for senior citizens and other populations. CDETA rehabilitates and develops market-rate commercial spaces in the downtown commercial district. CDETA was formerly a CHDO and has worked with funding from HUD, LIHTC, and private financing. Additionally, CDETA co-participates with organizations in workforce development programming.

[1] Síndrome de Inmunodeficiencia Adquirida (SIDA).

3. **Corporación para el Desarrollo Económico de Ceiba (CDEC)-Ceiba.** CDEC was founded in 1986. Currently it has a staff of six and provides economic development planning for business and microenterprises, housing construction, housing counseling, and workforce development services. CDEC is a certified CHDO and CDFI. CDEC draws funding from the Department of Labor, HUD, FEMA, and USDA.

4. **Corporación para el Desarrollo Económico, Vivienda y Salud (CODEVyS)-Arecibo.** CODEVyS was founded in 2000 and currently operates with a staff of 168 people who develop programs to support people with HIV/AIDS, disabilities, and victims of violence. They also provide housing counseling, enterprise incubation, and childcare services. CODEVyS was formerly a CHDO. They have drawn funding from Homeland Security, FEMA, Puerto Rico Department of Health, Puerto Rico Department of Justice, United Way, and the Angel Ramos Foundation. CODEVys is an affiliate of UNIDOSUS, the largest Latino nonprofit in the United States.

5. **Programa de Educación Comunal de Entrega y Servicio (PECES)-Humacao.** PECES, founded in 1985, currently has 104 employees and about fifty volunteers. PECES creates and manages social, economic, and youth educational programs, plus works on housing reconstruction. PECES was formerly a CHDO and is currently applying for CDFI certification. They have worked with funding from the Department of Justice, Department of Education, and FEMA, as well as various foundations in the United States and Puerto Rico.

6. **Ponce Neighborhood Housing Services (PNHS)-Ponce.** PNHS was founded in 1993, and currently has seven full-time employees, and two Americorps and five Summer Americorps Vista volunteers. PNHS offers housing counseling and reconstruction services, housing reconstruction loans, and community development planning. PHNS is a charter of NeighborWorks in Puerto Rico. In the past, PNHS was a certified CHDO (expired), and it is currently certified as a CDFI. PNHS has worked with HUD-CDBG and FEMA funding, and other funding from the Fundación Comunitaria de Puerto Rico and Hispanic Federation.

7. **Corporación para el Desarrollo de la Vivienda de Toa Baja (CDVTB)-Toa Baja.** CDVTB was founded in 1995 and currently has a staff of six people. It is chartered as a municipal corporation created by the Municipality of Toa Baja. It is also a certified CHDO. CDVTB is exclusively devoted to housing development and draws its funding from the private banking sector and through the sale of LIHTC.

8. **Sabana Grande Community and Economic Development Corporation (SACED).** SACED was founded in 2010. It has no permanent staff but contracts personnel for specific projects, and they are assisted by around thirty volunteers. The organization is involved in housing rehabilitation, drug prevention, education, and small business incubation. SACED has obtained funding from FEMA, and various foundations in the island.

9. **Corporación Desarrolladora de Vivienda de las Barriadas Israel y Bitumul (CDVI& B)-San Juan.** CDVI & B was founded in 1996, and is currently inactive, but it had a staff of three people. The organization was a certified CHDO, and it was exclusively devoted to housing and community develop-

ment. CDCVI & B has received funding from HUD (CDBG & HOME), private banks, the Municipality of San Juan, faith-based organizations, and Fundación Comunitaria de Puerto Rico.

10. **Fundación de Desarrollo Comunal (FUNDESCO)-Caguas.** FUNDESCO was founded in 1966 and has a staff of 32 people, with numerous volunteers assisting in specific various projects. The organization is dedicated to housing development and providing social support to various vulnerable populations such as HIV-positive individuals, homeless, victims of domestic violence, and senior citizens. In addition, FUNDESCO is active in vocational education services, health, and recreation. The organization has an extensive record of fundraising and managing federal funding from HUD, FEMA, EDA, as well from other sources including the Municipality of Caguas, FIDEVI, and the Fundación Comunitaria de Puerto Rico.

11. **Instituto para el Desarrollo Socioeconómico y de Vivienda de Puerto Rico, Inc. (INDESOVI)-Mayagüez.** INDESOVI was founded in 2005 and has a staff of 47 people. The organization is a certified CHDO and has created another limited liability corporation, Villa Dorado, LLC. INDESOVI is dedicated mainly to housing development, construction, rehabilitation, and management. In addition, they develop commercial space and are active in local economic development. INDESOVI has an extensive record obtaining and managing federal funding from HUD (CDBG; HOME; CDBG-DR); Low Income Housing Tax Credits; SBA; and FEMA. They have also drawn funding from private banks, the Municipality of Mayagüez, and the Fundación Comunitaria de Puerto Rico.

12. **Lucha Contra el SIDA, Inc.[2] (LUCHA)-San Juan.** LUCHA was founded in 1994 and has staff of sixty. The organization is a certified CHDO. LUCHA is dedicated to build permanent, rental, and transitional housing for various vulnerable populations: HIV/AIDS-positive, homeless, victims of domestic violence, recovering addicts, and at-risk families. At the same time, LUCHA maintains a strong infrastructure of social, mental, and medical supports for housing residents. LUCHA has acquired funding from HUD (CDBG-DR; CoC; CDBG); FEMA; Federal Department of Health Human Services; Fundación Comunitaria de Puerto Rico, Enterprise, and other private funders.

[2] Síndrome de Inmunodeficiencia Adquirida (SIDA).

APPENDIX 2

PRCDCs—Projects and Funding

Name of the Organization	Housing and Econ Development Projects	Sources of Funding
Programa de Educación Comunal de Entrega y Servicio (PECES)	Escuela Alternativa; Centro de Sostenibilidad Comunitaria; Programa Antorcha	PR Dept. of Education; PR Dept of Justice; PR Dept of Health; Medtronic Foundation; Fundación Banco Popular; Rotary Foundation; Walmart Foundation; United Way; Fundación Comunitaria de PR; Global Giving; Fundación Segarra Boerman
Corporación para el Desarrollo de Trujillo Alto (CDTA)	Egida Aires del Manantial; housing and commercial units in downtown Trujillo Alto; Assisted Living Centro Salvador	Oficina de Fondos Legislativos; PR Low Income Housing Tax Credits; HOME (HUD)
Corporación para el Desarrollo Económico de Ceiba (CDEC)	Portal de Ceiba (housing); Centro de Desarrollo Empresarial; Una Luz al Final del Camino (post-disaster relief and housing renovation)	PR Low Income Housing Tax Credits; SBA; FEMA; HOME (HUD); USDA Rural Development; PR Dept. of Labor; Fundación Comunitaria de PR
Ponce Neighborhood Housing Services (PNHS) (Affiliate of NeighborWorks USA)	Compra tu Casa; Rehabilitación de Hogares	Unidos por Puerto Rico; Fundación Comunitaria; Hispanic Federation;HOME (HUD);NeighborWorks.
Corporación Desarrollo Económico, Vivienda y Salud (CODEVyS)	CAPERNAUM;Manejo de Casos en Desastre (MDC); Ven a Mi, Exprésate (VAME) Iniciativa Comunitaria de Arecibo; Programa Incubadora Microempresa; Programa VALOR.	PR Dept. of Health; PR Dept of Justice; PR Dept of Education; FEMA; United Way; Fundación Angel Ramos; Otras Fundaciones
Asociación Mayagüezana de Personas con Impedimentos (AMPI)	Assisted Living: La Casa de AMPI/La Casa de Junny/ La Casa Doña Here; AMPI Pa' Puerto Rico; Proyecto de Comunidad La Chorra; CEMECAV; CEBRAIS.	Fundación Banco Popular de PR; Fundación Angel Ramos, United Way PR; Hispanic Federation; Fondo Legislativo de PR; Edward Life Science; HOME-HUD; FEMA
Corporación para el Desarrollo de la Vivienda de Toa Baja (CDVTB)	Golden Age Tower (Elderly Housing-Egida); Brisas del Campanero, I,II, III.	Low Income Housing Tax Credits (LIHTC); Private Banks; Loans.
Sabana Grande Community and Economic Development Corporation (SACED)	FEMA Disaster Case Management Program (DCMP); FEMA Drug-Free Communities Program (COMPASS); Incubadora Solidaria de Pequeños Negocios	FEMA; Foundations; Donations

APPENDIX 2 (CONTINUED)

PRCDCs—Projects and Funding

Name of the Organization	Housing and Econ Development Projects	Sources of Funding
Corporacion Desarrolladora de Vivienda de las Barriadas Israel y Bitumul (CDVI&B)	Villas del Paraiso I (Housing complex); Villas del Paraiso II (land acquisition) [Project stalled for permit conflicts, and finance issues, political redtate].	CBDG, HOME (HUD); Private Banks; Municipality of San Juan; Congregación MITA (faith-based); Fundación Comunitaria de PR; Fundación Angel Ramos; Legislature of PR (House and Senate).
Fundación de Desarrollo Comunal (FUNDESCO)	Albergue Los Peregrinos; Hogar La Piedad; Villas del Pelegrino; Remanso de Esperanza; El Salvador (Housing Plus projects); Miniempresa Hands for Work; CIMA/Cidra (childcare and family support services; Centro de Calidad de Vida-Trujillo Alto (Youth-and families at-risk supports).	CBDG (HUD); HOME (HUD); Section 811 HUD (Rental housing subsidy to support independent living of people with disabilities); FEMA; EDA; FIDEVI; Municipio de Caguas; Fundación Comunitaria de PR; Fundación Angel Ramos; PR Dept of Housing; Banks; Private Donations
Instituto para el Desarrollo Socioeconómico y de Vivienda de Puerto Rico, INC. (INDESOVI)	Compra tu Casa; Rehabilitación de Hogares	Unidos por Puerto Rico; Fundación Comunitaria; Hispanic Federation;HOME (HUD);NeighborWorks.
[Created Villa Dorado, LLC)	Urbanización Estancias del Río; Plaza Aguila; Plaza Casals; Paseo Danzas de Quinton; Vega Baja Urbano; D'Rio Court Apartments; San Miguel Apartments; Hogar Paraiso Dorado [Ongoing projects in Loiza, Carolina, Yabucoa]	Low Income Housing Tax Credits (LIHTC); USDA; CBDG, CBDG-DR, HOME (HUD); SBA; FEMA; Private Banks; Municipio Mayagüez; Joint partnerhsips with Fundación Comunitaria de PR; Fundación Ricky Martin; Fundacaión Somos una Voz.
Lucha Contra el SIDA, Inc. (LUCHA)	Manatiales de Vida-Centro de Cuidado Diurno; Renacer de Vida (transitional housing); Reencontrando el Sendero (transitory housing) Nuevo Horizonte (transitory housing); Remanso Elderly (elderly housing); Remanso de Paz (housing for disabled people); Sabana Village (multi-family housing); Gurabo Elderly (elderly housing); Lucero del Alba (permanent housing for homeless)	HUD (Continuum of Care Program (CoC) CBDG-DR; ; Fundación Comunitaria de PR; Enterprise; Municipality of San Juan; Health and Human Services.
Corporación para el Desarrollo de la Vivienda de Toa Baja (CDVTB)	Golden Age Tower (Elderly Housing-Egida); Brisas del Campanero, I,II, III.	Low Income Housing Tax Credits (LIHTC); Private Banks; Loans.

What Is Possible? Policy Options for Long-term Disaster Recovery in Puerto Rico

ARIAM L. TORRES CORDERO

ABSTRACT

Policymakers, practitioners, academics, and community leaders can often identify unjust outcomes resulting from disaster policies that fail to satisfy basic needs or that underserve disadvantaged populations. What is less clear is how to design and implement successful programs that result in better and more just outcomes. To shed light on this matter, this paper explores CDBG-DR governance models across different U.S. jurisdictions and examines strategies that promote equity by targeting the most vulnerable and prioritizing local needs, knowledge, and capabilities for long-term recovery. The paper uses a policy assemblage framework and draws on key stakeholder interviews and analysis of various secondary sources about disaster recovery planning and policy. Findings suggest that a great deal can be improved through (a) an equity-oriented interpretation of federal guidelines and the exercise of bureaucratic discretion, and (b) enabling networks to build local capacity for community and economic development. [Keywords: CDBG-DR, governance, disaster recovery, planning, advocacy, equity]

The author (ariamlt2@illinois.edu) is a Ph.D. candidate at University of Illinois, Urbana-Champaign and a Research Fellow for the Research Foundation of the City University of New York. His dissertation research focuses on disaster recovery planning and on how different civic sector organizations in Puerto Rico and in the diaspora develop alternative recovery pathways for vulnerable populations. Other research interests include urban environmental planning, community development, climate adaptation, and environmental justice.

Introduction

Puerto Rico is at a crossroads. September 2020 marked the three-year anniversary of Hurricane María—an event that altered the livelihoods of millions of Puerto Ricans in countless ways. As Puerto Rico transitions to long-term recovery, the prospect of billions of dollars in Community Development Block Grant—Disaster Recovery (CDBG-DR) and Mitigation (CDBG-MIT) funds is increasingly shaping planning and decision-making processes. If used properly, these funds could present an opportunity for communities to secure decent housing, adequate infrastructure, and economic recovery. If misused, at the very least, these funds will not reach the communities that need them the most.

Policymakers, practitioners, academics, and community leaders can often identify unjust outcomes resulting from disaster policies that fail to satisfy basic needs or that underserve disadvantaged populations. This indeed has been the case of Puerto Rico, as the paper shall explain later on. What is less clear is how to design and implement successful programs through appropriate planning processes that result in better and more just outcomes. To shed light on this matter, this paper presents a comparative case study research of CDBG-DR governance models in Puerto Rico, Louisiana, South Carolina, Florida, and Texas, and examines strategies that promote equity by targeting the most vulnerable and prioritizing local needs, knowledge, and capabilities for long-term recovery. Findings suggest that current federal guidelines for the use of CDBG-DR funds allow for a certain measure of discretion and interpretation that the Government of Puerto Rico can elect to exercise or not in order to develop more equitable programs aimed at producing a better and more just recovery. Further, the analysis shows that a common approach to achieving this goal is by harnessing local knowledge to enable networks that build capacity for community and economic development.

The next section provides a short review on the U.S. disaster policy framework and a brief account on how the institutional post-María recovery process has advanced thus far in Puerto Rico. After, the paper describes the research design, including methods and conceptual framework. It then presents the research findings from each case, followed by an analysis and discussion of planning and policy implications for Puerto Rico. Finally, the paper concludes with a call to action for policymakers, government officials, and planning practitioners.

U.S. Disaster Policy Framework

The main law that defines the U.S. disaster policy framework is the Disaster Relief Act of 1974. It was substantially amended in 1988 and titled the Robert T. Stafford Disaster Relief and Emergency Assistance Act (Stafford Act). Under the Stafford Act, the Federal Emergency Management Agency (FEMA) is the lead entity to coordinate the federal government's role in dealing with the effects of all domestic disasters. FEMA administers the federal government's main recovery assistance programs defined by the Stafford Act: Individual Assistance, Public Assistance, and Hazard Mitigation Assistance. Other federal government agencies with potentially significant roles and resources in post-disaster recovery include the U.S. Department of Housing and Urban Development (HUD), the Small Business Administration (SBA), the Economic Development Administration (EDA), and the U.S. Department of Agriculture (USDA) (Johnson and Olshansky 2017).

This recovery continuum progresses though four phases: preparedness, short-term (days), intermediate (weeks-months) and long-term (months-years).

In 2011, FEMA released the National Disaster Recovery Framework (NDRF), which was the first national recovery policy that defined measures of recovery success, including: individual and family empowerment, leadership and local primacy, pre-disaster recovery planning, engaged partnerships and inclusiveness, unity of effort, timeliness and flexibility, resilience and sustainability, and psychological and emotional recovery (FEMA 2016). Also, the NDRF uses the concept of "recovery continuum" to describe a sequence of interdependent and often concurrent activities that progressively advance a community toward its planned recovery outcomes. This recovery continuum progresses though four phases: preparedness, short-term (days), intermediate (weeks-months) and long-term (months-years) (see Figure 1).

Activities related to the post-disaster short-term recovery phase—also described as emergency response—focus primarily on saving lives and property, and on providing basic human needs and support services. Activities related to the intermediate or mid-term phase are those related primarily to providing interim solutions to housing, mobility, and the restoration of other essential services, aimed at returning to functional pre-disaster conditions. Activities related to long-term recovery are those of housing and infrastructure reconstruction, economic development, and hazard mitigation.

Long-term recovery activities across the U.S. have been largely centralized at the federal and state level, mainly driven by HUD's CDBG-DR funding (Johnson and Olshansky 2017). CDBG-DR is an allocation of funds from HUD that becomes available when the president declares a major disaster and there are significant needs left unmet by FEMA's individual and public assistance programs. After Congress appropriates CDBG-DR funds, HUD formally announces the CDBG-DR awards via press release and notices published in the Federal Register (HUD 2019).

CDBG-DR funds can be used in a variety of ways to address community development issues, including the restoration of essential services, the mitigation of the effects of future disasters, as well as "long-term recovery and reconstruction of businesses, homes, community facilities, and infrastructure" (Johnson and Olshansky 2017, 255). All CDBG-DR-supported programs must meet the criteria of at least one of the program's national objectives: (a) benefit low—and moderate—income persons or households, (b) aid and assist in the prevention or elimination of deteriorating areas, such as slums or blights, and (c) meet an urgent need (HUD 2019). Under applicable regulations or waivers and alternative requirements, general planning and program administrative costs are presumed to meet a national objective. Typically, HUD grants a waiver and alternative requirement to state CDBG-DR grantees to expand eligible planning activities to include non-project specific plans such as functional land-use plans, master plans, historic preservation plans, comprehensive plans, community recovery plans, development of housing codes, zoning ordinances, and neighborhood plans (HUD 2019).

Policy Problems in Post-María Recovery

To date, Puerto Rico's post-María recovery process has been plagued with policy failures and politics of injustice (see Currie 2019; Garcia 2019; Molinari 2019), resulting in an unreasonably elevated death toll (Kishore et al. 2018), the collapse of safety nets, and the displacement of thousands of citi-

Figure 1. Recovery Continuum

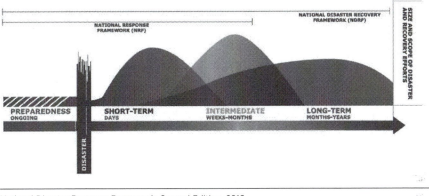

National Disaster Recovery Framework, Second Edition, 2016

zens (Wilson et al. 2019). During the short-term recovery phase, not all significant losses and casualties were identified and estimated appropriately, particularly those related to marginalized rural areas (Molinari 2019). This was due in part not only to the magnitude of the destruction, but also to the lack of preparedness by government units at all levels (FEMA 2018). In fact, in his testimony before the Committee on Homeland Security of the U.S. House of Representatives, Chris Currie, the director of Homeland Security and Justice, admitted that FEMA's lack of key supplies on Puerto Rico before the storm, their unqualified staff, and the many challenges with delivering emergency supplies affected the recovery process (Currie 2019).

Among the most visible policy problems leading to unjust outcomes of Puerto Rico's official institutional recovery process has been the marginalization of disadvantaged social groups. Two main issues here stand out. First, after María, FEMA developed new advisory flood maps as a mechanism to prevent the use of federal funds for housing reconstruction in flood zones areas without flood insurance. This has had great adverse implications for low-income coastal communities, limiting their opportunities to adequately participate in recovery programs and access recovery funds. Second, FEMA denied 58 percent of the total applications to the Individual Household Assistance program. Why? It often came down to proof of ownership, where many individuals either lack any documentation proving that they own their homes or their proof is incompatible with FEMA's requirements (García, Olshansky and Carrasquillo 2019).

Regarding transitions to the mid-term recovery phase, many stakeholders have consistently brought attention to systematic policy failures and local disaster recovery programs. To mention just a few, members of the U.S. Congress, Legal Aid Puerto Rico, and others have expressed grave concerns about the insufficient standards in regard to ensuing equitable access to recovery funds and about policy parameters that promote displacement (see Congress of the U.S. 2019; Legal Aid PR 2019). The Center for the New Economy has shed light on how federal relief and recovery spending in Puerto Rico has been mostly used to contract stateside private firms rather than local ones, limiting potential local economic development opportunities (Lamba-Nieves and Santiago 2018). The Center for Investigative Journalism has brought attention to the deregulated government contracting dynamics (e.g., no-bid contracts) and the associated corruption schemes (Flavelle, Malik and Smith 2017). Also, advocacy and professional organizations including the Hispanic Federation and the Puerto Rican Planning Society have claimed that opportunities for community involvement in key post-disaster planning processes (e.g., hazard mitigation, disaster recovery action planning, etc.) have been limited and restricted (García 2019).

Nevertheless, despite how events have transpired so far, Puerto Rico is still transitioning from an intermediate or mid-term recovery phase to long-term recovery and reconstruction. Although the implementation of current disaster policy and legislation has led to many unjust outcomes, research findings suggest that there is a great deal that can be improved through the interpretation of the federal policy rules and regulations and the exercise of bureaucratic discretion. This is particularly the case regarding action planning for the use of the CDBG-DR and CDBG-MIT funds.

Research Design

Planning scholar Libby Porter (2018) argues that any policymaking or planning activity that occurs in a context where colonial relations are present is saturated with complex and contested historical issues. This is true for Puerto Rico. Its territorial condition as defined in the U.S. Constitution and enforced by the U.S. Government and the Supreme Court directly shapes law, politics, and discourse, all of which have great effects on recovery processes. That is to say, Puerto Rico's colonial context directly shapes how the U.S. disaster policy framework is assembled and implemented in Puerto Rico.

Within this context, this paper applies a policy assemblage framework to explore options on how Puerto Rico might design and implement successful CDBG-DR programs. Understanding the uniqueness of Puerto Rico's relationship with the U.S., rather than the traditional approach of seeking for "best practices," the goal here is to identify what might work for Puerto Rico if the federal guidelines for the use of CDBG-DR funds are adapted to the local context in a way that is sensible to the multiple components and context-specific factors that need to be considered and strategically arranged to render better outcomes.

Policy Assemblage Framework

At its core, to focus on policy assemblage is to examine how multiple heterogeneous elements are arranged to create governable forms. These elements include arrangements of humans, materials, technologies, organizations, techniques, procedures, norms, and events (Baker and McGuirk 2016). According to Savage (2019), there are three foundations central to the policy assemblage framework: (1) relations of exteriority and emergence, (2) heterogeneity, relationality, and flux; and (3) attention to power, politics, and agency. Together, these foundations signal a coherency to assemblage thinking and allow researchers to see and explain things in ways that many established traditions in policy research do not.

The notion of relations of exteriority and emergence suggests that, rather than understanding a policy as a coherent thing or as definable as the sum of its constitutive components, an assemblage approach stresses that what is most important is understanding the "nature of interactions between components and the capacities such components exhibit when arranged in different ways" (Savage 2019, 4). Regarding heterogeneity, relationality and flux, the main idea is that assemblages are comprised of a multiplicity of component parts that have been arranged together in a particular way toward particular strategic ends. However, the relations between the parts are contingent rather than fixed. This means that the policy assemblage approach emphasizes the evolving nature of relationships and formations. Finally, attention to power, politics, and agency refers to the need to think in distinct ways about where power and agency comes from, how they are put to work in a particular policy assemblage, and how might they change if the elements comprising a particular assemblage are rearranged.

With these ideas in mind, the policy assemblage framework invites researchers to pay strong attention to politics and the relative capacities of individuals and organizations to exercise agency in relation to both the creation of policy and its enactments. Based on this framework, this paper explores cases across different U.S. jurisdictions to examine how their CDBG-DR governance models are arranged together in a particular way toward particular strategic ends.

Methods

The research design is based on a case study comparison that involved an analysis of CDBG-DR governance models in Puerto Rico, Louisiana, South Carolina, Florida, and Texas. These cases were selected through convenience sampling. The sample universe was defined as U.S. jurisdictions affected by hurricanes with experience managing federal disaster aid. Although contact was made to several different U.S. jurisdictions, the final selection was based on stakeholders' willingness and availability to participate in the study.

For insights into official institutional recovery and planning processes, the paper draws on key stakeholder interviews and analysis of various secondary sources about disaster recovery planning and policy collected between June 2019 and May 2020. The author conducted 48 semi-structured interviews to representatives from academia, civic sector organizations, and state, county, and city government officials (see Table 1). The article also draws on multiple secondary sources. Sources included institutional plans, academic and professional publications, news media, and public records, including notices of available funds (NOFAs), requests for applications/qualifications (RFAs/RFQs), among others.

Findings

This section is organized as follows. It begins by describing some of the basic elements available for CDBG-DR governance. It then presents the cases of the U.S. jurisdictions examined and their respective CDBG-DR governance models assembled for their priorities. At the end of the section, Table 2 presents a summary of all the CDBG-DR governance models examined.

...even when states are grantees or recipients, local governments can be actively engaged in the action planning process if given the opportunity

CDBG-DR Governance

HUD typically allocates funds to States given their capacity to administer funds across damaged areas. When this is the case, the CDBG-DR appropriation mandates that all funds must be spent to meet recovery needs in presidentially declared major disaster areas pursuant to the Stafford Act. Typically, appropriations further limit use of funds to the most impacted and distressed areas resulting from a major disaster. It is important to mention that, although HUD typically allocates funds to States, units of general local government (UGLGs) such as counties and cities could potentially be direct recipients or grantees. Further, as we shall see later on, even when states are grantees or recipients, local governments can be actively engaged in the action planning process if given the opportunity.

Grantees have many options when they consider their governance model for how CDBG-DR funds will flow to various types of projects. The three main models available are: (1) direct implementation, (2) partnerships, and (3) method of distribution. In a direct implementation model, the grantee develops or expands in-house capacity to directly administer the programs in all of the eligible impacted areas. This could be by a direct procurement of con-

Table 1. Interviews by Sector Across Study Sites

	Puerto Rico	Louisiana	South Carolina	Florida	Texas	Total
Government	3	4	3	2	2	14
Civic Sector	7	5	3	3	3	21
Academia	5	3	1	2	2	13
Total	15	12	7	7	7	48

tractors to manage or implement specific portions of a grantee program, or by distributing grant administration among peer state or municipal agencies to administer programs in their typical field of operations (HUD 2019). In a partnership model, the grantee delegates distinct responsibilities or programs to other state agencies, local governments, and nonprofits. Finally, the method of distribution allows for formulaic sub-awards to sub-recipient UGLGs to further define and administer projects and programs at the local level. It is important to mention these models are not necessarily mutually exclusive. Grantees can develop a hybrid governance model and combine different approaches.

Puerto Rico's CDBG-DR governance model

In Puerto Rico, since the entire archipelago was declared a major disaster area, the Commonwealth was designated as the grantee of approximately $20 billion in recovery funds made available by the U.S. Congress through CDBG-DR and CDBG-MIT appropriations. To administer these funds, the Governor of Puerto Rico appointed the Puerto Rico Department of Housing (hereinafter Vivienda). Vivienda was assigned the responsibility to develop the Puerto Rico Disaster Recovery Action Plan (DRAP) establishing how the CDBG-DR funds will be used, and another Action Plan establishing how the CDBG-MIT funds will be used. After assessing their organizational capacity, Vivienda decided to hire private contractors to help them design some housing and economic recovery programs, and one local nonprofit organization to help them design one planning program. With this approach to plan-making, Vivienda maintains control and closely oversees the program design process.

The first version of the DRAP centered on addressing urgent housing and socioeconomic needs and laying the foundation for the long-term recovery. This initial plan established four programmatic areas: Planning, Housing, Economy, and Infrastructure. In February 2018, HUD awarded $1.5 billion in CDBG-DR funds to support this effort. Later amendments to the plan added Multi-Sector as a fifth programmatic area. Across these five programmatic areas, the Action Plan presents a total of 25 programs: four in Planning, nine in Housing, seven in Economy, three in Infrastructure, and two in Multi-Sector. In total, approximately $10 billion in CDBG-DR funds will be available to support these efforts (DRAP Amendment Four 2020).[1] The remaining approximately $10 billion will be made available through CDBG-MIT allocations to design and implement the CDBG-MIT Action Plan.

According to the DRAP, Vivienda will utilize two different governance models for their 25 recovery programs: direct implementation and a method of distribution through subrecipient agreements. The concept of "subrecipient refers to a "public or private nonprofit agency, authority, or organization, or an authorized for-profit entity, receiving CDBG funds from the recipient (in this case Vivienda) to undertake activities eligible for such assistance" (DRAP Amendment Four 2020, 99). To administer the Housing Repair, Reconstruction, and Relocation (R3) Program, which is the main housing program and the largest recovery program in the DRAP, Vivienda adopted a direct implementation model with a procurement of contractors to manage specific portions of the program. For the rest of the programs, in housing and in the other programmatic areas, Vivienda adopted a method of distribution through subrecipient agreements.

Approximately 46 percent ($3.75 billion) of the second allocation of CDBG-DR funds ($8.22 billion) have been dedicated for housing recovery (DRAP Amendment Four 2020). Of this, 65 percent ($2.5 billion) are for the R3 program. Other housing programs include: CDBG-DR Gap to Low Income Housing Tax Credits Program (LIHTC) and Homebuyer Assistance Program, among others with less funds allocated.

In this centralized, top-down model, HUD and Vivienda control funding at all stages of the process.

In sum, Puerto Rico's CDBG-DR governance model follows a basic top-down approach, centralized at the federal (HUD) and state (Vivienda) level. In this centralized, top-down model, HUD and Vivienda control funding at all stages of the process. There is one action plan, administered by one central agency with external contractors performing specific functions of program design and implementation, as well as subrecipients assisting with certain program management functions. Through this approach, the amount of time allocated to community participation and consensus building is limited. Also, since the entire island was declared as a major disaster area, and no additional efforts were done to prioritize the most impacted and distressed areas, Vivienda can impose uniformity in planning and implementation.

Louisiana's Recovery after 2005 Hurricane Katrina

When thinking about other U.S. jurisdictions to draw lessons from, it is almost inevitable to examine the case of Louisiana after the 2005 Hurricanes Katrina and Rita. One can easily see numerous similarities, both in terms of the magnitude of the disaster and in the erratic recovery process. Just like Puerto Rico, Louisiana faced many bureaucratic obstacles, mainly due to their lack of capacity and to the lack of trust from the federal government (Johnson and Olshansky 2017).

After Hurricane Katrina, the Governor of Louisiana issued an executive order to create the Louisiana Recovery Authority (LRA) and charged it with securing funding and other resources, "establishing principles and policies for redevelopment, leading long-term community and regional planning efforts, ensuring transparency and accountability, and communicating progress, status, and needs of the recovery to officials, community advocates, and the public" (LRA 2010). The LRA was led by a board of directors whose 33 members were selected to be bipartisan, socioeconomically and racially diverse civic and national leaders who originated from affected communities. These volunteers met consistently nearly every month over the five-year life of the LRA, and the agency issued quarterly reports on its work, as required by the Louisiana legislature. The LRA also formed a series of task forces to develop and guide policy for a host of recovery issues, including "housing, economic and workforce development, infrastructure and transportation, public health and healthcare, the environment, human services, education, coastal protection, and long-term community planning" (Johnson and Olshansky 2017, 277).

Under the LRA, the two main recovery program management agencies were the Louisiana Office of Community Development (OCD) and the Governor's Office of Homeland Security and Emergency Preparedness (GOHSEP). The OCD established the Disaster Recovery Unit with lead responsibility for the administration of the CDBG-DR funds, while GOHSEP had lead responsibility administrating the FEMA's programs.

The State of Louisiana received approximately $13.4 billion in CDBG-DR funds, and their action plan identified four programmatic areas: planning, housing, infrastructure, and economic development. For the Housing programmatic area, also known as Road Home, the State assigned approximately $9 billion, close to 67 percent of their total CDBG-DR allocation. Within Road Home, four housing recovery programs were developed, all using a direct implementation model. To address their capacity limitations, the State hired private firms for the program design and implementation. Spaces and opportunities for the local non-profit sector were quite limited.

Louisiana's CDBG-DR Governance after 2008 Hurricanes Gustav and Ike

After the 2008 Hurricanes Gustav and Ike, the State of Louisiana determined that it was in their best interest "to allow the most impacted local governments, acting through subrecipient agreements, to decide which recovery programs they wanted to develop to meet their assessed unmet needs" (Interview, Hazard Mitigation Office, New Orleans, August 2, 2019). This time, they developed two different methods of distribution: (a) sub-awards to subrecipient UGLGs, and (b) subrecipient agreements through a competitive request for proposals (RFP) process.

According to the State of Louisiana Action Plan for the Utilization of CDBG Funds in Response to Hurricanes Gustav and Ike (Action Plan for Gustav and Ike), the State identified the parishes most affected and allowed them to define and administer their own projects and programs at the local level through sub-awards. Approximately 70 percent of the total CDBG-DR funds were distributed this way. For the rest of the affected areas, the state allocated 25 percent of the total CDBG-DR funds for competitive projects in the areas of affordable housing, agriculture, hurricane protection, coastal restoration, and fisheries (Action Plan for Gustav and Ike 2009, 6). Here, the State prioritized proposals that met the CDBG national objectives of benefiting to low- and moderate-income persons, the removal of slum and blight, and urgent need. Further, they prioritized proposals prepared by non-governmental or non-profit organizations, local governments, or governmental entities who presented community-driven projects that integrated the needs, desires, and resources of the residents in the reconstruction process.

South Carolina's CDBG-DR Governance after 2015 Hurricane Joaquin

The situation in South Carolina is quite different. In response to the flooding events caused by Hurricane Joaquin, in addition to the State of South Carolina, Richland County, Lexington County, and the City of Columbia are all direct recipients of CDBG-DR allocations. That is, within one state, there are four different grantees: the state and three UGLGs. This case of multiple grantees within one State is enabled by the Disaster Relief Appropriations Act of 2016 (Pub. L. 114-113, approved December 18, 2015).

HUD allocated $126.7 million in CDBG-DR funds to the State, $23.5 million to Richland County, $16.3 million to Lexington County, and $20 million to the City of Columbia. Each grantee has the responsibility of developing its own action plan and implementing their programs within their administrative boundary limits without overlapping. Stakeholders across all four jurisdictions attributed this to (a) the fact that Richland County, Lexington County, and the City of Columbia are all HUD Entitlement Communities that already had programs to manage CDBG, HOME, and Emergency Solutions Grants funds, and, more important, (b) political leadership, referring to political maneuvers of government officials and the congressional representative of those communities.

At the state level, South Carolina implemented a hybrid CDBG-DR governance model, including partnerships with nonprofit organizations and a method of distribution to prioritize the most affected areas outside Richland and Lexington. Also, they developed a nonprofit recovery fund—One SC Fund—to support nonprofit organizations providing relief and recovery assistance. Both Richland and Lexington adopted a direct implementation model, while the City of Columbia developed a hybrid approach, combining the partnerships model with a method of distribution through a competitive request for applications (RFA) process.

The approval of UGLGs in South Carolina resulted in new spaces and opportunities for local nonprofit and community organizations to get involved in rebuilding efforts. According to representatives of SBP, a 501 (c)3 nonprofit organization dedicated to disaster recovery in multiple states (including South Carolina), "when local governments have authority over housing recovery efforts within their jurisdiction, community development corporations (CDCs) and other nonprofit housing developers have greater access to official recovery planning processes and federal grants" (Interview with author, 25 October 2019).

Florida's CDBG-DR Governance after 2017 Hurricane Irma

Following Hurricane Irma, the State of Florida—as the sole grantee of CDBG-DR allocations—appointed the Department of Economic Opportunity (DEO) to develop the state action plan to administer the funds. The DEO established a governance model developing a method of distribution considering regional differentiation. Among the elements considered to determine regional differentiation were the level of impact of the hurricane, unmet urgent needs, and the geographic and socio-economic characteristics of the region. In total, three classifications for regional differentiation were established: (1) Monroe County, (2) Statewide, and (3) Smaller Developments. Once these classes were determined, the DEO developed specialized RFAs that established the entities that may participate in their different recovery programs and the mechanisms available for each one. The Statewide RFA targets more affluent impacted counties and requesting entities must combine CDBG-DR funds with Tax-Exempt Multifamily Mortgage Revenue Bonds (MMRB) and Non-Competitive Housing Credits. The Smaller Developments RFA targets less affluent impacted counties and requesting entities will receive increased support through CDBG-DR funds and capacity-building programs.

Approximately 69 percent of all CDBG-DR allocations were destined for housing recovery programs. The State's Action Plan divides their housing recovery budget into three programs: (a) Housing Repair and Replacement, organized with a direct implementation model, (b) Workforce Affordable Housing Construction, developed and implemented in partnership with the Florida Housing Finance Corporation (FHFC), and (c) Voluntary Home Buyout, with a method of distribution through subrecipient agreements to UGLGs designated as most impacted and distressed areas.

Regarding the Workforce Affordable Housing Construction Program, DEO and FHFC will provide two different funding mechanisms. The first mechanism includes leveraging CDBG-DR funds with other sources of funding, such as Low-Income Housing Tax Credits and Tax-Exempt Bond Financing, among others. The second mechanism is to utilize stand-alone CDBG-DR funds to provide zero-interest loans to create smaller, new multi-family developments. Both of these mechanisms are designed considering differentiation between counties, particularly the extent and character of unmet needs, county's capacity and assets. Further, both of these mechanisms provide spaces and opportunities for nonprofit housing developers, CDCs, and for joint ventures between for-profit and nonprofit community land trusts.

Texas CDBG-DR Governance after 2017 Hurricane Harvey

Following the 2017 Hurricane Harvey, the Governor of Texas recruited the Texas A&M University System's Chancellor and former State Comptroller John Sharp to lead the disaster recovery efforts and put together the state plans required by the NDRF. Within ten weeks of Hurricane Harvey, Chancellor Sharp and his team compiled a comprehensive flood infrastructure mitigation plan that requested $61 billions of federal aid to address related damages and needs (Sharp 2017).

To secure HUD's CDBG-DR funds, the Texas General Land Office (GLO), which has experience administering CDBG-DR funds since 2011, developed the State of Texas Plan for Disaster Recovery: Hurricane Harvey – Round 1 CDBG-DR Action Plan. This plan identified Harris County as a "most impacted and distressed" area and was allocated by the State, along with the City of Houston, a direct allocation from the State's CDBG-DR $5.024 billion allocation. Both Harris County and the City of Houston elected to develop their own local recovery programs, which required them to develop supplemental action plans to be submitted as a substantial amendment under the State of Texas Action Plan. As a result, the State Action Plan provided a three-way division of the non-administrative funds: $1.156 billion going to Harris County plan, $1.156 billion going to the City of Houston, and $2.51 billion staying with GLO for distribution to the rest of the state (Campbell 2018).

The primary goal of the Harris County Supplemental Action Plan was to give their residents opportunities to get involved in the recovery process as it pertains to CDBG-DR funds. This effort provides an ease of access to vulnerable populations. The plan focuses on housing recovery, combining, among other things, (a) the rehabilitation and reconstruction of public housing, affordable housing and other forms of assisted housing (e.g., Section 8 Housing Choice Voucher Program), (b) housing for vulnerable populations (e.g., housing for homeless and those at-risk of homelessness, etc.), and (c) strategies to minimize displacement.

ANALYSIS

Planning practitioners, academics, advocacy groups, and community leaders in Puerto Rico have consistently raised flags during the CDBG-DR action planning process regarding insufficient opportunities for community involvement, inequitable allocation of funds, and unjust outcomes resulting from recovery programs that fail to recognize regional differentiation and might force the displacement of disadvantaged populations. These con-

Table 2. Summary of CDBG-DR governance in five U.S. jurisdictions.

U.S. Jurisdiction	CDBG-DR governance model	Key insights
Louisiana (post-Hurricanes Gustav and Ike, 2008)	Subrecipient agreements with UGLGs and a method of distribution through RFPs	Provides direct allocations to local governments, giving deference to local knowledge and allowing them to design and run their own programs.
South Carolina (post-Hurricane Joaquin, 2015)	State: Partnerships and subrecipient agreements; Counties: Direct implementation; City of Columbia: Partnerships and a method of distribution through RFPs	In addition to the state, UGLGs act as grantees of federal appropriations. CDBG-DR governance is based on partnerships with nonprofit housing developers and community development corporations for housing recovery.
Florida (post-Hurricane Irma, 2017)	Partnerships and State-managed recovery with regional differentiation through RFPs.	This approach is rooted on joint ventures and partnerships between government agencies, for-profit and nonprofit organizations. Policy is attentive to different constituencies, necessities, and regional characteristics.
Texas (post-Hurricane Harvey, 2017)	Supplemental action planning.	Decentralized governance. Prioritizes most affected areas and redistributes resources from the state to county and city levels.
Puerto Rico (post-Hurricane María, 2017)	Centralized, top-down administration with private contractors and subrecipients.	Central action plan with external contractors performing specific policy design and implementation functions.

cerns and issues are tied to Puerto Rico's CDBG-DR governance model. As mentioned earlier, Puerto Rico's centralized, top-down approach limits the spaces and opportunities for community participation and consensus building. Also, since no efforts have been done to prioritize the most impacted and distressed areas, Vivienda imposes uniformity in program design, limiting regional or jurisdictional differences across the archipelago.

Applying a policy assemblage framework to this analysis helps direct our attention away from theoretical abstractions and ideal types, which are rife in political science and public policy studies, toward more materialist, relational, and bottom-up orientations in an effort to better understand the tangible stuff around HUD's CDBG-DR funds. It is true that post-disaster recovery planning across the U.S. has been fundamentally centralized at the federal and state level, largely driven by federal policies and funding allocations. This indeed tends to push states toward more centralized CDBG-DR governance models. Yet, after taking a closer look at how other U.S. jurisdictions assemble their CDBG-DR governance model, we can identify policy options still available for Puerto Rico.

But leadership should not be confused with centralized technocratic management.

Stakeholders across jurisdictions with knowledge on the field of hazard mitigation and disaster recovery action planning point to effective political and civil service leadership, as well as the exercise of bureaucratic discretion, in the interpretation of the federal rules and regulations for the use of CDBG-DR funds. But leadership should not be confused with centralized technocratic management. Excessive top-down control can render recovery programs overly rigid and exclude the local actors who better understand regional and local particulars that impact implementation (Jerolleman 2019).

Professional and advocacy groups like the Hispanic Federation, Legal Aid Puerto Rico, Puerto Rican Planning Society, Planners for Puerto Rico, and others have advocated for the creation of a multi-sectoral coalition of community leaders, private, and third-sector organizations, civil service, and government officials to design Puerto Rico's recovery agenda and define priorities for long-term recovery. To some extent, this might approximate

LRA's board and the task forces created to develop policy recommendations for a host of recovery issues. But there are also other approaches to CDBG-DR governance still available that might help increase community involvement and result in more equitable programs.

Policy options based on more decentralized and inclusive models for implementing recovery programs include partnerships with nonprofit organizations and methods of distribution through RFPs and RFAs rooted in joint ventures. For a more equitable housing and economic recovery, federal guidelines allow methods of distribution that prioritize the most affected areas and that take into consideration regional differentiation. Also, efforts that prioritize local needs by empowering local stakeholders in CDBG-DR action planning are more prone to result in more inclusive and equitable recovery processes. This could be through supplemental action planning agreements or subrecipient agreements with UGLGs that provide direct allocations for disaster recovery action planning.

A common pathway toward a more inclusive and equitable recovery process is building local capacity, focusing on empowering networks of civic sector organizations and local governments. Current policies and regulations do include provisions that, when enforced, can provide opportunities for this. Programs aimed at developing comprehensive community planning can serve to enhance participatory access, particularly where decisions regarding allocations of assistance and future development are concerned. One example of this is the Louisiana's Strategic Adaptations for Future Environments (LA SAFE) initiative, which was created and implemented as a joint venture between the State of Louisiana and the Foundation for Louisiana. LA SAFE is a statewide resilience policy framework focused on "helping communities plan for—and implement—safer, stronger, and smarter development strategies." Similarly, South Carolina developed the One SC Fund to support nonprofit organizations providing relief and recovery assistance.

To correct these trends, political, civil service, and the civic sector leadership can develop programs and initiatives that allow the civic sector to stay involved for long-term recovery.

It is broadly known that local governments and civic sector organizations play an important role after great disasters, providing spaces and opportunities for recovery to those most vulnerable (Contreras 2016; Khazai et al. 2006; Patterson, Weil and Patel 2010). However, as jurisdictions transition to long-term recovery, and most institutional efforts concentrate around CDBG-DR funds, much of the planning, design, engineering, and reconstruction work that state and municipal governments are required to do gets done by private consulting and construction firms. As a result, local communities lose spaces for active involvement, and nonprofits are held back providing social services and assistance, lacking the resources to sustain operations without financial assistance.

To correct these trends, political, civil service, and the civic sector leadership can develop programs and initiatives that allow the civic sector to stay involved for long-term recovery. The State of Florida, for example, does this through RFPs requiring joint ventures between for profit and nonprofit organizations, and through their partnership with the Florida Housing Finance Corporation. In the City of New Orleans, the Greater New Orleans Housing Alliance, a collaborative of home builders and community development organizations advocating for the preservation and production of affordable housing, developed the HousingNOLA 10-year Strategy and Implementation Plan. The implementation of this plan is funded by the Convergence Partnership, the City of New Orleans' Network for Economic Opportunity, the Ford Foundation, the Greater New Orleans Foundation's Metropolitan Opportunities Initiative, JPMorgan Chase Foundation, Surdna Foundation, and W.K. Kellogg Foundation (Greater New Orleans Housing Alliance 2015).

The Puerto Rico CDBG-DR Action Plan has two programs that, although largely centralized, might still provide opportunities to empower local networks. One is the Municipal Recovery Planning (MRP) Program with an allocation of $39 million that will be distributed across the 78 municipalities. Grants will be awarded to local municipalities through subrecipient agreements, and the amount of those grants will be determined by an award formula, which will consider factors including municipal population, land area, coastline length, area covered by water, and assessed damages data. The other program is the Whole Community Resiliency Planning (WCRP) Program with an allocation of $55 million. This program is managed by Foundation for Puerto Rico (FPR) by means of a subrecipient agreement with Vivienda. The goal of the program is to develop "comprehensive community recovery plans," which could allow communities to develop policies, planning, and management capacity that best meet their needs (García, Olshansky and Carrasquillo 2019).

Both of these programs—MRP and WCRP—present potential opportunities for local involvement and capacity-building. The extent to which they complement or contradict each other remains to be seen. The extent to which they harness local knowledge to enable networks that build capacity for community and economic development also remains to be seen. Further, the extent to which these efforts lead to the implementation of community developed projects, and the extent to which Vivienda will secure CDBG-MIT funds to support these efforts also remains unknown. Finally, the extent to which these programs relate to FEMA's municipal hazard mitigation planning program is still unclear, although professional groups state that so far "there is great disconnection" (Interview, Puerto Rican Planning Society, 6 June 2019).

Conclusion: Towards a Just Recovery

CDBG-DR regulations allows for a certain measure of discretion and interpretation that the Government of Puerto Rico can elect to exercise or not in order to develop more equitable programs aimed at producing a better and more just recovery. More decentralized, inclusive, and equitable CDBG-DR governance models provide greater spaces and opportunities for local involvement and are more prone to prioritize real and timely participation, the right to safe housing, and mitigation strategies that minimize displacements. Conversely, the lack of equitable access to resources and programs—including full participation in decision-making processes that govern resource allocation, future development, and other functions—hinders recovery.

To date, institutional recovery processes in Puerto Rico have demonstrated a lack of leadership, financial mismanagement, and corruption. Also, long-held local top-down management attitudes and mistrust from the White House and the U.S. Congress have shaped how local actors interact with federal policies, sometimes even subverting policy aims. In response, this paper constitutes a call to action, asking policy makers, government officials, nonprofit professional and community organizations, and other interested parties, such as diasporic communities who might have greater influence on Congress than local communities in Puerto Rico, to take a closer look at the policy options available for CDBG-DR governance and amend the current recovery trajectory. The pursuit of a more just recovery requires a strong push from multi-sectorial fronts and at various entry points in this recovery process: "from the congressional level, where recovery funds are appropriated, to agencies that establish the primary use of these funds and disbursement criteria, to the local project level" (Meléndez 2018).

Approaching these issues through a policy assemblage framework opens the door for us to see the role of various actors and agents at different levels of government and across different sectors of society in creating conditions of possibility for certain policy arrangements to emerge. Also, this framework sheds light on how the relationships between the agents and other policy components are contingent rather than fixed. As such, this paper invites all readers to pay strong attention to politics and the relative capacities of individuals and organizations to exercise agency in relation to both the creation of policy and its enactments.

The maneuvers referenced in this study are by no means easy to implement and might require significant structural and programmatic changes to the ways that disaster recovery is managed and resourced. The decision is not whether to change or not—the fact or reality is that change is inevitable. The decision is how to change in a manner that is equitable and that leads to a just recovery. The cases examined here show that incremental changes are possible; however, awareness and coalition building are crucial first steps toward the design and implementation of more inclusive and equitable policies. Further, what cannot be immediately changed, can be brought to light—and casting such a light on policy failures in clear and descriptive terms is a necessary precursor to change.

ACKNOWLEDGEMENTS
I am thankful to the Center for Puerto Rican Studies (Centro) for their financial support of the research described here. I also appreciate all the invaluable comments and suggestions from anonymous referees and other colleagues.

NOTES
[1] By the time this paper was published the DRAP Amendment Five had been approved with some substantial changes.

REFERENCES
Baker, Tom and Pauline McGuirk. 2016. Assemblage thinking as methodology: Commitments and practices for critical policy research. *Territory, Politics, Governance* 5(4), 425–42.

Campbell, Augustus. 2019. After the Storm: Understanding and Improving U.S. and Texas Disaster Recovery and Hazard Mitigation Policies. *Texas A&M Journal of Property Law* 5(2), 107–37.

City of Columbia. 2019. Action Plan Amendment Number 5. 2019. Accessed 24 May 2020. <https://dr.columbiasc.gov/wp-content/uploads/2019/10/CDBG-DR-SAPA-5.pdf/>.

Congress of the United States. 2019. PRDOH R3 Program Letter. Accessed 24 May 2020. <https://naturalresources.house.gov/imo/media/doc/PRDOH%20 R3%20Program%20Letter.pdf/>.

Contreras, Santina. 2016. Organizations and Participatory Development: Post-Disaster Recovery in Haiti. Ph.D. dissertation, University of California, Irvine.

Currie, Chris. 2019. Emergency Management: FEMA Has Made Progress, but Challenges and Future Risks Highlight Imperative for Further Improvements, Statement of Chris Currie, Director, Homeland Security and Justice, Testimony Before the Committee on Homeland Security, House of Representatives. In United States. Government Accountability Office, no. GAO-19-594T. United States. Government Accountability Office.

Federal Emergency Management Agency. 2016. National Disaster Recovery Framework. Accessed 24 May 2020. <https://www.fema.gov/media-library-dat a/14660149981234bec8550930f774269e0c5968b120ba2/National_Disaster_Recovery_Framework2nd.pdf/>.

_____. 2018. 2017 Hurricane season FEMA after-action report. Accessed 24 May 2020. <https://www.fema.gov/media-library-data/1531743865541-d16794d 43d3082544435e1471da07880/2017FEMAHurricaneAAR.pdf/>.

Fink, Sheri. 2018. Nearly a Year After Hurricane Maria, Puerto Rico Revises Death Toll to 2,975. *The New York Times* 28 August.

Flavelle, Christopher, Naureen Malik and Michael Smith. 2017. FEMA Probings $300 Million No Bid Contract for Puerto Rico Grid. *Bloomberg* 26 October.

Florida Department of Economic Opportunity 2020. State of Florida Action Plan for Disaster Recovery – Amendments 1 - 7. Accessed 11 April 2020. <https:// floridajobs.org/docs/default-source/office-of-disaster-recovery/hurricane-irma/action-plan---current-full-document/state-of-florida-action-plan-irma-final-1-16-20-english.pdf?sfvrsn=f52c40b0_2/>.

García, Ivis. 2019. Four plans for shaping the future of Puerto Rico. Accessed 24 May
      2020. <https://www.planning.org/blog/blogpost/9170787/?fbclid=IwAR20
      Oc4lbQE6V9l4fvnGq2_varEfS8O5Hp_EWYcR4ui6FOP77KTyzWJ78HE/>.
García, Ivis, Robert Olshansky and David Carrasquillo. 2019. Puerto Rico lurches to-
      ward recovery: Two years after Hurricane María a bottom-up community
      planning initiative is under way. *Planning* (August/September). <https://
      www.planning.org/planning/2019/aug/puertoricorecovery/>.
Greater New Orleans Housing Alliance. 2015. HousingNOLA 10 Year Strategy and
      Implementation Plan. Accessed 24 May 2020. <http://flux.modiphy.com/
      files/view/14208/>.
Jerolleman Alessandra. 2019. *Public Policy and Legislation. In: Disaster Recovery
      Through the Lens of Justice.* Cham, Switzerland: Palgrave Pivot.
Johnson, Laurie and Robert Olshansky. 2017. *After Great Disasters: An In-Depth
      Analysis of How Six Countries Managed Community Recovery.* Cambridge,
      MA: Lincoln Institute of Land Policy.
Khazai, Bijan, Guillermo Franco, J. Carter Ingram, Cristina Rumbaitis del Rio,
      Priyan Dias, Ranjith Dissanayake, Ravihansa Chandratilake and S. Jothy
      Kanna. 2006. Post-December 2004 Tsunami Reconstruction in Sri Lanka
      and its Potential Impacts on Future Vulnerability. *Earthquake Spectra*
      22(3), 829–44.
Kishore, Nishant, Domingo Marqués, Ayesha Mahmud, Mathew V. Kiang, Irmary
      Rodriguez, Arlan Fuller, Peggy Ebner, et al. 2018. Mortality in Puerto Rico
      after Hurricane Maria. *New England Journal of Medicine* 379(2), 162–70.
Lamba-Nieves, Deepak and Raúl Santiago. 2018. Transforming the recovery into
      locally-led growth: federal contracting in the post-disaster period. Center
      for the New Economy 26 September. Accessed 24 May 2020. <https://gru-
      pocne.org/wp-content/uploads/2018/09/Federal_Contracts_FINAL_with-
      cover-1.pdf/>.
Legal Aid Puerto Rico. 2019. Towards a just recovery: Recommendations to
      guarantee the right to housing in reconstruction after disasters. Ac-
      cessed 21 May 2020. <https://www.ayudalegalpuertorico.org/wp-con-
      tent/uploads/2019/06/JUST-RECOVERY-REPORT-JUNE-2019-ENG-
      Flattened.pdf/>.
Li, Tania M. 2007. Practices of Assemblage and Community Forest Management.
      Economy and Society 36(2), 263–93.
Louisiana Recovery Authority. 2010. Louisiana Recovery Authority, 2005 – 2010. Ac-
      cessed 15 January 2020. <http://lra.louisiana.gov/assets/docs/searchable/
      Quarterly%20Reports/FinalReportJune2010.pdf/>.
Meléndez, Edwin. 2018. Rebuild Puerto Rico: A Guide to Federal Policy and Ad-
      vocacy. Centro PB2018-02 October. Accessed 15 January 2020. <https://
      centropr.hunter.cuny.edu/sites/default/files/data_briefs/CENTRO_POLI-
      CYGUIDE_PB2018-02.pdf/>.
Molinari, Sarah. 2019. Authenticating Loss and Contesting Recovery: FEMA and
      the Politics of Colonial Disaster Management. In *Aftershocks of Disaster:
      Puerto Rico Before and After the Storm*, eds. Yarimar Bonilla and Marisol
      LeBrón. Chicago: Haymarket Press.

Patterson, Olivia, Frederick Weil and Kavita Patel. 2010. The Role of Community in Disaster Response: Conceptual Models. *Population Research and Policy Review* 29 (2), 127–41.

Porter, Libby. 2018. Postcolonial Consequences and New Meanings. In *The Routledge Handbook of Planning Theory*, eds. Michael Gunder, Ali Madanipur and Vanessa Watson. 167–79. New York: Routledge.

Puerto Rico Department of Housing. 2020. Puerto Rico Disaster Recovery Action Plan: Amendment Four. Accessed 24 May 2020. <https://www.cdbg-dr.pr.gov/en/download/action-plan-amendment-4-substantial-amendment/?ind=1585673841712&filename=Action%20Plan%20Amendment%204_Substantial_EN.pdf&wpdmdl=9145&refresh=5ec7e18e6da101590157710/>.

Sharp, John. 2017. Rebuild Texas: Request for Federal assistance Critical Infrastructure Projects. Accessed 21 May 2020. <www.houstontx.gov/postharvey/public/documents/10.31.2017_rebuild_texas.pdf/>.

South Carolina Disaster Recovery Office. 2019. South Carolina Action Plan for Disaster Recovery Amendment 8. Accessed 19 May 2020. <https://scstorm-recovery.com/wp-content/uploads/2019/07/SC-Severe-Storm-Amendment-8-6-26-19.pdf/>.

Texas General Land Office. 2019. State of Texas Plan for Disaster Recovery: Amendment 4. Accessed 19 May 2020. <https://recovery.texas.gov/files/hud-requirements-reports/hurricane-harvey/5b-apa4.pdf/>.

Torruella, Juan R. 2017. To Be or Not to Be: Puerto Ricans and Their Illusory U.S. Citizenship. *CENTRO: Journal of the Center for Puerto Rican Studies* 29(1), 108–35.

U.S. Department of Housing and Urban Development. 2019. CDBG-DR Policy Guide for Grantees. Accessed 19 May 2020. <https://files.hudexchange.info/resources/documents/CDBG-DR-Policy-Guide.pdf/>.

"Se conoce que usted es 'Moderna'": lecturas de la mujer moderna en la colonia hispana de Nueva York (1920-1940)

By María Teresa Vera-Rojas
Madrid and Frankfurt: Iberoamericana Vervuert, 2018
ISBN: 978-8491920038
390 pages; $37.00 [paper]

REVIEWED BY: Edna Acosta-Belén (eacosta-belen@albany.edu), University at Albany, SUNY

Scholarship on the history and evolution of the Puerto Rican and other Latino/a communities in New York City has expanded significantly, spanning over half a century since the emergence of Puerto Rican and Chicano/a studies, feminist/women/gender studies, and other interdisciplinary fields of academic inquiry. However, considering the vigorous levels of scholarship in these fields since their inception in the early 1970s, there are still a few important historical sources that have not received the proper attention they deserve. Foremost is New York's Spanish-language press during the first half of the twentieth century. A rich legacy of newspapers, magazines, journals, newsletters, and other periodical publications still remains largely untapped despite their unquestionable usefulness in revealing the issues, activities, conditions, and ideological positions that surrounded the daily lives of the various Latina/o groups in the city, and the wide range of female and male voices, their experiences, and subjectivities from a distant past. Among the best-known and long-lasting New York periodicals are *La Prensa* (1913-1963; and subsequently and to this day, *El Diario/La Prensa*), *Gráfico* (1927-1931), and *Artes y letras* (1933-1945)—all primary sources for María Teresa Vera-Rojas' comprehensive study, *"Se conoce que usted es 'Moderna'": lecturas de la mujer moderna en la colonia hispana de Nueva York (1920-1940)*. Compared to the other two periodicals, the daily *La Prensa* had a wider circulation and a bigger investment capital base, and was more connected to the media technologies of mass communications and advertising of the period. The last two publications were of a much smaller scale. *Gráfico* aimed primarily at a working class community audience, and *Artes y Letras* at a more professional readership interested in literary and artistic expressions. Both are also closely associated with their editors: *Gráfico,* with Puerto Rican journalist, community activist, and cigar roller Bernardo Vega (1885-1965), who bought and edited the paper from 1928-1929; and *Artes y Letras,* with its Puerto Rican feminist founder, editor, and writer Josefina Silva de Cintrón (1895-1986).

Initial efforts to rescue Spanish-language periodicals from oblivion were propelled by the launch of the *Recovering the Hispanic Literary Heritage of the United States* project in 1992, headed by Puerto Rican scholar Nicolás Kanellos at the University of Houston. The project's success in identifying and recovering an impressive number of these publications in New York City and throughout the United States (see Kanellos 2011; Kanellos and Martell 2000) inspired Vera-Rojas and a few other scholars to engage in the rescue and critical analysis of the journalistic and creative writings of some of the most prolific authors of the city's *colonia hispana* published in these periodicals (see Acosta-Belén 1993; Colón 1993, 2001; Colón López 2002). Among Vera-Rojas' earlier publications were a series of scholarly articles rescuing, contextualizing, and analyzing the journalistic writings of a few of the most prolific women contributors to some of these periodicals. The author's initial interest in their writings began with her doctoral dissertation at the University of Houston, which collected and analyzed the scattered journalistic writings of Clotilde Betances Jaeger (1890-187?), grandniece of the nineteenth century Puerto Rican patriot Ramón Emeterio Betances, and a frequent contributor to the aforementioned and several other Spanish-language newspapers of the 1920s and '30s. In subsequent published work, Vera-Rojas also brought to public light the writings of another Puerto Rican woman regularly writing for the Spanish-language press, María Mas Pozo (1893-1981?), who besides her journalistic writings in these newspapers, also contributed as a reader submitting several letters of opinion to the "De nuestros lectores" section of *La Prensa* (see Vera-Rojas 2014, 2011-2012, 2010). Some of the most memorable journalistic writings of these two women are their published debates in the column "Charlas Femeninas" of *Gráfico* in 1929 (April 13, 20, May 18, June 8, 15, 22,), which addressed their different positions on and meanings of what constitutes being a "mujer moderna" or a "Mujer Nueva" within the context of their specific geographic and cultural locations, and undergoing rapid and dramatic social transformations occurring in the modern cosmopolitan milieu of New York City during the post-World War I, Roaring Twenties era.

Both women journalists reappear in Vera-Rojas's new book—an insightful, well-documented exhaustive theoretical analysis of the extent to which discourses and visual representations of the modern or new woman introduced and propagated in the Anglo-American mainstream press and other media (i.e., Hollywood films, radio broadcasting). Generally embodied by the paradigmatic "flapper" female, these discussions of the contemporary woman of the time were also reproduced in the Spanish-language periodicals selected for her study. By extracting from the aforementioned newspapers, articles written by women journalists and those taken from regular columns and pages targeted to a female audience (e.g., "Charlas Femeninas" in *Gráfico;* "Para la mujer" in *La Prensa*), along with letters from women readers, photographs and other illustrations, and advertisements, the author appraises the influence of heavily publicized Anglo-American representations and paradigms of beauty, fashion, and behaviors of the modern woman on "las mujeres de la colonia hispana," in order to analyze the process and forms of subjectivitization that intervene in the experiences of femininity of these readers. Vera-Rojas skillfully and at length shows that as readers of these publications and responders to the content of the frequent articles and columns aimed at a female audience, these women's subjectivities reveal "la conjunción, reapropiación y resignificación" (p. 17) of broadly circulated paradigms and representations of femininity and the modern woman in mainstream U.S. society, and their negotiations with the norms, traditions, and restrictions exerted by their own cultures and communities.

During the period at hand, dominant discourses, representations, and paradigms of what it means to be a modern woman were circulated by consumer and marketing patterns and strategies of the mainstream English-language press and other prevailing media of the period. These ideas and images were also partially reproduced in the Spanish-language press, both visually and discursively to women consumers through targeted advertisement and columns or pages focused on women's beauty, fashion, products related to health and hygiene, and new technologies to improve housework, women's bodies and physical appearance. The author considers as well as the content of letters these women readers sent to these newspapers, and the journalistic articles written by regular women contributors to the three selected newspapers. This occurred in part as a response to the need of these community newspapers, especially the smaller ones, to acknowledge the "modernizing trends" of the times and appeal to a larger number of readers within the "colonia hispana," but also to increase their own advertising revenue by opening their pages to U.S. companies and businesses seeking to promote their products and further boost their profit margins by extending their marketing efforts to the city's various ethnic communities.

Veras-Rojas' new book both reflects more recent research interests on new and dissident subjectivities and sexualities that challenge binary constructs of women's representations, identities, and discourses about femininity and feminism, while giving continuity to her earlier scholarly interests in women's writings in the Spanish-language press. This latest study stands out first, for making an important contribution to what is still a scarcity of research on the lives, experiences, and subjectivities of "las mujeres de la colonia hispana" (at the time, mostly Puerto Rican women, followed by a visible presence of Spanish and Cuban women and a smaller sector of women from a wide range of other Latin American/Caribbean nationalities) during the first three decades of the twentieth century; and, second, for its solid theoretical framing and incisive and sound critical analysis to demonstrate that the subjectivities and identities of these women were far from being monolithic. On the contrary, through the various chapter discussions, the author makes frequent theoretical detours to remind readers of the heterogeneous, contradictory, and intrinsically complex nature behind the constructions of identities and processes and forms of subjectivization. Some of these contradictions are exposed by the numerous discursive and visual examples she carefully extracts from the three selected newspapers. These include articles written by women (and a few men) authors on issues of femininity and feminism, the nature and character of women, their role in the public and private spheres, women's individual freedom and various social and cultural constraints, and being members of society at a time of significant modern transformations but, when compared to men, still subjects of unequal treatment and limited rights in multiple areas.

The sequence of the various book chapters begins with intricate theoretical expositions about the presence of women in newspapers, as writers, readers, and subjects, with numerous references to the cultural and gender studies literature dealing with the power and control of the mass media industry in a consumer society such as the United States, in regulating and marketing the construction of women identities and bodies, and in circulating imaginaries and paradigms of the "modern woman." These theoretical interventions are a prelude to formulating and contextualizing the particular actual "experiencias de modernidad y subjetivación de las mujeres hispanas." Chapter Two shifts the focus to the readings and readers unearthed from the three different Spanish-language periodicals; all claiming in some way to be "portavoces" of the concerns and cultures of "la raza" or "la colonia hispana." Of particular interest are the ways in which *Artes y Letras* manages to blend "feminismo, hispanismo, and ciudadanía" (p. 112), largely due to the feminist outlook of its prominent founder and editor, to become a defender of "la raza hispana," women's equality, and, as stated by the author, a more positive and strategic approach to "la liberación e identidad de la mujer moderna" (p. 112).

The first part of Vera-Rojas' book title ("Se conoce que usted es 'Moderna'") is explained at length in Chapter Three, "Imaginarios de la Mujer Moderna." The remark is part of a response to a question posed to Aimée, the woman in charge of the section "Consultorio de belleza" of the weekly *Gráfico* by one of her readers (published in the June 15, 1929 issue, page 10). As the title of Aimés's column indicates, this printed space was open to women readers to visit and consult by sending letters seeking advice or answers to their beauty-related inquiries and problems, which were then regularly answered in the newspaper. This particular reader wanted Aimée to tell her if there was a problem in changing the color of her face. The first part of the columnist's answer was the written interjection: "Su problema es muy nuevo y se conoce que usted es 'Moderna.'" Aimee's reaction to and implicit assumption about the reader's question, was that there was nothing wrong with wanting to darken your skin color, either by using natural sun rays or sun lamps at the beauty parlor (also an assumption of the reader's whiteness). Her response gave a seal of approval to this reader's potential transgression of old-fashioned norms of beauty and beautification practices, now being facilitated in modern society by new products and technologies (in this case, the sun lamp). Answering a different question from another reader worried about the propriety of not wearing stockings in the summer and thus being perceived as antisocial, Aimée, again, seizes the defiant women's spirit of the times: "No se preocupe del qué dirán. Sea una individua y no una esclava de la tradición" (pp. 151–2).

Both Chapters Three and Four follow a similar pattern of theoretical contextualizing and discerning analysis, this time focusing on the socioeconomic, political, and cultural transformations, and also the capitalist modernizing drive during the World War I postwar decades, after the achievement of women's suffrage validated more than seven decades of prior struggles for voting rights, more freedoms, and equal treatment. Suffrage increased women's visibility and participation in the nation's socioeconomic, political, and cultural life during this period. All of these rapid changes also led to new imaginaries about what it meant to be a modern woman in terms of beauty, fashion, behavior, and bodies, and the author deftly examines how these new imaginaries are regulated and controlled in a capitalist mass consumer culture. Vera-Rojas' theoretical incursions look at the way new technologies regulate and propagate norms of femininity and different aspects of women's corporal beauty (Chapter IV), and also promote consumption are of interest to specialists in these fields, even when occasionally they sidetrack readers from the main focus of her study—that is, to problematize the intricate forms of subjectivitization that intervene in the experiences of femininity of "las mujeres hispanas de la colonia," and the ways in which these women negotiate the ideas, representations, and paradigms of modern women in Anglo American society with the norms, traditions, and restrictions of their own native cultures and communities.

Cultural contradictions among "las mujeres de la colonia," about what it means to be a modern woman sharing two different cultural contexts, as well as their diverse positions on a variety of women-related issues, become more evident when Vera-Rojas focuses in Chapter Five on the content of Betances Jaeger and Mas Pozo debates, which discussed divergent views on women's newly acquired rights and freedoms, their roles in the domestic and public spheres, and as individuals and social actors subject to the traditions and values of their cultures and communities and the influences of mainstream U.S. society and the "American way of life." The two authors were central to the debates about the notions of "la Mujer Moderna" or "la

Mujer Nueva" because of their published debates and original articles about the role and rights of women in the domestic and public spheres, as read in *Gráfico* in 1929. There were obvious ideological differences and standpoints between the more progressive Betances Jaeger, a defender of equality between the sexes and individual freedom, and a more conservative Mas Pozo, who rejected the trivial aspects of modernity and the modern woman in US society and was critical of what she perceived as a frivolous obsession with beauty, fashion, and consumerist practices. At the same time, Mas Pozo was also subscribing to more traditional views of women's moral duties and role as protector of the family and household, and "suprema artista que modela las almas" (p. 301). Thus, these two women were also very much attuned to ongoing discussions about the changing roles of women during the post-World War I years and the multiple implications for the present and future of women, their families, their communities and nations, and, indeed, all of humanity in a changing world.

In the book's introduction, the author had initially addressed the importance of the widespread presence of the "flapper" in the pages of *Gráfico* as a paradigm of the modern woman. A more detailed discussion of this character is the focus of Chapter Six. Of particular interest is the section on the "flapper latina" and her subversive performances. This acculturated version of the "flapper" was heavily criticized by Jesús Colón and a few other male writers as an exaggerated and caricaturesque version of the Anglo-American original. Thus, the numerous visual representations and allusions to the "flapper" in *Gráfico* illustrate the contradictions between the defense of more traditional roles and values of "las mujeres de la colonia hispana" by some of the weekly's male editors and writers (such as Alberto O'Farril, Erasmo Vando, Bernardo Vega, and Jesús Colón), who were often critical of the values and behaviors of Anglo- American modern women, and their potential harmful influence on the community's women, while the newspaper itself repeatedly publicized these images.

The theoretical considerations that frame the analysis and argumentation in some parts of Chapters Five and Six cogently reveal the complex, contradictory, and fluid aspects of the discourses and representations that influence the formation of subjectivities and identities. Nonetheless, it was unfortunate that some of the numerous photographs and illustrations inserted in the various chapters were often too small in size and hard to fully appreciate, partly due to the less than adequate visual quality of the microfilm originals. It would have meant adding a few more pages to the book, but the publisher should have recognized the need to enlarge some of this visual material because of the overall importance and centrality of some of these images. In closing, Vera-Rojas demonstrates once more that the Spanish-language press represents an invaluable source for researchers. The media of the time enables us to grasp the wide range of issues, concerns, viewpoints, and numerous cultural, political, and social activities that engaged the early *colonias* and *barrios* built by Puerto Ricans and other Latina/o nationalities during their formative stages. Thus "las mujeres hispanas," as readers of Spanish-language newspapers, become modern consumers and negotiate, re-appropriate, or resignify hegemonic discourses or influences to "modernize" their personal appearance and domestic and social lives, or to become a modern woman. These social changes involve class, race, and ethnic considerations and distinctions that the author is quite cognizant of. In her concluding remarks, Vera-Rojas reminds readers that "pensar a las mujeres hispanas como sujetos modernos no [es] solo pensar la feminidad como una experiencia moderna, sino, sobretodo, inscribir la subjetividad de las inmigrantes hispanas como parte de los cambios y las experiencias que han dado forma a la modernidad" (p. 368).

Scattered, sometimes incomplete or blurred by the microfilming process or the poor quality of the original, and still mostly neglected, many of the columns, editorials, creative literature, photographs, cartoons, and ads in these periodicals, provide indispensable threads for weaving the story of individual and collective lives of the "colonia hispana" and its external interactions with the New York City environment, and the respective countries of origin of its diverse population at different historical moments. Drawing on a vast array of sources, with this study Vera-Rojas makes it clear, once again, that these periodicals are indispensable. They allow us to reconstruct and preserve a historical memory of the origins and evolution of the presence, productive lives, and experiences of Latinas/os in the United States and for assessing their import to their present and future conditions and challenges.

REFERENCES

Acosta-Belén, Edna. 1993. The Building of a Community: Puerto Rican Writers and Activists in New York City, 1890s-1960s. In *Recovering the U.S. Hispanic Literary Heritage*, eds. Ramón Gutiérrez and Genaro Padilla. 179–85. Houston: Arte Público Press.

Colón, Jesús. 1993. *The Way it Was and Other Writings*. Edited by Edna Acosta-Belén, and Virginia Sánchez Korrol. Houston: Arte Público Press.

_____. 2001. *Lo que el pueblo me dice...* Edited by Edwin Karli Padilla Aponte. Houston: Arte Público Press.

Colón López, Joaquín. 2002. *Pioneros puertorriqueños en Nueva York: 1917-1947*. Edited by Edwin Karli Padilla Aponte. Houston: Arte Público Press.

Flores, Juan, 1993. *Divided Borders: Essays on Puerto Rican Identity*. Houston: Arte Público Press.

Kanellos, Nicolás. 2011. *Hispanic Immigrant Literature: El sueño del retorno*. Austin: University of Texas Press.

_____ and Helvetia Martell. 2000. *Hispanic Periodicals in the United States: Origins to 1969. Brief History and Comprehensive Bibliography*. Houston: Arte Público Press.

Vera-Rojas, María Teresa. 2010. Polémicas feministas, puertorriqueñas y desconocidas; Clotilde Betances Jaeger y sus "Charlas femeninas" en el *Gráfico* de Nueva York (1928-1930). *CENTRO: Journal of the Center for Puerto Rican Studies* 22(2), 4–33.

_____. 2011-2012. Alianzas transgresoras: hispanismo, feminismo y cultura en *Artes y Letras. Latino(a) Research Review* 8(1-2), 175–98.

_____. 2014. Lecturas desde el margen: en torno a las cartas de María Mas Pozo en el diario *La Prensa* de Nueva York. *CENTRO: Journal of the Center for Puerto Rican Studies* 26(2), 80–109.

Tiempos binarios: La Guerra Fría desde Puerto Rico y el Caribe

Edited by Manuel R. Rodríguez Vázquez y Silvia Álvarez Curbelo
San Juan: Ediciones Callejón, 2017
ISBN: 978-1615052615
414 pages; $24.00 [paper]

REVIEWED BY: Pedro L. San Miguel (sanmiguelupr@gmail.com), Universidad de Puerto Rico (Profesor Jubilado)

"El siglo XX comenzó con la utopía futurista y terminó con la nostalgia". Con este epígrafe inicia Jorge Lizardi Pollock su colaboración en el libro colectivo *Tiempos binarios: La Guerra Fría desde Puerto Rico y el Caribe*. La nostalgia, por cierto, tiene múltiples expresiones en el mundo contemporáneo, entre ellas los incontables *remakes*, secuelas o precuelas de películas y obras literarias. Florece también en las propuestas intelectuales y, por supuesto, en las ideologías y los movimientos políticos. Para demostrarlo, basta con mencionar la propensión a enaltecer a ese Santiago Matamoros moderno que conminaba a sus seguidores a convertirse en "eficaces, violentos, selectivos y frías máquinas de matar" (Ernesto "Che" Guevara *dixit*). O quienes erigen como modelo a seguir a esa, sin duda, futurista "Revolución de Octubre" que terminó, no obstante, trocándose en uno de los totalitarismos más feroces de la historia. Corrientes como éstas se nutren de esa visión nostálgica invocada por Lizardi Pollock. Quizá sin ser consciente de ello, quienes la patrocinan terminan por suscribir esa lógica maniquea que marcó los "tiempos binarios" de la llamada Guerra Fría. Siguen siendo, pues, *cold warriors*, no *avant la lettre* sino después de finiquitado el acontecimiento.

El libro que comento parte, precisamente, de una postura crítica tanto de los sucesos que definieron la Guerra Fría como de las maneras de concebirla, estudiarla y representarla. Que esta obra esté cimentada sobre tales pilares no debe extrañarnos ya que sus editores, Silvia Álvarez Curbelo y Manuel Rodríguez Vázquez, son académicos notables; sobresalen, precisamente, por el aliento crítico que caracteriza sus indagaciones sobre el pasado. A ellos se han sumado investigadores que brindan una gama de análisis sobre los "tiempos binarios" de la Guerra Fría, teniendo como eje a Puerto Rico, si bien trazando líneas de conexión con el contexto más amplio de la región caribeña. Esto, de por sí, le confiere un valor agregado a este volumen, ya que contribuye a romper con los localismos que tradicionalmente han caracterizado a las investigaciones efectuadas en la mayoría de los países del Caribe.

En este comentario me concentraré en aquellos trabajos que, a mi entender, resultan particularmente iluminadores. Destaco, para empezar, la "Introducción" del volumen, sugerentemente titulada "Tiempos binarios: Miradas múltiples", rótulo que establece la pauta en la confección de la obra. Entre otras cosas, en este breve texto se hace un llamado a entablar un "diálogo entre las historiografías de Puerto Rico y Estados Unidos" (p. 9). Tal ha sido —me consta— uno de los objetivos centrales de la labor historiográfica de Rodríguez Vázquez. Continúan los editores requiriendo investigaciones sobre la Guerra Fría que trasciendan el mero estudio de sus expresiones más formales o más patentes, como las relaciones internacionales, de las cuales los conflictos diplomáticos o armados —que aunque Fría se denominó a la tal Guerra, la misma no careció de instancias muy ardientes— son manifestaciones. Otra importante aportación de esta "Introducción" estriba en señalar la relación entre el desarrollo de la Guerra Fría y la producción de los saberes, relación evidente en el uso de la caída del muro de Berlín como "metáfora del colapso de un sistema de saberes que sustentaba ideologías inmutables y prácticas de poder" (p. 14). La propuesta conceptual de los editores se sintetiza —en sus propias palabras— en "la necesidad de trascender la causalidad ideológica, el determinismo geoestratégico y el reduccionismo territorial" (p. 14), esto en función de recuperar la "complejidad e indefinición" de un proceso histórico que abarcó virtualmente a toda la humanidad.

El trabajo que inicia el volumen, "Un mundo perplejo: La discursiva del gobernador Luis Muñoz Marín en tiempos nucleares, 1946-1964", constituye una puesta en escena de las propuestas conceptuales indicadas. En su rastreo, su autora, Álvarez Curbelo, ofrece una imagen compleja del político puertorriqueño, históricamente denostado por una izquierda fundamentalista —puertorriqueña y latinoamericana— que, a mi juicio, posee una visión estereotipada y hasta pueril de Puerto Rico, su historia y su situación. Lejos de los binarismos que, por un lado, endiosan a Muñoz Marín, artífice de la transformación económico-social y política de Puerto Rico, o que, por otro lado, lo satanizan como un mero "títere del imperialismo americano", en este enjundioso texto, su autora identifica líneas de argumentación en el ideario del líder político, no sin dejar de señalar las tensiones en su discursiva. A todo esto subyacía un profundo temor "al eclipse de la civilización" debido a la bomba atómica. Tal parecer, por demás, estaba lejos de seguir al pie de la letra las prescripciones del poder político de Estados Unidos —como podrían pensar quienes ven en Muñoz Marín a un simple monigote gringo—; estaba, por el contrario, firmemente anclado en lo que eran sus concepciones acerca de la democracia y de la búsqueda de un sistema político y económico capaz de enfrentar las necesidades de las grandes masas de su país y, por extensión, de toda América Latina.

Que la Guerra Fría incidió directamente sobre la vida de los puertorriqueños, es el asunto que aborda Rodríguez Vázquez, el otro editor del libro, en su trabajo "Imaginar el desastre: Aprensiones nucleares, desvaríos radioactivos y Defensa Civil en Puerto Rico durante la Guerra Fría, 1960-1965". Recurriendo a conceptos como "Guerra Total", "utopía de la seguridad" e "imaginario de la catástrofe", el autor rastrea minuciosamente los esfuerzos de la Defensa Civil, entidad gubernamental que intentó difundir entre los puertorriqueños "una pedagogía del desastre" (p. 91), asociada a la "construcción de una ciudadanía que exigía compromiso y responsabilidad ante las amenazas de una guerra impredecible e incorpórea" (p. 104). Este texto —producto de una escrupulosa investigación y estructurado de manera ejemplar—, por otro lado, no deja de tener una dimensión irónica, perceptible en la contradicción entre ese esfuerzo por proteger a la población de un ataque nuclear y unas alternativas que, a todas luces, hubiesen resultado inútiles ante tal eventualidad.

Referido también al ámbito puertorriqueño, Lizardi Pollock, en "Daños colaterales: Utopía, ciudad y suburbio en tiempos de Guerra Fría (1942-1972)", indaga los imaginarios urbanistas durante tres décadas. Aquí también se percibe una gran ironía, patente en el hecho de que —en palabras del autor—, "entre los conflictos de la pasada centuria", fue la Guerra Fría "el que más extendió su presencia arquitectónica" (p. 209). Su presencia, no obstante, tuvo "mayor visibilidad y presencia en la arquitectura civil y doméstica que en la propiamente militar" (p. 210). Una de las vertientes de ello radicó en las disputas entre desarrolladores y constructores, por un lado, y aquellas entidades y funcionarios gubernamentales que aspiraban a establecer ciudades amables que tuvieran como fin esa "vida buena" que tanto pregonó

Luis Muñoz Marín. En ese escenario coludieron "el desarrollismo en manos privadas y los pulsos utópicos con su afán de un bien común fundado en la ciudad" (p. 233), ya que esto último implicaba un control estatal de recursos y una centralización en la planificación urbana, a lo que se oponían quienes apostaban por un urbanismo libre de tales trabas, por lo que atacaron los impulsos reformistas acusándolos de "comunistas". Trazar esta tensión constituye el hilo central del trabajo de Lizardi Pollock, texto que por momentos posee un dejo poético que le brinda un atractivo adicional.

En lo que a la isla de Puerto Rico se refiere, hay otros textos que por razones de espacio meramente gloso a paso acelerado. En "La criatura del mar encantado: Medios y mediaciones de la Guerra Fría en Puerto Rico, 1945-1950", Eliseo Colón Zayas discute el papel de los medios de comunicación en el surgimiento de un imaginario colectivo en torno al conflicto entre EEUU y la URSS —si bien me resulta difícil de percibir cómo la película *Ben Hur* (1959) mostraba, como alega este autor, "las virtudes de la religión bíblica como el núcleo del capitalismo y la democracia estadounidense" (p. 176). Por su parte, Malena Rodríguez Castro, en "Frías batallas, ardientes escaramuzas: Guerra y cultura en Puerto Rico", sondea la impronta de dicho conflicto en la vida cultural. Uno de los méritos de este trabajo es que evidencia lo difícil que resultaba para los intelectuales escapar a la dicotomía ideológica que implicaba dicha pugna; resultaba especialmente arduo a quienes intentaron trascenderla, planteando opciones culturales y políticas que quedaran fuera de los extremismos que ella suponía. Ubicada también en el ámbito cultural, Mara Pastor Rodríguez, en "Desorientes familiares: La Guerra de Vietnam en la poesía puertorriqueña del setenta", estudia este asunto en varios poetas, incluyendo tanto a figuras canónicas como a escritores menos conocidos. De este último conflicto se ocupa también Manuel A. Avilés-Santiago en "War! What it's good for? Absolutely nothing: Testimonios de soldados sobre la Guerra de Vietnam", que recurre a la historia oral con la intención de descifrar qué significó dicha experiencia para los puertorriqueños que combatieron en esa salvaje conflagración.

En lo que al ámbito caribeño respecta, Javier Figueroa de Cárdenas, en "Negociando el futuro: Cuba y Estados Unidos al finalizar la Segunda Guerra Mundial, 1944-1952", explora las relaciones entre estos dos países, resaltando las intrincadas negociaciones para ubicar el azúcar cubano en el mercado estadounidense. Y Carlos Altagracia Espada, en "«Un problema, un reto y una oportunidad»: Puerto Rico y la transición dictadura-democracia en la República Dominicana, 1961-1965", examina el papel del denominado "Grupo de Puerto Rico" —el gobernador Luis Muñoz Marín, el rector de la Universidad de Puerto Rico, Jaime Benítez, y el historiador y funcionario público Arturo Morales Carrión, entre otros— en la coyuntura crítica luego del ajusticiamiento del tirano Rafael L. Trujillo. Altagracia Espada muestra cómo el "Grupo de Puerto Rico" buscó afanosamente una salida política a dicha crisis, tratando de evitar una opción militar —que fue la que prevaleció—, lo que resultaría perjudicial tanto al modelo político-social impulsado por ese Grupo como a la proyección de Estados Unidos en toda América Latina. El resultado sería la anulación de una vía política que evitase los extremismos implicados por la Guerra Fría, vía que se conceptuaba entonces como Izquierda Democrática.

Como conclusión, sólo me resta invitar a acercarse a esta obra, que seguramente provocará interrogantes, polémicas y debates. Los editores y colaboradores de este volumen han contribuido al saber, que debe tener como objetivo central cuestionar la realidad. Y esto debe conllevar, en primer lugar, cuestionarnos a nosotros mismos y, por ende, cuestionar las maneras en que tratamos de comprender y dar sentido a dicha realidad.

Population, Migration, and Socioeconomic Outcomes Among Island and Mainland Puerto Ricans: La Crisis Boricua

By Marie T. Mora, Alberto Davila, and Havidan Rodriguez
Lanham: Lexington Books, 2018
ISBN: 978-1-4985-1686-0
242 pages; $95.00 [cloth] / $39.99 [paper]

REVIEWED BY: Maura I. Toro-Morn (mitmorn@ilstu.edu), Illinois State University

"La Crisis Boricua" is a central concept that organizes the empirical analysis of this new book by three well-known scholars in the fields of economics and sociology. The research team of Marie T. Mora, Alberto Davila, and Havidan Rodriguez offers readers an exhaustive and compelling analysis of the socio-economic problems facing Puerto Ricans in both the U.S. and Puerto Rico. They visited the Island as a research team, met with local scholars, and took lots of pictures (the pictures are identified and highlighted in Appendix C). Their analysis was done before Hurricanes Irma and Maria hit the Island, so the book opens with the author's addendum on Hurricane Maria. As they submitted the book to the publishers, they knew that "La Crisis Boricua showed no signs of relenting." Indeed, as the authors of this book anticipated and we all know by now: Hurricane Maria devastated Puerto Rico, making migration, yet again, as an important way of dealing with the immediate aftermath of the storm and beyond. As this book shows, before Hurricane Maria, migration was a safety valve for Puerto Ricans across social classes. A research brief from the Center for Puerto Rican Studies, written by Edwin Melendez and Jennifer Hinojosa, confirms that the impact of Hurricane Maria on population dynamics was unprecedented: they estimated that from 2017 to 2019, Puerto Rico nearly lost 14 percent of its residents. In other words, Puerto Rico lost the same population, in a span of a couple of years after Hurricane Maria, as the Island lost during a prior decade of economic stagnation (Meléndez and Hinijosa 2017).

In fact, Florida became the place of choice for those seeking temporary refuge from the storm. Today, we know that Florida has surpassed New York for the first time in history as the state with the largest concentration of

Puerto Ricans. I empathize with the authors in this respect because I was also writing about Puerto Rican migration to Illinois when hurricanes Irma and Maria hit the Island. We now have a new historical benchmark through which to understand a host of social, political, and economic issues. The migration of Puerto Ricans and its consequences matter to the authors of this book and this reviewer.

The empirical findings offered in this book are relevant now because they describe the constellation of factors that engulfed the Island prior to the hurricane season of 2017. In this respect, the book has much to offer. In the interest of self-disclosure, I must share that I had first seen their work when sociologist Williams Velez organized a group of us to present our work at the 2014 annual meeting of the Puerto Rican Studies Association, which took place in Denver. Some of the essays of that panel presentation were assembled for a special volume of the *Centro Journal,* published in 2017.

"La Crisis Boricua" is one of those terms that keeps gaining intellectual clarity as scholars construct and deconstruct it in the larger context of Puerto Rican history. We are clearly at a point in the scholarship about Puerto Rico where new benchmarks of analysis are emerging, making this new corpus of work all the more relevant and interesting. A new taxonomy of analysis may be evident here: La Crisis Boricua before Hurricane Maria; La Crisis Boricua after Hurricane Maria. For sure, "La Crisis Boricua" is a term that is here to stay. This is both a point of praise and criticism that I wish to address in this book review. Puerto Rican scholar Nelson Maldonado Torres (2019) invites scholars to think about the meaning of crisis, disaster, and catastrophe, words used frequently to describe the situation in Puerto Rico, a task I heed as I review this book.

What is La Crisis Boricua? For those of us interested in how intellectual work is produced, La Crisis Boricua is now a concept that keeps expanding as the situation in Puerto Rico worsens politically, economically, and now, we must add, environmentally. In fact, one must praise the authors because they have offered a very good overview of key issues that anchor La Crisis Boricua. For better or worse, the concept is now a convenient explanation for the social ills of the Island, its residents, and those in la Diaspora.

The book opens with an excellent historical overview, now customary for books about Puerto Rico and Puerto Ricans. The historical background offers readers an overview of the socio-historical location of Puerto Rico, first as a colony of Spain and now a colony of the U.S. One wonders when that kind of historical overview is no longer necessary to frame any writing about Puerto Rico. Given current events and how little Americans still know about Puerto Rico, such historical background continues to be needed. The historical overview covers the modernization program, and here the authors make an effort to address one of the gender dimensions of the economic development plan, namely, the sterilization of Puerto Rican women as a population control policy. The remainder of the chapter describes Puerto Rico's demographic transition through labor force participation rates, poverty, and mortality. Unfortunately, the discussion of labor force participation rates are not addressed by gender, thus missing a great opportunity to continue to drive the point that the development model was deeply gendered in execution, implementation, and consequences. (If they didn't want to crunch the numbers, there is really good work done by Puerto Rican feminists that would have been worth referencing here.)

Chapter Three, "The Year of the Perfect Storm and the Onset of La Crisis Boricua," addresses the constellation of factors shaping the unfolding of the crisis. They placed 2006 as a critical year to understand the developing crisis because that was the year in which Section 936 of the Internal Revenue Code expired. In other words, corporations were no longer exempted from paying corporate income taxes, an important underpinning of the much studied and debated development program Operation Bootstrap. This is also the year that the government imposed the "island's first sales tax on an increasingly economically disenfranchised population." Although the end of Section 936 did not happen overnight, the overall effect was the loss of jobs as corporations moved their operations to more attractive locations. As they put it, the corresponding loss in bank deposits, reduced access to credit among Island residents and businesses leading to debt defaults. In a span of a decade, the island's economy deteriorated significantly. The 2008 recession exacerbated social problems in Puerto Rico. A weakened labor market, higher unemployment rates, and declining labor force participation placed people in a lot of stress and pushed people to migrate. The next dimension of the crisis played out in the front pages of the *New York Times* as Puerto Rico tried to shake off recession problems, and years of mismanagement and poor decision making by local politicians finally caught up with them. The Puerto Rican government had amassed so much debt that it could not meet its financial obligations. Bankruptcy was not an option due to the status of the Island as a "territory." In 2016, President Obama signed into law the Puerto Rico Oversight, Managements and Economic Stability Act, Promesa, an acronym sadly lacking in meaning. As if these issues were not enough, Puerto Ricans also faced a significant loss of public sector jobs, escalating energy prices, and a severe housing market crisis.

To make matters even more complicated, a deteriorating health care industry stretched to its limits lost personnel in great numbers. Who is going to care for the health and well-being of Puerto Ricans, given the high levels of stress that poverty and unemployment produce? This was a pressing question then; is it still one today? The authors cite research conducted by the Puerto Rico College of Physicians and Surgeons, which shows that in 2016 the number of doctors in Puerto Rico declined by 36 percent, from 14,000 to 9,000. What happened to these doctors? They left the Island for better jobs in the U.S. In 2015, 500 physicians left Puerto Rico, a number up from 365 in 2014. Are local medical schools replenishing these doctors? Unfortunately, Puerto Rico is now facing what is known as the "graying of Puerto Rican doctors," a set of circumstances resuling in a smaller number of older doctors serving a larger share of patients. These doctors themselves are of retirement age. In the conclusion of the chapter about La Crisis Boricua, they authors note that the crisis exposed decades of unsustainable economic policies, mishandling of public funds, and the inability of government officials to secure Puerto Rico's future, underpinned by over a century of dependence on the United States.

The impact of La Crisis Boricua is the focus of Chapters 4, 5, 6 and 7, in which the authors describe the consequences through demographic and econometric analysis. They lay out the demographic profile of Puerto Ricans migrants. To answer the question of who migrates, they turned to two sources: the Puerto Rican travelers Survey (TS) and the American Community Survey (ACS). The first most striking observation is that women represented half of the migrants in both the TS (48 percent) and the ACS (50.9 percent). They also observed work to be the primary reasons for moving. They addressed the brain drain question, although they do not call it as such, by looking at skillbased migration patterns (p. 63). Here they found that skill-based migrations were volatile. In other words, they found that in 2006, in the early years of the crisis, those with higher levels of education were leaving the Island in greater numbers, but this tendency is not sustained throughout the crisis. As the crisis deepened, they note that less educated Puerto Ricans were also pushed to move. They point out that "as 'La Crisis Boricua' deepened, the initial pressures might have pushed less educated individuals into migrating, but over time, this crisis also began impacting middle and higher-skilled individuals (including doctors), especially after the mainland recovered from its Great Recession" (p. 66).

It is in this context that they raised a relevant question: How permanent were these moves? Data for return migrants show that some people went back. They report that "educated and older Puerto Ricans tended to be the ones to return to the Island during La Crisis Boricua" (p. 75). They also note that lacking English language skills increased the odds of returning, but women were less likely to return compared to men. Here, we find confirmation of the term, introduced many years ago by anthropologist Jorge Duany, Puerto Rican migration may be a "vaiven" shaped by larger socio-economic forces, as well as personal,and familial ones.

Where are these migrants going? Are they going to traditional areas or new settlements? Overall, they report that Puerto Ricans are going everywhere, but from 2006 through2014, they were headed to Florida, Pennsylvania, New York, Massachusetts, Texas, and New Jersey. Texas had the strongest employment and earnings prospects for Puerto Ricans. In other words, they are going to places where there are established communities (Pennsylvania and New York), but also new destination points too. In this respect, they confirm what has been made evident in the last decade of work about Puerto Rican migration—scholarship that was first published in the Centro Journal and that some key pieces are absent from their reference list—Florida is the "preferred destination" for migrants.

Jorge Duany, Elizabeth Aranda, Patricia Silver were the scholars who first reported on the movement and development of Puerto Rican communities in Florida. Florida has been the destination of choice for Puerto Ricans for over a decade. One must ask: When does a new destination become an established community? Although Florida did not offer the salaries found in Texas and Pennsylvania, Florida was the preferred site for movement for Puerto Ricans during the crisis. As I mentioned above, we now know that Hurricanes Irma and Maria consolidated Florida as the preferred site for migrants across the board. Given that Illinois is considered a traditional destination community, I was surprised and disappointed that there was no discussion that focused on Illinois. Illinois was evident in some of the tables but not in the discussion of findings.

How attractive is New York, a mostly traditional destination, in relation to newer places? They report that young and educated Puerto Ricans were more attracted to Texas. They also note that Texas has been more aggressive in the recruitment of teachers, nurses, and other skilled workers. Given what we know about how networks of migration work, it is also probable that Dallas and Orlando are also more attractive than New York. They found that half of Puerto Ricans bound for Texas, and four out of ten of those going to Florida and New York, are going to work. As demographers, they frame the movement of people using the traditional push and pull forces as a way to theoretically organize their research findings with respect to migration. This is a relatively well-traveled road in terms of scholarly work that has established these trends.

As someone who has devoted her career to studying gender in the migration process of Puerto Ricans to the U.S, I was particularly happy to see a whole chapter devoted to women's migration and social mobility outcomes. First, they report that women tended to leave for family reasons, not work. Feminist scholars in the field of migration have problematized the binary of work- and family-related migrations because that imposes an artificial division to the reasons why women migrate. Women migrate and do the reproductive work that supports their families; this is work that is not paid but that supports families across communities. In this sense, their analysis tends to be reductionist. When looking at Island-born and mainland-born women and men, they report that mainlanborn men and women had higher employment-population ratios and labor force participation rates than Island-born men and women (p. 132). Of course, the labor markets Puerto Rican men and women are entering across states tend to differ greatly. So, when they report that Puerto Rican women in Texas, a preferred destination for young educated Puerto Ricans, had an earning disadvantage compared to men, one must explore this issue with further research, something they recognized as necessary. We know that Puerto Rican women have historically struggled to support their families in the U.S., many becoming part of the working poor or living below poverty levels at higher rates than other minority groups. Here they observe that double-digit differences existed between Island-born Puerto Rican men and women in Massachusetts and Pennsylvania and New York, compared to considerably narrower rates they found in Texas and Florida. Indeed, they recognize that gender differences matter and that more work is needed to further explain the precarious condition of women and families in traditional settlement areas. In reporting poverty rates, they examine comparisons with non-Hispanic whites, but I wonder: If they had compared poverty rates among Latino groups, would differences in poverty rates have been more telling? One is left wondering about the limits of demographic analysis to truly give us a sense of poverty as a social problem for those that were pushed by the Puerto Rican crisis.

Chapter Eight, "Shaping Business and Political Landscape on the Mainland," offers readers a sharp contrast from the discussion about poverty. A strength and a weakness of this book is indeed the wealth of demographic information. Here they use data gathered from a survey of business owners (SBO). I found this portion of the book intriguing because the focus on poverty, poor labor market outcomes, and unemployment as markers of Puerto Rican communities tend to obscure other areas of work. The material is intriguing because it shows Puerto Ricans as generators of employment and possibilities for themselves and other Latinos. Here women also play an important role, too. There has been a history of Puerto Rican entrepreneurship in U.S. communities, but it has been eclipsed by the attention to the social problems we have faced in the process of incorporation. For example, in 2012, Puerto Ricans owned 258,221 businesses, placing third behind Mexican Americans (1.6 million firms) and Cubans (281, 982). Yet between 2007 and 2012, the number of businesses owned by Puerto Ricans increased by 65 percent (p. 143). Intriguingly, they report that the "growth rates in the total number of paid employees, total payroll, and average salary paid to employees were higher for Puerto Rican-owned establishments than the other groups. Equally intriguing, the number of businesses owned by Puerto Rican women increased by 116.2 percent for the same period. They tempered the readers' excitement by reminding us the growth tended to be in one category, labelled "other services," which is frequently associated with higher closure rates. But one is left sufficiently excited at the prospects that new research can help us understand how women enter into self-employment and entrepreneurial activities of their own. While conducting research in Chicago, I interviewed several Puerto Rican women business owners; it strikes me that this is an area begging for new research. What kinds of business do Puerto Ricans tend to have? How do they create capital? Who do they employ?

What are the characteristics of these businesses? Do they offer Puerto Ricans pathways into self-employment? As anticipated, Florida and New York were the states with the largest number of Puerto Rican owned businesses for both 2007 and 2012. In Florida, "Puerto Rican owned businesses generated 4.8 billion in sales, $725 million in payroll, and 22, 911 jobs in 2012" (p. 149). To be sure, when compared to Cuban firms, the group that has been celebrated as the most successful with businesses and entrepreneurship, Puerto Rican firms tended to be small and low revenue. They pressed this issue further by looking at self-employment rates. Here, they observed that Puerto Ricans had lower self-employment rates than other Latinos groups. What we know about self-employment has been derived by studies of the ethnic enclave. It is assumed that living in an ethnic enclave increases the tendency to be self-employed. In this respect, that did not appear to be the case for Puerto Ricans. (p. 155). As they put it, "self-employment propensities among mainland-born Puerto Ricans intensified outside of the enclaves relative to those in enclaves over time" (p. 155). Newer destinations offered more opportunities for businesses than traditional ones. Given the earlier and exciting reports about women's entrepreneurship, the question needs to be asked: Are women more likely to be self-employed than men? Indeed, "Puerto Rican women were more likely than their non-Hispanic white counterparts to be self-employed" (p. 157). They observe that self-employment may be beneficial for women because it offers the most flexibility, but it is clear that this topic needs to be studied more thoroughly. This chapter ended with a brief discussion of the role of growing Puerto Rican populations and their potential political influence in federal elections. In Florida, for example, Puerto Ricans are now the second largest Latino group in the state, and for the last election they voted primarily Democrat. When you combine their presence with the larger voter turnout that has been evident in past elections, Puerto Ricans could shape the political landscape for congressional races.

In the conclusion of the book, the authors recognize that La Crisis Boricua, exacerbated by the new policies put in place as part of the PROMESA policies and other economic factors, is poised to create more migrations. As the Island's population ages, those left behind will be the elderly and those that cannot move due to illness or other factors. As the book went to press, the authors could not determine the impact of the Trump's administration on La Crisis Boricua, but they proposed the notion that there are policy implementations that could slow the Puerto Rican exodus. For example, they proposed that stimulating employment, reducing shipping costs through deregulation efforts, and lifting the Jones Act of 1920 can help create a more attractive business environment and encourage more businesses to come to Puerto Rico. They also proposed debt restructuring as another way to alleviate financial burdens on the Island's residents. It is evident that a conclusion cannot be offered since the crisis in Puerto Rico has become a humanitarian one. One factor they fail to notice, in the book's conclusion, is the role of the diaspora in helping to call attention to the unfolding crisis in Puerto Rico in the aftermath of Promesa and in the offering of aid. Chicago's Puerto Rican Agenda held regular press conferences denouncing the establishment of Promesa, its policies, and the underlying political situation facing Puerto Rico. The Puerto Rican community in Chicago was also the first to offer aid in the face of the negligent federal government response (see for example, Alicea and Toro-Morn 2018). A question that future researchers must research is: What role do diasporic Puerto Ricans have in the economic recovery of Puerto Rico?

The authors described La Crisis Boricua as a "perfect storm." It first shows up in the title of Chapter Three, and then it is used throughout the book. I must admit that the metaphor can prove exhausting because there is nothing perfect or supernatural about what is facing Puerto Ricans today and what has been happening for the last 20 years. In other words, La Crisis Boricua is one that, as the author's pointed out, has been in the making for decades. Thus, one is left wondering: What makes it "perfect"? Perfect for whom? Who is accountable for the decisions underlying the debt, the policy decisions, the investments, the budget cuts? I recognize that these questions are beyond the scope of the book. Indeed, this will be the work of future historians: to name the policies, the administrators, the kakistocracy of policymakers that benefitted and contributed to the making of La Crisis Boricua. Similarly, the impact of "la crisis" is evident in the Island and abroad. In this way, this book sets a good foundation for future scholars and future research in traditional and new destination areas. Demographic data paint a powerful profile, but it cannot get at the subjectivities and the experiences of women, men, and children in these families. There is, of course, only so much a book can be addressed in one volume. This one packs quite a punch of demographic data.

In closing, I want to come back to Nelson Maldonado Torres' essay, in the book *Aftershocks of Disaster: Puerto Rico Before and After the Storm* (2019), edited by Yarimar Bonilla and Marisol Lebron. Here he tries to bring clarity to the terms that are now frequently ascribed to Puerto Rico: crisis, disaster, and catastrophe. Maldonado Torres (2019, 333) writes that crisis "refers to a state of affairs that requires a decision because it is no longer stable." He adds that crisis "maintains a view of the past, its value, and the possibilities of the present." The etymology of disaster connects such an outlook to something "ill." "misguided," or given to "ill fortune." As Maldonado Torres sees it: "Disaster is not invested in the value of the past...after a disaster a gap opens up within hegemonic discourse and there emerge provocations" (2019, 334). Yet catastrophe stands in sharp distinction from crisis and disaster because it does not evoke decision or fate. He argues that if you follow the etymology of the word, it means an "unexpected downturn of events." He argues that catastrophe "challenges all existing cognitive frameworks and requires new modes of thinking." According to Maldonado Torres (2019, 339), "Hurricane Maria is a catastrophe inseparable from the catastrophe of Puerto Rican colonialism (a colonialism that continues in liberal, conversative, neoliberal and neofascist times) and the catastrophe of modernity/coloniality."

I read this book in late December, when the Island was shaken by a 4.7 earthquake, followed by one registering a 6.4, on January 7th, 2020. These earthquakes were mostly felt in the southwestern part of Puerto Rico. The Island is now in the midst of what geologists call an earthquake swarm, shaken by tremors every day. The earthquakes have created yet a new layer of stress, devastation, and, one might say, without hesitation added a new catastrophe.

The social consequences of these catastrophic events are now being analyzed by social scientists in the Island and the diaspora. In this respect, Mora, Davila, and Rodriguez's book represents an important building block to understanding the making of the crisis; their review and evaluation of the social dimensions of the crisis allows us to see the recent past with clarity. More analysis is needed to isolate specific policies and their impact on Puerto Ricans. The demographic and socio-economic profile they have offered is rich with details that frame future research questions as we delve into new questions about Puerto Rico. But I would propose the idea, with which they may disagree, that to continue to call it a "crisis" is now somewhat limiting.

REFERENCES

Alicea, Marisa and Maura Toro-Morn. 2018. Puerto Rican Chicago dice presente: Preliminary reflections on community responses to Hurricanes Irma and Maria. *Latino Studies* 16, 548–58.

Maldonado-Torres, Nelson. 2019. Afterword: Critique and Decoloniality in the Face of Crisis, Disaster, and Catastrophe. In *Aftershocks of Disaster: Puerto Rico Before and After the Storm*, eds. Yarimar Bonilla and Marisol LeBrón. Chicago: Haymarket Books.

Meléndez, Edwin and Jennifer Hinojosa. 2017. Estimates of Post-Hurricane Maria Exodus from Puerto Rico. Centro Research Brief 2017-01. Center for Puerto Rican Studies, Hunter College, CUNY. <https://centropr.hunter.cuny.edu/research/data-center/research-briefs/estimates-post-hurricane-maria-exodus-puerto-rico/>.

Latinx: The New Force in American Politics and Culture

By Ed Morales
Verso Books, 2018
ISBN: 978-1784783198
368 pages; $24.95 [cloth]

REVIEWERS: Darrien Salinas (Darrien.Salinas@student.tamuk.edu), Texas A&M University – Kingsville; and Nick J. Sciullo (Nick.Sciullo@tamuk.edu), Texas A&M University – Kingsville

Ed Morales's *Latinx: The New Force in American Politics and Culture* focuses on the history of Latinx identities. In this ten-chapter book, Morales discusses what Latinx means, how Latinx cultures of the past have shaped what Latinx people understand their identity as today, and where these notions of identity could lead us in the future. His central argument is that identifying as Latinx is a unique political identity that contains an idea of "mixed-ness" or "hybridity," while also challenging the black/white racial binary so common in American history.

Although we know race is an "idea or phenomenon that has been created, invented, or constructed by people in a particular society or culture through communication" (Sorrells 2016, 54), in order to support racial hegemony, it seems that racial tensions have only escalated since Donald Trump's election. Morales is not afraid to address Latinx people being looked down upon and classified as *other*. Make no mistake, this is due to the rising tension between Donald Trump's draconian border politics and hateful rhetoric toward immigrants, as well as the rise of alt-right hate groups. Morales writes through this hate to produce a meaningful analysis of what being Latinx, and even American, means today.

The book begins with a thorough discussion of colonialism and the origins of the Latinx community. Some readers may find this a slow start to a book that is otherwise dynamically written with references to art, popular culture, politics, social movements, language, and media. The beginning chapters are necessary though to properly contextualize Morales's later discussion of *mestizaje, mestizo*, and *border thinking*. Rather than proceed chapter by chapter, this review will focus on the most salient discussions Morales, who has reported on Puerto Rico for over 20 years, addresses. This review will also address the importance of the book to thinking about Puerto Rico, Puerto Rican identity, and related concepts of the relationship between Puerto Rico and the United States, a common feature of Morales's other writings. Lastly, some brief criticisms will be addressed in the spirit of productive engagement.

Morales deftly discusses otherness or double consciousness, a concept coined by W.E.B. Du Bois, and its relation to migrant and border thinking in the United States of America. The focus on the duality of migration, being home and foreign, Latin and American, counted and contested, is central to this book, and many readers familiar with race writing will find these discussions relatable and interesting. In this way, Morales links this project not only to much of the work in Latinx studies, but also that in critical race theory and other race-related projects.

This idea of otherness, or looking at the self through the eyes of someone else, tends to bleed into the politics of migration and border thinking in the United States. Morales argues double consciousness allowed African Americans to "see through the illusions of America's benevolence," and it allowed black people to "shape their cultural character" (p. 138). This development of awareness gives the double consciousness an opportunity to oppose established racial hegemony and recontextualize what it means to be black. On that note, this same concept can be applied to border thinking. As Morales discusses in Chapter Five, relying on the work of Gloria Anzaldúa, border thinking incorporates elements of intersectionality and is a way to positively construct one's multiple subject positions. As he discusses the concept of border thinking, Morales uses it as an area to push forward his central argument of America's changing racial binary and introduces this notion of an "uncontrollable border" (p. 139). He points out that Latinx people are seemingly viewed as "other," where the notion of otherness is overdetermined, being a mixture of culture, race, colorism, and many other factors. Many Americans distrust outsiders and the unknown, and this fear propels them to label anyone foreign as an alien, as an existential threat, while knowing that the migrant worker is only temporary. Unsurprisingly, the media has been detrimental for many migrants, which only reignites the hateful rhetoric arguing they pose threats to national security (Sorrells 2016). Morales argues border thinking is useful to relay awareness about migrants' multiple identities while also resisting categorization and disrupting power relations (p. 142).

One of the central sites of categorization is what Morales terms "linguistic terrorism." It is the idea that speaking a foreign language is intolerable, which fuels xenophobia. One need only scroll through Twitter briefly to find a video of a white person yelling at someone speaking Spanish to speak English. Morales argues that these incidents are a result of deep-seated paranoia that the person is speaking about them, and this paranoia drives them to high levels of discomfort. Morales also states that many Latinx people feel shame over their inability to speak English as first-generation immigrants, but by the second or third generations there is a shame that they cannot speak what could have been their native language (p. 144). This compounds the idea that many Latinx people must work harder to fit into modern-day America, especially if they have Mexican lineage, as they are often deemed too white for Mexico, yet too Mexican for America. The lines of language policing cast a dark shadow on Latinx people living in the United States.

The second highlight is his focus on art with numerous references to the Latinx art scene, the hybridity of the art, and its cultural significance. Throughout this book, Morales makes numerous references to his childhood and the art scene in which he grew up. Here his Nuyorican roots lend credibility to his argument and mark him as a relatable Latinx writer with interest and experience in all that he has written. Since Morales has taught and written about Latinx music for years, including in *Rolling Stone,* it is not a surprise that his focus, when discussing his childhood, is the music and art around him. Morales notes that Latinx art has been used as a tool for ethnic stereotyping, namely when Cuban music made an entrance in America's music scene. He also uses this part of *Latinx* to emphasize the connection Puerto Rican music had in the ethnic music industry, and how it quickly became marginalized by the mainstream media (p. 91).

While the focus of the book is largely Latinx music, he also analyzes paintings. He references *casta* paintings, paintings created in the 18th century by the Spanish, to establish a racial hierarchy. These paintings highlight acceptable racial mixing. Morales does an excellent job of intertwining the caste system with early tales of Spain's arrival to the new world. Most notably, his reference to the story of La Malinche illustrates the subordination indigenous men endured at the hands of the Spanish. Morales states, "These indigenous men had little hope in continuing their influence outside of a model of intermarriage that would make their offspring white enough to move higher in the casta hierarchy" (p. 35).

The third highlight is Morales's discussion of "white-passing" and the privilege that comes with Latinx people who are white-passing. This idea of being white enough to be granted certain social privileges is a topic that Morales frequently ventures back to throughout *Latinx*. Of course colorism is felt by Latinx people around the United States today, with white-passing and those with lighter skin often accruing privileges that those with dark skin cannot. Numerous stories of colorism and Puerto Rican identity also emphasize how both individuals living on the Island and those living on the mainland struggle with racisms, assumptions about their identity, and difficulty getting others, including other Latinx persons, to accept their Latinidad (Campoamor 2017; Salazar 2019). Morales argues that whiteness is the marker for persistent racial discrimination and that a large number of Latinx people tend to "seek white privilege rather than critique it" (p. 166). This is likely to be a controversial argument for at least some studying Latinx culture, but it is also certainly worth debating. He reinforces this phenotypical dilemma by discussing Ted Cruz and Marco Rubio's 2016 presidential campaigns and their relation to those oriented toward a white culture, a position reinforced by their light skin and Cuban identity--Cubans in the United States have often maintained conservative or Republican politics. As white-passing Cubans, both men seemed to be able to disregard their Cuban ancestry and alienated Latinx cultures by perpetuating myths about violent border towns and migrants. Morales does not shy away from arguing that their whiteness coincided with the Republican Party's "white supremacist rhetoric" (p. 197).

Those interested in Puerto Rican studies will find Morales's own story and analysis of Nuyorican identity rewarding (pp. 98–118). Morales covers familiar territory with his discussion of the Young Lords and *The Diaspora Strikes Back*, but also includes references to song and poetry that may be less familiar to readers. His mention of Felipe Luciano's "Jíbaro, My Pretty Nigger" leaves one contemplating Monumento al Jíbaro Puertorriqueño in Salinas, Puerto Rico, and its startling whiteness as one darts down El Expreso

Luis A. Ferré while at the same time hearing Mos Def introduce Luciano on Def Poetry Jam. Puerto Rican identity is never far from Morales's work. His discussion of hybridity owes much to Nuyoricaness and what he understands as a close relationship with the Chicanx movement (p. 131).

It would be impossible to read any chapter of this book and not think about what it means to be Puerto Rican, given the Island's complex relationship with the United States. Puerto Rican hip-hop fans will no doubt appreciate his reference to the late Big Pun (p. 248), although there is much more to say about Puerto Rican identity and hip-hop than Morales does. One need not look further than Nuyorican identity to understand border thinking and the way it can bring together and articulate the multiple subject positions of being in New York, with Puerto Rican ancestry, a complex racial identity, outside and inside at once, and a history of colonization in which we find chains on the individual now living on the lands of another colonizer. Morales's story and analysis of Nuyorican identity marks his book as deeply personal and also emphasizes how applicable the lessons of *Latinx* are to Puerto Ricans and Nuyoricans.

One flaw with this otherwise fine book is its lack of discussion of machismo culture, an often-problematic set of ideals about what masculinity is and should be that is so common among and many Latinx cultures. While the idea of machismo is briefly mentioned halfway through the book, there is no contextualization of this characteristic of Latinx cultures. The reader neither gets the historical context nor Morales's personal experience in a way that would help the reader understand better how gender functions in Latinx culture. This is a book that embraces a word that dismantles gender in language, such as the use of "x" in the name "Latinx," intended to make the term inclusive (p. 306). Morales seems excited by and appreciative of the strategy, but by not mentioning a prominent part of Latinx culture, he is doing his work a disservice. He could have included a chapter to address this topic, which would have woven together his nuanced understanding of race, national origin, and other identity characteristics in the modern United States. Machismo culture is well studied in the Latinx community and is described as a "hyper-masculine idealization of men in Latino communities, wherein masculinity is conflated with desire for relations with women and dominion over women and less masculine men" (Collins, 2018, p. 42).

This book succeeds at challenging the black/white racial binary by arguing, among other ideas, that Latinx culture is more than race, but only briefly reflects on gender inclusivity. If we are to truly understand Latinx culture, then we must pay more attention to gender.

Latinx: The New Force in American Politics and Culture is highly recommended for undergraduate Latinx studies, political science, communication, sociology, and cultural studies courses. It is a book that delivers a detailed history of racial mixing and its complexity in constructing a Latinx identity. Morales is a thoroughly enjoyable writer, with a writing style and references to pop culture that keep the reader engaged. To read further on machismo culture, readers will find "How Machismo Got Its Spurs—in English: Social Science, Cold War Imperialism, and the Ethnicization of Hypermasculinity" (Cowan 2017) a good starting point as Cowan traces the emergence of machismo as a term and how it is intertwined in Latin American gender systems. Criticism aside, this is a book worth reading and will perhaps stand with Eduardo Galeano's (1997) *Open Veins of Latin America* as a classic exploration of Latinx culture.

REFERENCES

Campoamor, Danielle. 2017. I'm a mixed-race woman but everyone thinks I'm white — which hurts my pride but gives me privilege. *Bustle* 7 February. Retrieved from <https://www.bustle.com/p/im-a-mixed-race-woman-but-everyone-thinks-im-white-which-hurts-my-pride-but-gives-me-privilege-32955/>.

Collins, Joshua C. 2018. Navigating Machismo: The Exemplary Knowledge and Transformative Learning of Three Gay Latino Men. *New Horizons in Adult Education & Human Resource Development* 30(4), 42–53.

Cowan, Benjamin A. 2017. How Machismo Got Its Spurs—in English: Social science, Cold War Imperialism, and the Ethnicization of Hypermasculinity. *Latin American Research Review* 52(3), 606–22.

Galeano, Eduardo. 1997. *Open Veins of Latin America: Five Centuries of the Pillage of a Continent.* 25th Anniversary Ed. New York: Monthly Review Press.

Salazar, Miguel. 2019. The problem with Latinidad. *The Nation* 16 September. Retrieved from <https://www.thenation.com/article/archive/hispanic-heritage-month-latinidad/>.

Sorrells, Kathryn. 2016. *Intercultural Communication: Globalization and Social Justice.* New York: SAGE.

CARIBBEAN STUDIES

Revista bianual del Instituto de Estudios del Caribe
Universidad de Puerto Rico

ÍNDICE • CONTENTS • SOMAIRE
Vol. 45, Nos. 1-2 (January-December 2017)

*Special Issue: Language Contact, Creoles, and Multilingualism:
Stigma, Creativity, and Resilience*

Suscripción Anual

Instituciones $50.00 / Individuos $25.00

Cheque o giro postal pagadero a
Universidad de Puerto Rico

INSTITUTO DE ESTUDIOS DEL CARIBE
UNIVERSIDAD DE PUERTO RICO
9 AVE UNIVERSIDAD STE 901
SAN JUAN, PR 00925-2529

Tel. 787-764-0000, ext. 87738
caribbean.studies@upr.edu

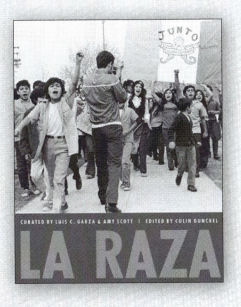

La Raza

Edited by Colin Gunckel

Exhibition curated by Luis C. Garza and Amy Scott

La Raza, launched in 1967 in the basement of an Eastside Los Angeles church, was conceived as a tool for community-based organizing during the early days of the Chicano movement. The photographers for the newspaper and subsequent magazine played a critical role as artists, journalists, and activists, creating an unparalleled record of the determination, resilience, and achievements of the Chicana/o community during a period of profound social change.

This volume presents over one hundred photographs drawn from the more than 25,000 images in the CSRC's _La Raza_ Photograph Collection and from the exhibition _La Raza_, curated by Luis C. Garza and Amy Scott, at the Autry Museum of the American West. The accompanying essays offer not only scholarly assessments of the role of Chicana/o photographers in social movements and art history but also personal perspectives from _La Raza_ photographers.

Design by William Morosi

Distributed by the University of Washington Press

 UCLA Chicano Studies
Research Center Press
www.chicano.ucla.edu

 Distributed by University of
Washington Press
www.washington.edu/uwpress

Centro Publications

2020 CATALOGUE

NEW
Liberalism and Identity Politics: Puerto Rican Community Organizations and Collective Action in New York City
José E. Cruz
ISBN 9781945662089 | LCCN 2017006438
$24.99; $9.99 Kindle

This book is a recollection and analysis of the role of ethnic identity in Puerto Rican community institutional development and collective action in New York City between 1960-1990. The book demonstrates that through institutional development and collective action, Puerto Ricans articulated and promoted a liberal form of identity politics in which ethnic identity and the idea of group rights provided a platform for the production of both individual and collective goods.

Not the Time to Stay: The Unpublished Plays of Víctor Fragoso
Víctor Fragoso; Edited, Translated and with an Introduction by Consuelo Martínez-Reyes
ISBN 9781945662249 | LCCN 2018034538
Pbk. 2018; 244 pages
$24.99; $9.99 Kindle

Not the Time to Stay brings to light for the first time the marvellous work of Puerto Rican playwright Víctor Fragoso. Eight plays, edited and translated by Consuelo Martínez-Reyes, portray the socio-cultural issues Fragoso sought to expose: the choice and difficulties of migration, the clash between American and Puerto Rican societies, the oppression suffered by Latinos in the USA, homelessness, and domestic violence, among others. Fragoso played a key role in the New York City theatre scene in the 1970s, and in the overall interrogation of Puerto Rican and Latino identities in the USA.

NEW
Patria: Puerto Rican Revolutionary Exiles in Late Nineteenth Century New York
Edgardo Meléndez
$24.99

Patria examines the activities and ideals of Puerto Rican revolutionaries exiles in New York City at the end of the nineteenth century. The study is centered in the writings, news reports, and announcements by and about Puerto Ricans in the newspaper *Patria*, of the Cuban Revolutionary Party. The book looks at the political, organizational and ideological ties between Cuban and Puerto Rican revolutionaries in exile, as well as the events surrounding the war of 1898. The analysis also offers a glimpse into the daily life and community of Puerto Rican exiles in late nineteenth century New York City.

Centro Publications

2020 CATALOGUE

FORTHCOMING FALL 2019
Fighting on Two Fronts: Puerto Rican Soldiers in the Korean War
Harry Franqui-Rivera
$24.99

Tens of thousands of Puerto Rican soldiers took part in the Korean War as combat troops. Many of these soldiers fought as part of the 65th U.S. Army Infantry Regiment, "el sesenta y cinco." Its men were known as the Borinqueneers. During the war, the 65th became a national icon on the island and among the growing Puerto Rican communities in the mainland. The island-based press and political figures made reference to the 65th as a catalyst for forging a modern person and a modern Puerto Rico, while the community in New York highlighted the Puerto Rican soldiers' heroic efforts and sacrifices to counter racial discrimination. The Borinqueneers helped established a bridge between New York and the island. These Puerto Rican soldiers' service required them to fight on two fronts. They fought relentlessly North Korean and Chinese soldiers in fierce combat. They also fought brutal racial discrimination within the U.S. Armed Forces. Their story is a neglected chapter in the history of the Puerto Ricans.

Race, Front and Center: Perspectives on Race Among Puerto Ricans
Edited by Carlos Vargas-Ramos
ISBN 9781945662003
LCCN 2016030601. Pbk. 2017; 403 pages **$24.99**

Race, Front and Center is a collection of essays that captures in a single volume the breadth of research on the subject of race among Puerto Ricans, both in Puerto Rico, in the United States and in the migration between the two countries. Its twenty-two chapters divided into seven sections address the intellectual, aesthetic and historical trajectories that have served to inform the creation of a national identity among Puerto Ricans and how race as a social identity fits into the process of national identity-building.

Before the Wave: Puerto Ricans in Philadelphia, 1910–1945
Víctor Vázquez-Hernández
ISBN 9781945662027
LCCN 2016047262. Pbk. 2017; 129 pages **$19.99**

This book recounts the genesis of the Puerto Rican community in Philadelphia during the interwar years (1917–1945). It connects the origins of this community to the mass migration of the post-WW II years when Puerto Ricans consolidated their presence in Philadelphia (1945–1985). This study compares the experiences of Puerto Ricans with that of the Italians, the Polish, and African Americans in Philadelphia during the early twentieth century.

Centro Publications

2020 CATALOGUE

Rhythm & Power: Performing Salsa in Puerto Rican and Latino Communities
Edited by Derrick León Washington, Priscilla Renta and Sydney Hutchinson
ISBN 9781945662164
LCCN 2017038687. Pbk. 2017; 88 pages   **$12.00**

The story of New York salsa is one of cultural fusion, artistry, and skilled marketing. A multi-disciplinary collective of scholars illuminate how immigrant and migrant communities in New York City—most notably from Puerto Rico—nurtured and developed salsa, growing it from a local movement playing out in the city's streets and clubs into a global phenomenon.

State of Puerto Ricans 2017
Edited by Edwin Meléndez
and Carlos Vargas-Ramos
ISBN 9781945662126
LCCN 2017021705. Pbk. 2017; 138 pages   **$20.00**

This book provides an updated overview of some of the most salient subjects and themes about the Puerto Rican population in the United States at present. It highlights the continued mobility and expansion of the Puerto Rican population throughout the country, including state-to-state migration, migration from Puerto Rico in light of the economic crisis in the island, as well as the role of service in the armed forces in anchoring new areas of settlement.

Almanac of Puerto Ricans in the United States
Editors Jennifer Hinojosa and
Carlos Vargas-Ramos
ISBN 978-1945662072
LCCN 2017002040. Pbk. 2016; 167 pages. **$20**

Learn more about the recent changes in the Puerto Rican community on the mainland United States through national and state-specific demographic data. The almanac compiles information on social, economic, and civic conditions of the Puerto Rican population in nine key states, and includes maps, tables, and descriptions of the population nationwide.

The Bodega: A conerstone of Puerto Rican Barrios (The Justo Martí Collection)
Carlos Sanabria
ISBN 978-1945662065. Pbk. 2016; 43 pages. **$15**

This photo book is a compilation of photographs of bodegas in 1960s New York City shot by Cuban photographer Justo Martí. The photos are part of Centro's Justo Martí collection, which documents the life and activities of the individuals, families and organizations that made up the Puerto Rican experience in New York.

Centro Publications

2020 CATALOGUE

Gilberto Gerena Valentín: My Life as a Community Activist, Labor Organizer, and Progressive Politician in NYC
Edited by Carlos Rodríguez Fraticelli; Translated by Andrew Hurley; With an Introduction by José E. Cruz
ISBN 9781878483744; 2013; 315 pages.   **$20**

Gilberto Gerena Valentín is a key figure in the development of the Puerto Rican community in the United States, especially from the forties through the seventies. He was a union organizer, community leader, political activist and general in the war for the civil-rights recognition of his community. In his memoirs, Gilberto Gerena Valentín takes us into the center of the fierce labor, political, civil-rights, social and cultural struggles waged by Puerto Ricans in New York from the 1940s through the 1970s.

Puerto Ricans at the Dawn of the New Millennium
Edited by Edwin Meléndez
and Carlos Vargas-Ramos
ISBN 978187848379-9. Pbk. 2014; 319 pages.   **$24.99**

This edited volume features chapters by Centro researchers and outside scholars presenting new research on social, economic, political and health conditions of the Puerto Rican population in the United States and highlighting the improvements and the challenges in this rapidly changing and growing community.

Soy Gilberto Gerena Valentín: memorias de un puertorriqueño en Nueva York
Gilberto Gerena Valentín; Edición de Carlos Rodríguez Fraticelli
ISBN: 9781878483645—ISBN: 9781878483454 (ebook); 2013; 302 pages.
$20 (print); $6 (ebook)

Gilberto Gerena Valentín es uno de los personajes claves en el desarrollo de la comunidad puertorriqueña en Nueva York. En sus memorias, Gilberto Gerena Valentín nos lleva al centro de las continuas luchas sindicales, políticas, sociales y culturales que los puertorriqueños fraguaron en Nueva York durante el periodo de la Gran Migración hasta los años setenta.

Centro Publications

2020 CATALOGUE

The AmeRícan Poet: Essays on the Work of Tato Laviera
Edited by Stephanie Alvarez and William Luis
ISBN: 9781878483669; 2014. Pbk. 2014; 418 pages.   **$24.99**

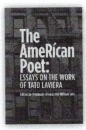

A collection of thirteen essays, an introduction and a foreword by fifteen established and emerging scholars. The essays discuss diverse aspects of Laviera's life and substantial body of work that includes five published collections of poetry, twelve written and staged plays, and many years of political, social, literary and healthcare activism. The book also includes four unpublished poems and the play King of Cans.

The Stories I Read to the Children: The Life and Writing of Pura Belpré, the Legendary Storyteller, Children's Book Author, and New York Public Librarian
Pura Belpré; Edited and Biographical Introduction by Lisa Sánchez González
ISBN: 9781878483805—ISBN: 9781878483454 (Kindle). 2013; 286 pages.
$20 (print); $7.99 (Kindle)

The Stories I Read to the Children documents, for the very first time, Pura Belpré's contributions to North American, Caribbean, and Latin American literary and library history. Thoroughly researched but clearly written, this study is scholarship that is also accessible to general readers, students, and teachers. Lisa Sánchez González has collected, edited, and annotated over 40 of Belpré's stories and essays, most of which have never been published. Her introduction to the volume is the most extensive study to date of Belpré's life and writing.

The State of Puerto Ricans 2013
Edited by Edwin Meléndez
and Carlos Vargas-Ramos
ISBN: 9781878483720; 2013; 91 pages.   **$15**

The State of Puerto Ricans 2013 collects in a single report the most current data on social, economic and civic conditions of the Puerto Rican population in the United States available from governmental sources, mostly the U.S. census Bureau.

Made in the USA
Columbia, SC
02 February 2021